D0815010

Diary of a
French Missionary

Diary of a French Missionary: Penang during the Japanese Occupation
Copyright © 2021 Serge Jardin & Areca Books
Published in 2021 by Areca Books Asia Sdn Bhd
70 Lebuh Acheh, 10200 Penang, Malaysia
www.arecabooks.com

Edited by Manasi Dhanorkar, Khoo Salma Nasution and Yew Jen Khai.
Design and layout by Malvina Anthony.
Printed by Phoenix Press Sdn Bhd, Malaysia.

Published with the support of the French Embassy in Malaysia

All rights reserved. No part of this publication may be reproduced, stored in a retrieval system, or transmitted in any form, or by any means, electronic, mechanical, photocopying, recording or otherwise, without the prior permission of the copyright holder.

Perpustakaan Negara Malaysia   Cataloguing-in-Publication Data
Rouhan, Marcel, Father
    Diary of a French Missionary: Penang during the Japanese Occupation/
    Written by Marcel Rouhan (MEP), Translated, introduced and annotated by Serge Jardin
    ISBN 978-967-5719-43-1
    1. Rouhan, Marcel, Father–Diaries.
    2. Pulau Pinang (Malaysia)–History–Japanese Occupation,1941–1945.
    3. Malaya–History–Japanese Occupation, 1941–1945.
    I. Jardin, Serge.
    II. Title.
    959.595113

Cover photo: Episcopal Consecration of Mgr Adrian Devals, Bishop of Malacca. Penang, 15 April 1934.
First row (seated, from left): Fr Renard, Fr Rouhan, Mgr Deswazière, Mgr Perros, Mgr Devals, Mgr Falière, Mgr Ruaudel, and Fr Burghoffer.
Second row (standing, from left): Fr Baloche, Fr Fourgs, Fr Ouillon, Fr Perroudon, Fr Girard, Fr Cardon, Fr Perrissoud, Fr Michel, Fr Dupoirieux, and Fr François.
Third row (standing, from left): Fr Duvelle, Fr Auriol, Fr Bélet, Fr Paul, Fr Olçomendy, Fr Edmond, Fr Bonamy, Fr Sy, Fr Dubois, and Fr Barnitus.
Fourth row (standing, from left): Fr Seet, Fr De Souza, Fr De Silva, Fr Lee, Fr Koh, Fr Piffaut, and (far right) Fr Souhait.
Bulletin de la Société des missions étrangères de Paris, 1934 (between page 368 and page 369)
GALLICA, BIBLIOTHÈQUE NATIONALE DE FRANCE DIGITAL LIBRARY GALLICA.BNF.FR

Areca Books is a publisher based in Penang, Malaysia. The imprint has a reputation for pioneering works that celebrate *genius loci* and sense of place. Its richly illustrated publications are enduring contributions to the fields of cultural heritage, social history, visual arts and the environment, appealing to both popular readers and academic researchers of Malaysia and Southeast Asia.

Diary of a French Missionary

PENANG DURING THE JAPANESE OCCUPATION

WRITTEN BY
MARCEL ROUHAN (MEP)

TRANSLATED, INTRODUCED AND ANNOTATED
BY SERGE JARDIN

ARECA BOOKS

College General in Pulau Tikus: Four directors standing
on a balcony looking over a group of students.
Photograph by Kristen Feilberg, circa 1868.

ROYAL COLLECTION TRUST / UNITED KINGDOM (RCIN 2702891)

Contents

Abbreviations

AA	Anti-Aircraft
B	Blessed, the station between Venerable and Saint
BB	plural of B
BMA	British Military Administration, the interim administrator of British Malaya from the end of World War II to the establishment of the Malayan Union (August 1945–April 1946): nicknamed the Black Market Administration or the Black Market Association
BMV	Latin, Beata Maria Vergine, meaning Blessed Virgin Mary
CBE	Commander of the Most Excellent Order of the British Empire
CG	French, Collège Général
CIC	Commander-in-Chief
CSC	Chinese Swimming Club
Fr	Father (Priest)
HQ	Headquarters
IIL	Indian Independence League
IJS	Infant Jesus Sisters, or Dames of Saint Maur
INA	Indian National Army
MEP	French, Missions Étrangères de Paris, meaning Paris Foreign Missions Society
MP	Military Police
MBRAS	Malaysian Branch of the Royal Asiatic Society, formerly, Malayan Branch of the Royal Asiatic Society
Mgr	Monseigneur, a title and an honorific in the Roman Catholic Church
NB	Latin, Nota Bene

NS	Negeri Sembilan, one of the four Federated Malay States
OBE	Officer of the Most Excellent Order of the British Empire
PAR	Precautionary Air Raid
PPC	Peace Preservation Committee, which replaced the PSC after the arrival of the Japanese
PSC	Penang Service Committee, headed by Manicasothy Savaranamuttu, which kept peace and order in Penang in the short interim period between the British evacuation and Japanese occupation
PW	Province Wellesley which, together with Penang island, formed the British Straits Settlement of Penang
RAF	Royal Air Force, the United Kingdom's aerial warfare force formed towards the end of the First World War
RIP	Latin, Requiescat In Pace, Rest In Peace
SFI	Saint Francis' Institution, school in Malacca
SFX	Saint Francis Xavier Church, Malacca
SS	plural of St
St	Saint
SSVF	Straits Settlements Volunteer Force
SXB	Saint Xavier's Institution Branch school in Penang.
SXI	Saint Xavier's Institution, a boys' school in Penang
TB	Tuberculosis
WWI	WW1, First World War (1914–1918)
WWII	WW2, Second World War (1939–1945)

Foreword

I t is a joy to see this precious diary of the Director of the Collège Général in Penang translated and published in this way.

The College is one of Malaysia's oldest institutions, playing a critical educational role throughout East Asia for two centuries. Yet, because for most of its life it was a French Institution, it has seemed to rest obscurely in the shadows of Malaysia's national story.

This publication, with its excellent introductory history of the College, should remedy that. The diary itself is a remarkable record of an institution that was a monument to continuity even in *Malaya Upside Down*.

Anthony Reid
Historian

Acknowledgements

Dr Bernard Patary, the historian who discovered the Diary in the College General archives while working on his PhD thesis;

Father Stanley Antoni, Rector, College General, who opened the door of the archives for me; Jude Manickam, Administrator, College General, and Juliana M. Michael, Librarian, College General, for their kind assistance;

Agnès Krassinine de Soultrait for acting as a go-between;

Br Ambrose Loke, for sharing his knowledge about the Christian Brothers;

Andrew Hwang for his knowledge on the SSVF;

Ayako Endo-High and Clement Liang for translating some Japanese expressions;

Chen Yen Ling for her research on the Infant Jesus Sisters;

Colin Goh for sharing his sources on the Catholic church;

Fr Joseph Reulen, MEP, for his input on the College General;

Khoo Salma Nasution, from Areca Books, for her interest in the book, which made its publication possible, and her knowledge which contributed to improving the book;

The Areca Books team for all the pre-publishing work they put in;

The French Embassy in Malaysia for the material support, especially HE Frédéric Laplanche, the former Ambassador for his keen interest in the French Memory in Malaysia and Roland Husson, the former Counsellor for Cooperation and Cultural Affairs;

Anthony Reid, Historian, for his kind words of support;

for their availability and willingness to share their knowledge, their sources, and their time, and to take the trouble to correct some of my mistakes, thank you.

The shortcomings, of course, are mine.

Seminaire général indigène pour l'Extrême-Orient, à Penang (Malaisie)
Séminaristes Chinois, Birmans, Siamois, Annamites, Tonkinois
Asiatic General Seminary, Penang'

College General, Penang (Malaya), with
ninety-seven Chinese, Burmese, Siamese,
Annamese, and Tonkinese seminarists. Five
French priests are seated in the front row: Justin
Pagès, the Superior (centre), and four directors.
To the Superior's immediate left is Henri
Michel, while Georges Denarié is among the
other three directors. Photo taken circa 1920.

MISSION ETRANGÈRES DE PARIS / FRANCE

❧ Introduction ❧

A French Missionary in Penang

During the Japanese occupation of Malaya, a French missionary kept regular record of the events and experiences faced by the Fathers and students of the College General and, to a lesser extent, by the larger Catholic Community in Penang. This Diary was not an official document (administrative, diplomatic or military), but a private one. It was not meant to be published, but most probably maintained as a memoir, to aid the author's memory in case he needed to answer questions after the war. The diary mostly dwelled on matters of daily survival in time of war, the experience of students and teachers in a religious boarding school.

War is an abnormal situation. This Diary deals with the period of the Japanese occupation and the immediate prewar and postwar periods (1938–1946). Contrary to common belief, not all the 'White Men' disappeared during the war. Not all escaped before the arrival of the Japanese troops, or died fighting, or spent the war in the Changi prison in Singapore or some other prisoners' camps. Some stayed put. Among them were the Catholic missionaries.

American, British, and Canadian citizens who served as Protestant missionaries were considered enemy subjects and arrested at the start of the Japanese occupation. However, the Catholic missionaries, especially the French, were spared, because the French Government of Vichy was friendly with the Germans and, by extension, with the Axis powers. The French colony of Indochina was also friendly with Japan. Therefore, they spent the war among the local people, sharing their difficulties, their hopes and their struggles.

A unique document

Quite a few documents have already been published on the subject of the Japanese occupation of Malaya, Penang included, from autobiographies to novels. This French missionary's diary may have been written from a European perspective, but it is not another testimony from a prisoner of war, nor an afterthought written to explain the defeat of the British. It is the Diary of an outsider – neither the coloniser nor the colonized, but the citizen of a neutral country – a 'Neutral', as such a person was called. In contrast to official records, vernacular sources are mostly oral, and rarely written down, but this is a vernacular written account – a diary kept during the war.

For all these reasons, I believe this Diary is an exceptional and unique document. As it was written in French, I thought it would be worth translating into English – for the Penangites of course, but also for anyone interested in Catholicism or war history, and for the curious readers of Malaysian history at large.

So many questions

The most crucial issue in the Diary is the seminary and the Community's survival in times of war, but there was also the challenge of preserving the institution for which the Missionaries were responsible. Perhaps the most important concern – even if it was never mentioned – was the safety of so many young people, so far from their families to whom the Fathers were answerable.

The Diary helps us to understand many questions. How to find food and what was the effect of rationing? What were the consequences on people's health? Why did a black market exist and what about the prices? How to deal with the lack of news and its corollary, rumours? What about public safety and how to carry on with life?

The Diary also provides insights into human behaviour during an extraordinary time, when one has to choose between acceptance and resistance. This constant struggle at times takes on a religious dimension. What were the necessary adaptations brought by war and what were the changes in store for the future?

Some limits, however

While most chronicles of WWII cover the Japanese invasion, the occupation and the surrender, this Diary covers a broader period. The war did not start with the occupation and did not end with the surrender. The Diary narrates the first signs of war in 1938. After the war was over, the situation was far from satisfactory under the British Military Administration; as a matter of fact, life never reverted to the way it was in pre-war times. With the British occupation, Malaya entered a new era on 1 April 1946 as the Malayan Union.

The College General is located on Penang Island, but events and people from Malaya and beyond are mentioned. While some directors (as the teachers were called) and seminarians crossed the Penang Channel to Province Wellesley, Cameron Highlands and Singapore, the author of the Diary never left the island during the period concerned.

Being the director of a Catholic institution, the writer presents a unique voice. He was not just a Neutral, but also a Frenchman and a priest. Of course, his writing carries with it the subjectivity of his background.

A comprehensive presentation

In introducing the translation of the Diary, I consider it necessary to present the institution (the College General), and to introduce the document and its author.

I shall also highlight a few salient points which make the Diary a remarkable socio-historical document. The predominant thinking in times of war is *Primum superesse, deinde philosophari* or 'first to stay alive, then to philosophise'. This was a period of insecurity which did not end with the return of the British. *Primum panem, deinde philosophari* or 'first some bread, then philosophy', means that the Diary dwells in length on food and husbandry, rations, prices and the black market, and sources of income. The Diary also mentions newspaper reports, radio announcements, rumours, health, leisure, transport, weather, among other issues. Finally, the Diary chronicles a Community facing historic events that would bring imminent change to the institution of the College General, as well as to Malaya.

In addition to the translation, I thought it would be useful to add a short chronology, as well as glossaries and notes to help the reader comprehend the text, and to provide some additional information about the Missions, the people and the places mentioned in the Diary. Finally, I have also proposed a list for further reading that can provide a better understanding of the Diary's context.

A BRIEF HISTORY

Birth and disappearance

The history of the College General is closely linked to the history of the Missions Étrangères de Paris (MEP). In fact, the College General in Penang was a flagship of the Society of Foreign Missions of Paris.

At the beginning of Portuguese maritime expansion in the early fifteenth century, Rome granted the Portuguese Crown permission to expand the church to Asia. This Royal Patronage (*Padroado Real*) was eroded from the seventeenth century, when Portugal was overtaken by England and Holland, both Protestant countries, as the dominant power in Asia.

As early as 1622, Rome founded the Sacred Congregation for the Propagation of the Faith (*Propaganda Fide*) for the purpose of taking over control of the church. In France, a French Jesuit, Alexandre de Rhodes, was a strong advocate of this policy; he repeatedly emphasised the need to send missionaries to Asia, where he had spent thirty years. By the time his efforts finally bore fruit, he had already left France for Persia in 1654.

The MEP was founded in 1658 by two priests, Pierre Lambert de la Motte and

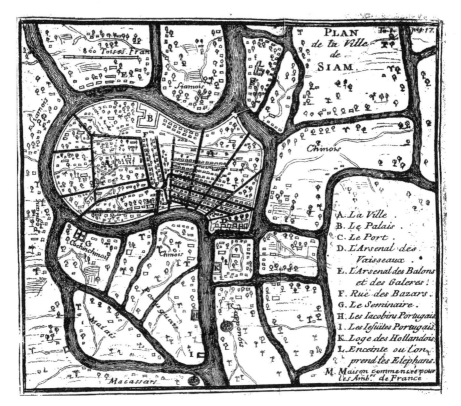

The location of the College (Le Séminaire) of the Missions Etrangères de Paris in Ayutthaya, Siam, around 1687. Simon de La Loubère, *Du royaume de Siam, Tome premier*, Paris: Jean Baptiste Coignard, 1691.

GALLICA / BIBLIOTHÈQUE NATIONALE DE FRANCE

François Pallu. Rome immediately ordained them as bishops, bearing the newly-coined title 'Apostolic Vicars', responding directly to the Pope while circumventing the authority of the King of Portugal. They were also the first missionaries, unrestricted by the geographical boundaries of the *Real Padroado,* to embark on their respective Missions. Lambert de la Motte left in 1660 for Cochinchina and François Pallu in 1662 for Tonkin. Both met in Ayutthaya, the capital of Siam, where they decided to settle down.

One of the objectives of the MEP was to train the local people to form a clergy. It led to an obvious decision to create a seminary. The capital of Siam, centrally located, easily accessible and politically stable, seemed a good choice. Application was made to the king, who offered a large plot of land on the bank of the Chao Phraya river. In 1665, the Seminary of Saint Joseph welcomed its first students. As they were drawn from neighbouring countries, Goa, Macao and Tonkin, the interdiocesan seminary became known as the College General.

The first priest was ordained in 1667. Ten years later, the College General had both a Major Seminary, with about thirty students divided between the studies of philosophy and theology, and a Minor Seminary, with about sixty students essentially

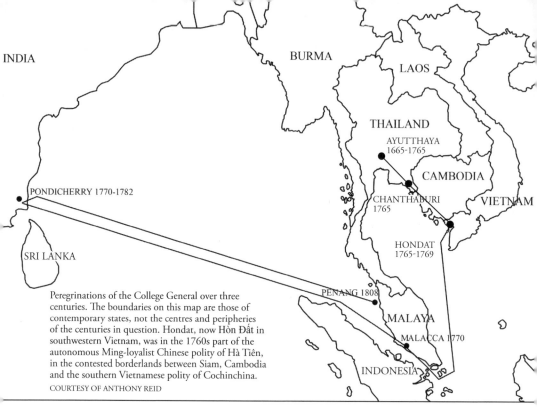

INDIA
BURMA
LAOS
THAILAND
AYUTTHAYA
1665-1765
CAMBODIA
CHANTHABURI
1765
VIETNAM
PONDICHERRY 1770-1782
HONDAT
1765-1769
SRI LANKA

Peregrinations of the College General over three
centuries. The boundaries on this map are those of
contemporary states, not the centres and peripheries
of the centuries in question. Hondat, now Hòn Đất in
southwestern Vietnam, was in the 1760s part of the
autonomous Ming-loyalist Chinese polity of Hà Tiên,
in the contested borderlands between Siam, Cambodia
and the southern Vietnamese polity of Cochinchina.
COURTESY OF ANTHONY REID

PENANG 1808
MALAYA
MALACCA 1770
INDONESIA

devoted to learning Latin. Indeed, Latin served as the language of education up until the Second Vatican Council in 1965. The teachers were called 'directors', while the headmaster was styled 'superior'. The students came from Burma, China, Cochinchina, Japan, Malaya, and Siam. For a century, the College General went through many vicissitudes (including a brief period when its directors were imprisoned during the Siamese Revolution of 1688–1690), but it remained in Siam.

When a fire destroyed its premises in 1677, the seminary was rebuilt in Mahapram (Bang Ban), four kilometers west of the capital, and took the name of Holy Angels Seminary. The comings and goings between the two sites continued until 1765, when the Burmese besieged Ayutthaya for 22 months, and finally destroyed the city.

The College General first found refuge in Chanthaburi on the Gulf of Siam, then in Cancao (Hà Tiên) (a port located in Cambodia on the border with Cochinchina), before settling in Hon Dat. In 1767, Pierre Pigneau de Béhaine, who had just been named Superior, was accused of being complicit with the Siamese and imprisoned with the other directors of the College General. Soon after the directors were freed, the Cambodians, who massacred the Vietnamese, destroyed the seminary in 1769. On 11 December, a Chinese junk left Cancao with 43 'boat-people'.

On 3 January 1770, the survivors reached Malacca, but were welcomed by neither the Dutch Protestants nor the Portuguese Catholics. Finally, a Portuguese man offered his house against the will of his community. The College General spent two months in Malacca, but the cost of living was high and their savings were running out. At the end of February, the São Jorge, a Portuguese ship carrying Armenians en route to India, took on Pierre Pigneau de Béhaine but had only enough room for 12 students. The others were spread over three Muslim boats which provided free passage to India.

Finally, in 1770, the College General settled in Veerampattinam, seven kilometers south of Pondicherry. The students were reduced from 39 to only 18 in 1778. Paris decided to close down the College General, as it was too remote from most of the Missions, which were beginning to open their own seminaries.

The choice of Penang

Claude Ledontal, Procureur of the MEP in Macao, was the true architect of the revival of the College General. He was familiar with all the Missions, without being attached to any. He received the support of the Missions which experienced religious persecutions, particularly in China and Vietnam – the need for a College General to be established in a safe zone was obvious to them. Catholic Manila was approached; however, a request sent to the King of Spain in 1802 had yet to receive an answer in 1807. Malacca was considered, but the Dutch were deemed too Protestant and the Catholics too Portuguese.

It was finally Penang Island, under the dominion of the British East India Company, which was chosen as the location of the new seminary. Pulau Pinang (island of the areca palm tree) enjoyed Pax Britannica and had a healthy climate. It was well located and easily accessible from all Missions (across India, China and Southeast Asia). A Catholic community was already thriving there.

Chased out of Siam in 1779, a small group of Catholics led by Antoine Garnault visited Phuket and Malacca, but finally settled in Kuala Kedah in 1781. This is where the meeting took place with Captain Francis Light, who had just established a British colony on Penang Island in 1786. As superintendent of the 'Prince of Wales Island', as it was called, Captain Light distributed land to encourage settlers. Captain Light's wife, Martina Rozells, was a Catholic Portuguese Eurasian, and Antoine Garnault received a large plot in the city centre. Light then offered Garnault passage to Pondicherry for his episcopal ordination.

The new College General opened in 1808 in two abandoned houses lent by the English. In 1809, Michel Lolivier, the first Superior of the College, bought two houses (one for the directors and one for the seminarians) and a plot of land by the seaside, in a small village called Pulau Tikus (meaning 'rat island'), west of the city. He also purchased four houses in town to provide a rental income to the College General. In 1811, the College General had twenty students, all of them Chinese from Sichuan. One day, the College General was attacked by 'pirates', and Lolivier defended it with a rifle in his hand. In 1812, when a fire destroyed the four houses, the financial situation became disastrous. Soon after, the College General started receiving funds from the Society for the Propagation of Faith, founded by Pauline Jaricot in Lyon in 1822, dedicated to financing the Missions. This Society remained, till the end, a pillar of financial support for the College General.

With the arrival of François Albrand to succeed Lolivier (who died in 1833), the College General enjoyed a period of prosperity. Religious persecution in Cochinchina resulted in an influx of students. The site of the burnt-down houses was sold, and land was bought for planting nutmeg trees; when attacked by disease in 1860, they were replaced with coconut trees. Albrand also started a rice field, constructed a new building with a chapel, and set up a small printing house. Then, for health reasons, he returned to Paris, where he was a director before becoming the Superior of the MEP Seminary. He was replaced by Claude Tisserand in 1839.

The Vicariate of Western Siam, covering today's Malay Peninsula and Singapore, was established in 1841. From 1843 to 1845, the College General had a director named Pierre Favre, who started the construction of the Saint Francis Xavier Church in Malacca in 1849 and the construction of the new Assumption Church in George Town in 1857. Later, when he was teaching Malay at the School of Oriental Languages in Paris, Favre gave us the first reliable tools – dictionaries and grammar rule books – for learning Malay in French.

In addition to the funding, the relations of authority between the Superior of the College General and his bishop became a recurring problem. At times, the very utility of the College General was in doubt. As it received only pupils from China and Vietnam, the College struggled to be 'General'. The signing of the Franco–Chinese treaty in 1844 opened five Chinese ports to French trade. This marked the end of religious persecution, but it also meant that the source of Chinese students would soon dry up. When Tisserand was discharged from the Superiorship in 1847, he went on to found a Minor Seminary named the College Sainte-Marie. Locally known as St Mary's College, it was located in Permatang Tinggi ('Matang Tinggi') in the plantation area of Province Wellesley.

In the mid-nineteenth century, the situation stabilised. In 1848, there were five directors for 154 students, the highest number ever: 44 from Western Cochinchina, 78 from Eastern Cochinchina, six from Tonkin (these three missions are located in today's Vietnam); ten from Western Siam; ten from Sichuan, four from Yunnan and two from Kuy-Tcheou (Guizhou) – the last three being missions in China. In addition to China, Malaya and Vietnam, students from Cambodia, Korea and Burma arrived, then from Siam in 1849 and from Borneo in 1867. The College then became truly General.

The revolution of 1848 in France did not help the financial situation of the College General. In that year, land was acquired in Tanjung Bungah, three kilometers west of Pulau Tikus, to build a country house called Mariophile. This land was cultivated. In 1849, the new Superior, Sylvestre Thivet, was fatally impaled in a tiger pit. In 1850, Paris took over the material direction of the College General, leaving the spiritual direction to the Bishop of Malacca. In 1855, a new chapel was completed, along with two new wings. It was during Joseph Laigre's Superiorship (1869–1885) that Roman centralisation was reinforced with regard to spirituality (the permanent wearing of the cassock, the Gregorian liturgy, and the use of Latin), in parallel with the strengthening of Parisian centralism on material aspects (appointments, allocations and auditing of accounts). Recognised by Rome and protected by Paris, the diversification of recruitment in the seminary continued. The College General received its first Japanese student in 1869.

With the Franco–German war in 1870, funds disappeared. The staffing was reduced. The progress of the Missions and colonisation would seem to go hand in hand throughout history, but in fact, the consequences of colonisation were negative for the College General. With colonial peace, religious persecutions disappeared and regional seminaries flourished. In Pulau Tikus, the College General was enlarged, a pond was dug, the chapel was renovated, and a rice field opened. In 1884, a new chapel was started at Mariophile, the country residence of the College General, built in brick in Roman style and completed in 1885. The chapel still stands today. Its main altar is surmounted by a statue donated by the Governor of the Straits Settlements, Sir Frederick Weld. The Father's House was added in 1928. In 1885, plans were made to rebuild the College General (apart from the newly-renovated chapel), and these plans were approved the following year. The work was financed with a loan from Paris headquarters.

Laigre died in 1885 and was replaced by Edmond Walleys who, despite the decline in student numbers, began the expansion work: this included three main double-storey buildings facing the sea, with colonial-style arcades around a large yard planted with *angsana* trees (*Pterocarpus indicus*). The different spaces were consistent with life in a seminary: prayer, study, relaxation, body care and sleep. The spaces reserved for the directors were clearly separated from those of the students. Sénateurs were also separated from Supersénateurs.

At the end of the nineteenth century, the College General experienced a paradoxical situation. Never before did it have such beautiful, large premises with a capacity for 150 students, but in reality, it had only 20 students and three directors. The arrival of a Tibetan student in 1902 did not change anything. What should be done? To transform the College General into a seminary solely responsible for higher education, to close it, or to sell it? The decision had to be taken quickly. Some rich

Chinese wanted to buy the buildings in order to convert them into a hospital.

Paris chose the first solution and the College General was saved. In 1905, a law of laicity was passed in France, imposing the separation between Church and State, which meant that religious congregations were not allowed to teach. A way had to be found to prepare the priests intellectually up to par with the secular, technical and scientific schools of the Republic. In 1906, while waiting to clarify the MEP's position, 36 students and two directors from the Parisian seminary landed in Penang.

The declaration of war in 1914 resulted in the departure of all the young missionaries who were conscripted. Finally, in 1921, the College General became a Major Seminary only. The civil war in China favoured the return of students to Penang. The diversification of students continued: the first Indian arrived in 1923, and the first Laotian in 1924. Sent to Penang as director in 1925, Marcel Rouhan became the Superior in 1930.

Running the College General before the War

In 1931, the College General had 117 students from 24 missions. The administration of the College General was simple. The directors were appointed by Paris, and so was the Superior, after consultation with the directors. Besides, the directors formed a Deliberative Council which took their own decisions, by voting if necessary. The Council chose from among the directors a Procureur to manage the material aspects of the College General. The students were sent by the Missions.

The Council could dismiss a student for indiscipline. Daily life was very precisely organised, not only with regards to matters of education and religious services, but also with respect to maintenance routines and leisure activities. Each student had a place allocated in the dormitory, the refectory, and the chapel. Students had two daily breaks. They were always expected to keep company with a minimum of two others. They were allowed to smoke. They could swim in the sea and go for walks, but always accompanied by a director.

From 1830 to 1988, the College trained 2,266 students. Two out of five students became priests. Malaya, Singapore, and Sarawak provided 435 seminarians: 218 Chinese, 120 Indians, and 97 Eurasians. Out of the 174 who became priests, 62 per cent were of Chinese origin, 25 per cent of Eurasian origin, and 13 per cent of Indian origin. Up to a dozen nationalities had been represented in the College General, but on the eve of the war only seven remained: Burma, Cambodia, China, Laos, Malaysia, Thailand and Vietnam. The countries no longer represented were India, Indonesia, Japan, Korea and Tibet.

The College General reflected the cosmopolitanism of the Asian Catholic

Missions. During this period, most students came from the region close to Penang. Burma, Malaya, and Siam sent a cumulative total of 1,000 students, while Indochina (Vietnam, Cambodia and Laos) sent 678 students, and China sent 455 students. Korea, India, Indonesia, Japan, and Tibet sent only a few students each.

The directors did not belong to a religious order. The MEP was an association of priests, all French-speaking, including two Belgians and one Italian apart from the French. Between 1807 and 1968, the College General received 61 priests as directors. The vast majority of directors were younger than 25 years old when they arrived in Penang. Two-thirds of the directors did not stay more than 10 years at the College General. Exceptions were Henri Michel and Marcel Rouhan, who each stayed two decades, and Georges Denarié and Pierre Piffaut, who each remained four decades.

The profiles of the College General priests were no different from that of other missionaries. The typical priest came from a practising Catholic family, modest in means and large in size, from a small town in a rural setting. While 'Paris' appears in the name Missions Étrangères de Paris and the headquarters are located there, not a single director of the College General actually came from there.

On average, missionaries from Paris studied for five years, either in their bishopric or in the Paris seminary, before leaving for Penang. François Pallu, co-founder of the MEP, stipulated in 1665 that the missionary should: 'study the character of the peoples in which he must be sowing and germinating the seed of the Gospel'. The learning of languages was equally important, but as the missionary would only learn of his destination the day before his departure, the study of languages would be taken up during the journey. In addition to English, a College General director was expected to know at least one Asian language. Latin was the language of communication and teaching, but the Latin proficiency of the local young pupils was so poor that it was necessary for the missionary to acquire vernacular languages. It is important to mention here the MEP's contribution to the French knowledge of the languages of Asia.

The curriculum of the College General was no different from that of a Major Seminary in France. It strictly followed the *Propaganda Fide* in Rome, even in the way Latin was pronounced. Until the 1960s, Latin was the language of communication, and it was only after 1904 that students were allowed to use English to learn the language. The duration of the course was six years: two years of Philosophy (including cosmology, criteriology, logic, metaphysics and theodicy), followed by four years of theology (along with canon law, church history, sacred liturgy, and plain chant). During the war, Japanese language was added as a subject. The year was divided into three trimesters, and each trimester was followed by a month-long break (April, August and December). Twice a year, the seminarians sat for exams, both oral and written.

Even in the twentieth century, liturgical practice in the College General was far from being well adapted to local culture, although such adaptation was already advocated by the Jesuits in the seventeenth century. As a concession to the East, however, a gong replaced the bell in Mariophile, which rang so powerfully that it was sometimes possible to hear it in the College General, three kilometers away. When it expired in 1935, a replacement was sought in Singapore, because in Penang 'among the curiosity merchants, one asks exaggerated prices'.

When it came to food and drink, temperance was the cardinal virtue. Of course, the basis of the diet was rice, and one ate more fish than meat. Penang being an island, resources were scarce and expensive. This is why, very early on, the College General developed its own agricultural production. In the second half of the nineteenth century, the College General had a coconut plantation and a rice field. Its proximity to the sea provided an excellent opportunity for the seminarians to practise fishing. The kitchen staff were mostly Chinese. If abstinence from drinking wine was the custom in Siam, it seems never to have been followed in Penang. The purchase of red wine and brandy was regularly mentioned in the correspondence. The French directors likely considered alcohol a form of medicine.

In France, there is a saying, 'a good priest does not take a bath', but Malaya's climate made it necessary to do so several times a day. Modesty was the rule, and the lower abdomen had to remain covered even when taking a bath. Seminarians were also responsible for the cleanliness of the College General. It seems that the results varied according to the Superior and the directors. From 1878, the College General enjoyed running water. Twice a week, seminarians had to empty the buckets of the pit latrine as the septic tank did not arrive until after the Second World War. In terms of personal grooming, the hair was expected to be kept short while the beard was the signature of a French Missionary. After WWI, it was compulsory for both directors and seminarians to wear the black cassock. However, due to the climate, the white cassock prevailed in the 1930s. In the chapel, one was expected to wear shoes, long pants and a black cassock.

The Procureur sent the accounts annually to Paris, from where most of the funds originated. Revenues came from four different sources. The first source was European funds from the Paris headquarters and from Rome where the *Propanganda Fide* controlled various associations which financed the missions. The second source consisted of gifts, legacies and paid masses. The sale of agricultural products acted as the third source of income. Besides rice, nutmegs, rambutans, durians and mangosteens, coconut palms, bananas and pineapples, rubber trees (*Hevea brasiliensis*) were planted in the early twentieth century. After World War II, the College General was famous for its honey.

In 1920, the College General owned eight hectares of land in Pulau Tikus and

80 hectares in Tanjung Bungah. And finally, the College General had income from bank interest and its own assets. The bulk of this income came from the rental of land and buildings: the houses numbered 1 to 24 on College Square, five houses on Kelawei Road, five houses by the sea in Tanjung Bungah built in 1938, and one more bought in 1943. The expenses were essentially operational.

Finally, the economic activities remained modest. The College General never tried to create an economic organisation inspired by Christian values as an alternative to the prevailing liberal economic system. The involvement in the economic world was just a way to finance the operations of the College General.

During the war and after

On the eve of the war (15 October 1941), the College General enumerated 64 students from 12 Missions. On 4 December, the College General moved to Mariophile, the country house, and stayed there until 18 February 1945. This was the date when the College General returned to Pulau Tikus and a small group of Malayans and two priests went to Matang Tinggi in Province Wellesley. Neither the College General in Pulau Tikus nor Mariophile was ever bombed by Japanese planes in 1941 or Allied planes in 1945.

Even before the occupation, shelters were built and night watch was organised. As soon as the Japanese forces landed on 19 December 1941, the Community started to grow vegetables and rear chickens.

On 8 January 1942, at the end of the holidays, classes resumed but only part-time, as part of the day was occupied with securing food. On 10 March 1942, one student passed away because of typhoid, the only death recorded at the College General during the period of the war. In June, all the French still living in Malaya, except for the missionaries, were sent to Indochina. About the same time, the Infant Jesus Sisters opened a girls' school in the College General as their Convent was occupied by the Japanese Navy.

In May 1943, for the first time, the Japanese authorities started to look closely at the College General and other religious educational institutions. A report Father Rouhan wrote to the Japanese authorities enumerated 55 students (5 Annamite, 15 Burmese, 13 Chinese, 3 Eurasian, 11 Indian, 0 Malay and 8 Thai students) at the College General. In August 1943, the College General was one of the biggest schools in George Town, accommodating 1,000 students, with Brothers and Sisters teaching side by side in addition to laic teachers.

In his report to the MEP HQ in Paris, dated 15 October 1945, Father Rouhan wrote: 'by November 1943, we received enough information from outside to understand that the course of events had become favorable to the Allies'. On 28

December 1943, Father Michel (considered an enemy alien because he was Belgian) was arrested and interned in Singapore.

In early January 1944, the first direct intervention from the Japanese authorities in the College General's educational programme took place. Of the three demands made, only one – the teaching of Japanese language – was ever implemented; however, this was abandoned before the end of the occupation. The Labour Service Corps was started, but the College General eventually managed to get out of the requirement to send its students. After the landing of the Allies in Normandy in June, fearing that they would be interned, the Fathers requested Monseigneur Devals, the Bishop of Malacca, to dispatch a local priest to take over the College General in case of emergency. Father Aloysius arrived on 4 August. An Allied plane was sighted over Penang Island for the first time on 5 November.

On 11 February 1945, Mariophile was finally requisitioned by the Japanese Navy. The Community moved back to Pulau Tikus but the students from the Malacca Mission, together with two directors, settled in Matang Tinggi. The Brothers in the Novitiate next door shared the fruits of their garden and their fish catch, while the Sisters cooked for the Community. At the time, the College General housed three schools in one: a seminary, a convent and a government primary school. On 12 August, the Japanese forces surrendered; on 30 August, the group from Matang Tinggi returned, and was sent to Mariophile to take care of the property, by then abandoned by the Japanese occupiers. On 3 September, the British landed. The running of the government primary school was soon taken over by the Brothers, and classes continued on the College General premises until the end of the year. By 15 October 1945, the College General was reduced to 36 students from 10 missions; however, the number of directors remained unchanged.

After the war, life slowly returned to normal, and student numbers slowly recovered to 80 to 100 students representing ten different nationalities, an average sustained until the end of the 1950s.

In 1948, a State of Emergency was declared in Malaya due to the communist insurrection. In 1949, the Chinese Communist Party took over China, resulting in a reluctant exodus of missionaries. The winds of independence were blowing across the old empires, stirring the spirit of liberation in the British, French and Dutch colonies in Southeast Asia. As early as 1955, the Catholic Church created the archbishopric of Singapore–Malacca and the bishoprics of Kuala Lumpur and Penang, with two local bishops, respectively Monseigneur Dominic Vendargon and Monseigneur Francis Chan. The new ecclesiastical province, thus formed, had 90 Catholic schools, with 1,500 teachers for 52,000 students. Among them were 44 local priests and 60 missionaries from the MEP.

Life in the College General went through a slow but irreversible transformation.

Students were permitted to take the bus alone and to buy drinks and food with their pocket money (10 dollars a month, instead of the earlier 5 dollars). The College General began to modernise in line with the policies and pronouncements of the Second Vatican Council, which met from 11 October 1962 to 8 December 1965. Letters were no longer opened by the Superior. The cassock – white because of the climate – was only worn during office hours or outside the College General. The students started to learn English and were allowed to go to cinema. They were invited to participate in parish life and to practice ecumenism by encountering Protestants. The College General bought bicycles for the students and invited outsiders to give conferences.

The celebration of the tri-centenary of the College General (1665–1965), towards the end of the Vatican Council, was simultaneously an apotheosis and a swan song. Latin was abandoned and directors could be recruited from the local clergy. The students were allowed to have their own personal radio receiver sets. They started to learn democracy by electing a student representative to the Council. Finally, the altar in the chapel, originally *ad orientem* towards the apse, was turned around so that the priest would face the Community.

On 1 September 1966, the College General became a regional seminary. By 1971, Father Achilles Choong became the first non-European to be appointed Superior. In 1978, the last French director left Penang. In 1983, the Seminary moved definitively from Pulau Tikus to Tanjung Bungah (Mariophile). The following year, the Pulau Tikus property was sold, then destroyed, and is today replaced by Gurney Plaza, retaining only a few *angsana* trees. The money generated from the sale was used to build three seminaries, one each in Kuching, Penang and Singapore. In 1989, new buildings were added in Mariophile and the Seminary inaugurated its new campus in 1995.

In memory of more than 2,000 students trained and 900 priests ordained throughout its history, the Penang Seminary continues to be known today as the College General.

THE DOCUMENT AND ITS AUTHOR

About the author

The Diary's authorship is anonymous. Obviously, it was written by one of the seven directors who were present at the College General during the period considered (1931–1946). We can exclude Philippe Meissonnier, who arrived only in 1935 and was in Bahau, the Agricultural Catholic Settlement, from the beginning of 1944 until the end of the war. Henri Michel was arrested and spent a few months in

Singapore from 1944 until the Japanese surrender. René Paroissin and Pierre Piffaut went to Matang Tinggi, Province Wellesley, in February 1945. We are then left with Georges Denarié (director from 1917 to 1958), Hubert Monjean (director from 1923 to 1949) and Marcel Rouhan. The temptation is great to eliminate the last in the list, because the author of the Diary mentions 'Father Rouhan' and profiles him as 'the Superior'. It might be common in the Malay language to refer to oneself in the third person, but it would be very unusual to do so in French.

The dates of service, however, favour Marcel Rouhan as they closely correspond to the period the Diary was kept. Father Rouhan arrived in Penang as director in 1925 and became the Superior of the College General in 1930, while the Diary was started on 29 March 1931. The last page of the Diary ended on 9 September 1946 and Marcel Rouhan left for France on 19 November in the same year. I believe that if the writer took the trouble to hide behind the third person, it was for reasons of safety. The consequences of the Japanese discovering the Diary would be dire, as the information contained therein could incriminate the author or other persons mentioned in the Diary.

The author inadvertently betrayed himself with a *lapsus calami*. On 20 April 1943, when the College General was making space for extra classrooms at the request of the Japanese authorities, he wrote: 'The BMV statue at the main entrance is parked in my office.' The office referred to was the Superior's office; from this we can conclude that the author was Marcel Rouhan.

Father Rouhan was born in 1896 in Aix-en-Provence, in the South of France. Conscripted during the Great War, he rose to the rank of Second Lieutenant. He entered the MEP's Seminary in 1921 and went to study in Rome at the Pontifical Gregorian University, where he was ordained as a priest on 6 June 1925. On 14 September the same year, he sailed to Penang where he served as a director from 1925 until 1946. He became the Superior in 1930. On 19 November 1946, he returned to France.

The manuscript

The Diary of the College General (1931–1946) is a notebook with a black hard cover. The Diary started on 29 March 1931, and it was interrupted on 9 January 1944. The Diary was then continued in two small exercise schoolbooks with brown paper cover (printed for the College General by Thean Wah Factory in Penang). They are respectively dated, from 10 January 1944 to 16 January 1945, and from 17 January to 17 March 1945. On 17 March 1945, the Diary was continued in the black hard cover notebook until 10 August 1945. The pages from 11 August to 20 September 1945 are missing. Finally, the Diary was resumed in a small exercise schoolbook (brown paper cover) on 21 September 1945 until 9 September 1946.

Altogether, I translated 286 hand-written pages.

Some notes were added at a later date. In March 1940, a note was added 'to see 3 July 1940'; in July 1940, an observation 'up to September, no one has come yet'; in the entry for 18 December 1941, a hand-written note was added on November 1945; on 5 March 1942, a remark was inserted to say that an ordination which took place abroad was 'known only after the war'. The Diary was apparently not written daily, but a few days at a time. For example, on 2 January 1944, the remark 'we shall be sure of that, only two days later' was not an addition, but stood in the middle of the text.

The Diary was started on 29 March 1931, but I have only translated the entries from 12 August 1939, when the Community left for Mariophile for holidays, shortly before the war started on 3 September 1939 on the Western front. Before that, the Diary was mostly about arrival and departure, the expulsion and ordination of seminarists, as well as maintenance work at the College General and at Mariophile. Visits from MEP's priests and bishops were mentioned. Before 12 August 1939, I included only two entries, 29 September 1938 and 10 April 1939, related to the coming war. I also translated the postwar entries up till the end of the Diary when life had very slowly returned to normal.

The Diary followed the movement of the students, and gave the reasons for their departure. It was important, for financial reasons, to know when a student arrived and left, in order to split the cost between the College General and the Missions. The Diary was also an aide-mémoire for writing reports. The Superior knew it was a matter of time before he would have to report to Paris. For that reason, the Superior was compelled to keep track of unique events and information during those exceptional times.

The Diary illustrates two different approaches. Before the war (1931–1939), the Diary is totally silent about events of the outside world, with exceptions being the death of Pope Pius XI on February 1939 and the election of Pie XII a month later. With the coming of the war, worldly preoccupations – daily life as well as major events – took the centre stage. For that reason, the author of the Diary recalled the conditions of the time and justified the decisions made.

Our author needed to protect his institution and his function, so he preferred to remain anonymous and kept his Diary in a safe place. After 9 January 1944, one entry mentions: 'This notebook is packed away at the College for safety reasons and the Diary is continued on loose sheets which will be inserted here.' From 10 January, it was noted that 'The Diary is continued on loose sheets because the notebook has been placed in relative safety. We start writing again today.' As the necessary precautions had been taken, the writing of the Diary reflects a degree of freedom which might be absent from a letter or a report destined to be shared.

About the translation

The orthography of local names is quite variable. For example, the name of the College General's tailor is sometimes written as Chong Tsam, and sometimes as Siong Tsann.

Interestingly, the author used English words in some instances, like rubber, lorry, and estate, and a variety of words from other languages, including Latin, Japanese, Hokkien and Malay. All non-French words in the French text appear in italics in the translation.

In order to avoid any confusion, the time is transcribed as 1:00 to 24:00, as it is usually written in French, instead of am and pm.

Following the original text, the settlements are spelt as 'Malacca' and 'Penang' instead of Melaka and Pinang.

A SOCIAL HISTORY

To survive in times of war

Primum superesse, deinde philosophari: First, stay alive, then, philosophise. The most important preoccupation in times of war is to stay alive. One should note that a state of war or military occupation continued throughout the full length of the Japanese occupation, and this was followed by a period of British military occupation.

Running the College General was not a personal initiative or an individual enterprise. The leaders had heavy responsibilities: seven adults were in charge of more than fifty teenagers and young adults. They were also safeguarding the physical, intellectual and spiritual integrity of an institution, by managing the buildings and lands, running the seminary, and administering the sacraments of the Catholic faith.

The first threat of war was the bombing. As early as 1939, a plan for constructing bomb shelters in Mariophile was considered. Work started in early 1941, under the supervision of Father Rouhan who had served as Second Lieutenant during WWI; in the same year, the blackout drills were commenced. For safety reasons, the Community left the College General and relocated to Mariophile which was further out of town. The College General would return to Pulau Tikus in February 1945, after the Japanese Navy requisitioned Mariophile.

In fact, the College General was lucky to escape destruction, and so were all the Catholic churches in the state and the Sisters' schools. The unlucky ones were the Lasallian Brothers who lost St Xavier's Institution during the Allied bombings in 1945.

On 2 January 1942, the Japanese commanding officer, Major General Manaki, summoned the senior community leaders to Asdang House, where he proclaimed a list of 38 decrees. The Military Commander was now in charge. The Japanese wartime administration had taken over all the lands and properties of the former British administration. Anyone who did not cooperate with the Japanese authorities was likely go to jail or end up dead, and their properties confiscated. Anyone who helped the Japanese authorities would be safe. Temporarily, the dollar could still be used, and was on par with the Japanese currency. Motor cars had to be surrendered. The Asdang House declaration specifically ordered people to report 'any military weapons', 'bad Chinese characters or Communist', or 'saboteurs'.

The rules of the game had been laid out. This gave the community leaders a good idea of what was in store for the people in the years to come. The Japanese military commander issued a decree:

Whether you live or die will be in accordance to our wishes... Japanese soldiers are currently fighting… do not indulge in any luxuries, be satisfied with the bare minimum. You must bear hunger… Do not wander about the street unnecessarily. Do some work. There is plenty to be done. You will be told what you have to do hereafter by proclamation or decree. Obey the commands of the Military authorities. Any evil doer will be severely punished … You must only fly the Japanese flag, and that only when told to do so. Resume your normal life...

The Diary selectively quoted sections of the above decree which pertained to property. 'Normal life' meant living in fear of being spied upon, and under constant watch of the police. The Fathers, especially the Superior, were summoned at will by the Education Department, the Navy and the Police. On 14 July 1942, the French Fathers, the Annamites, and Burmese seminarists were registered with the police as Neutrals; the Diary states what was forbidden and what was permitted. Unhappy with the cooperative efforts of the Neutrals, the police sent for them on 25 January 1943.

The most violent episodes of the Japanese occupation were the Sook Ching ('purge through cleansing'), a systematic killing of perceived hostile elements among the Chinese population by the Japanese occupants. Following the second wave of Sook Ching, on 17 October 1942, the Kempeitai searched the College General and Mariophile but found nothing. During their next visit a year later, the Kempeitai was angry to find a matchbox with a patriotic Chinese inscription and a map of Burma. Police visits to search for radio sets were not as alarming, but much more frequent.

On 5 January 1944, the Head of Education was displeased to note that the students were unable to speak Japanese, the College General was not keeping Tokyo time, and the Indian students were not joining the Indian National Army.

At the end of 1943, the Japanese authorities created a Labour Service Corp. The students of the College General were fortunate to escape compulsory conscription. The Brothers were 'levied 20 men (out of the 60 who are in the Novitiate)', but the conscription was never implemented and 'the affair was happily resolved afterwards.'

The worst fate, of course, was to be arrested. On 14 July 1942, the Brothers in Taiping were denounced for converting a Communist; they were held in a Kuala Lumpur jail for a month. The following year, five Brothers from Kuala Lumpur were taken in and sent to Singapore. On 3 October 1943, the College General's tailor, suspected of providing food to British soldiers in hiding, was arrested and beaten up. By mid-March 1944, a priest of Bukit Mertajam, named Joachin Teng, was locked up for a week. On 4 October 1944, the College General's *kepala* was also detained for a week. Even the Superior was once apprehended by a patrol for walking alone near the forest.

Some Catholic missionaries were first put under house arrest, but eventually sent to the internment camps in Singapore when the tides of war deemed that they were no longer 'neutral'. When Italy surrendered in September 1943, the Italian Sisters were taken in. After Portugal authorised the Allies to use the Azores in October 1943, the Portuguese priests were arrested. As a Belgian citizen, the College General's Procureur Henri Michel was taken to Singapore in December 1943. On March 1945, it was the turn of the American Brother, Michael Blais, to be interned in Singapore. The same month, all the 'first-generation' Eurasians were swept up by the police – altogether, 96 families in Penang and three Brothers. Finally, after the capitulation of Germany, even the Germans stationed in Penang ended up in Singapore internment camps in January 1945.

Following the Allied landing in Normandy, the College General requested the bishop to send a local priest to the College General in case the French priests were arrested. As the Superior wrote: 'We are always on the alert, our suitcases ready, and we expect an arrest from one moment to the next.' In August 1944, Ignatius J. Aloysius became assistant to the Superior and the Procureur.

Primum panem, deinde philosophari

First, to eat; then, to philosophise. Besides avoiding arrest and trying to stay alive, the basic preoccupation of the College General was to stay alive without going hungry. Their concerns were no different from the rest of the population. When food rationing was imposed, the black market, inflation and farming became the topics of the day – the number of entries thereof in the Diary speaks volumes about the constant preoccupation with food.

The first ingredient to disappear from the market was wheat flour. Our bread eaters looked for alternatives like potatoes, corn or tapioca for making bread flour.

Finally, bread was replaced with porridge, tapioca or *ragi* as the staple. It seems that wheat flour for baking regular bread only reappeared in Penang in March 1946.

On the whole, the College General did quite well during the occupation. Except for the last six months spent in Pulau Tikus, the College General had access to a huge piece of land in the Tanjung Bungah countryside, where Mariophile was located. If having the students meant there were 50 mouths to feed, it also meant there were a hundred arms to do the work. During the first six months of the occupation, food supply was still adequate and prices were reasonable. But when the situation deteriorated, the land became essential for growing fruits and vegetables.

By the end of 1943, the French Fathers still enjoyed a glass of wine with each meal and, thanks to the goats, the College General had enough milk for the invalids. By 1944, salt and sugar were scarce. Even rice had to be replaced with dehydrated rice (cooked and dried) in order to be able to provide a daily meal of rice. The 'ordinary' diet was

> ...per person per day: tapioca in the morning with banana; rice, fish or meat, vegetables from our garden at noon; in the evening *sagu*; the next day, beans boiled in the morning, with banana; at noon, *cangee* with fish (either fresh or dried), vegetables from the garden; in the evening, tapioca.

Having a garden was a blessing, with 'our 500 banana trees and more, we have a profusion of bananas at our disposal.' This supply would disappear when they moved back to Pulau Tikus. On 29 June 1945, the Community was treated to durians from Balik Pulau, thanks to Mother Saint-Louis from the Infant Jesus Sisters.

By September 1945, the students stopped going out to fish as the BMA provided free meat and fish. They discovered refrigerated meat which was 'not bad at all'. One month later, the College General slaughtered a cow because beef disappeared and pork was too expensive. Luckily, the garden yielded a lot of vegetables. The day after Christmas, a rice shortage was announced. On 13 August 1946, the army stopped giving free rations of bread and biscuits to the College General, and on the same day, the Town Council did not renew the free water agreement the College General had enjoyed since 1934. On the positive side, for the first time since the start of war, the College General received communion wine from Australia produced by the Jesuits. At $1.15 per bottle, the price was reasonable, but the $2 duty was not so sweet.

Throughout the occupation, and in the period immediately after, the order of the day was rationing.

The main item of rationing was rice. In May 1942, the monthly ration was 4 *gantang* per person. One month later, it was reduced to 3 *gantang*. By March 1943, the ration decreased to 2.1 *gantang*, and in August it was again reduced to 2 *gantang*. The rations were even smaller for women and children. The size of rations was proportionately reduced for everyone in Balik Pulau and Province Wellesley, for the reason that 'in these places everyone can have land to cultivate, which is not possible in town.' Furthermore, the rice did not arrive regularly. By November 1944, the rations decreased further. To add salt to injury,

> It seems that instead of weighing the rice distributed to the dealers, the Government measures it to the *gantang*, and the *gantangs* are not filled when measuring. When the dealers come to distribute, they weigh (6 *katis* = 1 *gantang*) and do not get their full measure.[1]

By the end of the war, the ration was reduced to 1 *gantang* per person. The rationing did not end in August 1945. In October, the rice was distributed free, but the quantity was far from sufficient (2 *gantang* for an adult male in November and December) and still very irregularly distributed.

Besides rice, items rationed included sugar, coconut oil, matchboxes, sweet potatoes, and fish. The quantities were slowly reduced. The 4 *tahils* salt ration was knocked down to 2 *tahils* per person. That ration being insufficient, the students started to boil sea water to make salt. On 10 December 1944, Father Rouhan wrote:

> Coconut thefts are multiplying, too; but people plead extenuating circumstances. The coconut rations are reduced to one per month and per family...

The practice of rationing implemented together with price control gave birth to a terrible, but unavoidable, scourge: the black market. On 25 November 1943, Father Rouhan wrote:

> The control of coconuts (sales and prices), of vegetables, of fish (price only) will badly affect the supply. Not a coconut or a sweet potato on the market. People are flustered. Secretly, a coconut sells for $0.60 and more. At the official price we only buy... fish heads.

In 1944, the Japanese authorities created official trusts to distribute vegetables and fish, but these items disappeared as soon as these organisations were created. In January 1945, pork was sold the same way, 'and almost overnight pork meat disappears from the market.' Finally, these trusts were dissolved in July 1945, because they 'were boycotted and everything was going to the black market.' It seems that everything was available, with the right contact and at the right price.

> As contraband, we can have it [fish] more often, starting from two dollars per *kati* in our neighborhood; in town it goes up to 15 dollars. And the pig up to 19 dollars per *kati*, a coconut 50 cents... We buy 3 piculs of rice for more than 5 thousand dollars... It's obviously a black market!

The poor people were withdrawing half of their ration and, after selling it to the black market, they bought the second half of the ration with a profit to keep. Father Rouhan gave practical advice: 'Better to have food in the store than notes in

---

1 The discrepancy came from the fact that the government was using *gantang* as a measure of volume while the dealers were using it as a measure of weight.

the safe'. As paper money had no value, it was better to buy and sell.

We buy, despite the astronomical prices, a lot of fish, corn, *ragi* and dried *mee* especially... and we shall sell it with great profit after a while.

In 1945, the black market spread to the telephone operators for, without greasing the palms of the phone operators, the line would always be engaged when anyone tried to make a call.

The black market did not stop with the capitulation of Japan. Under the British Military Administration, official prices for foodstuffs may have been low, but due to insufficient quantities, the black market was flourishing. On 16 November 1945, 'rice at $180 a *gantang* instead of $5 was recorded.' This continued even after the 'Black Market Administration' was replaced by the civil authority. On 21 July 1946, it was noted that,

The rice ration given by the government in recent weeks is pathetic, 1 *kati* per person per week. On the other hand, the rice black market at 4 dollars per *gantang* is flourishing. We can have as much as we want and this rice arrives by the ferry at Michell Pier, brought by Chinese ladies, old or young, by children even, with bags or baskets containing less than 20 katies, to escape the regulations on the transport of rice, as everyone knows. The rice comes from Kedah and Siam.

A logical consequence of scarcity and rationing, hand in hand with the workings of the black market, was inflation. In general, food prices increased steadily during the Japanese ooccupation, and started to decrease slowly afterwards. The price of rice started to rise as early as April 1941, with the disappearance of Siamese rice, and hiked astronomically at the end of the war.

A one-*pikul* bag of rice cost $12.50 in January 1942, 15 dollars in May, and 20 dollars in June (compared to 40 dollars in Singapore and 4 dollars in Kedah), 230 dollars in February 1944, 264 dollars in November; the price reached 1,600 dollars in 1945 and was back to 60 dollars in October.

A coconut was 50 cents in 1943, $2 in early 1945 and $5 by mid-year; at the end of 1945, it was down to 25 cents (the price in 1942).

The price of one egg rose from 7 cents in January 1943 (compared to 20 cents in Singapore) to 60 cents in early 1944, and to $1 by the end of the same year. A *kati* of pork cost $2 in 1943, $5 on 7 April 1944, $8 on 22 April 1944, $20 in November 1944, $27 on 2 January 1945, and $45 on 31 January 1945.

Everything became pricey. In 1943, a bottle of Whiskey cost $60, even an empty brandy bottle cost $3, and a typewriter ribbon was worth $45. A cup of coffee at the *kedai* was 80 cents in 1944. The price for a bicycle rose from $1,000 to $18,000 in July 1945. Official prices were ignored by the business community. On 19 October 1945, Father Rouhan wrote,

No pork to buy, the pork sellers refuse to open shop for four days because some of them were arrested for selling above the controlled price.

People's lifestyles changed as food was hard to come by and prices were high. Everybody became a part-time farmer, using every available piece of land to produce food. The Japanese administration's policies indeed encouraged this trend, especially in 1944 when the problem became more acute, with the administration at one point threatening to cancel the supply of food. They also distributed plants and seeds, and created Agricultural Settlements.

The College General was lucky to own a big piece of land. Farming started as early as 22 December 1941 under the direction of Father Denarié, who bought chickens to start a henhouse the very next day and purchased goats on Christmas Day.

By 1942, the planting of vegetables and fruits was in full swing. Five hundred banana trees were planted in Mariophile. By the end of the year, thousands of sweet potatoes and tapiocas were planted. The yield of the latter turned out to be much better than the former. Less noxious species of tapioca were selected, and finally sweet potatoes and maize were abandoned in favour of tapioca. In 1943, a large plantation of durian and cashew was started. The following year, the football field was not spared; half was covered with banana and the other half with pineapple. The College General obtained permission to harvest, for personal use of its members, 300 coconuts per month instead of 50. In 1943, the farm counted 14 goats and five cows, as well as some rabbits. Guinea pigs and ducks were also doing well.

In February 1945, when the Japanese authorities took over Mariophile, the College General lost the investment they had put into the farm and had to start all over again in Pulau Tikus, on a much smaller piece of land. Part of the College General started to look like Noah's Ark. A henhouse was built under the veranda of the study room. By July 1945, altogether 33 goats, four cows and two piglets were sharing the College General with the humans. Finally, more vegetables were harvested, especially *kangkong*, coriander, *bayam* and Jerusalem artichoke. The sweet potatoes were more productive here than in Mariophile, but the long beans were attacked by many insects. The real bonus was the mature fruit trees: rambutan, mangosteen and coconut trees.

Besides farming, the seminarians and students of the College General managed to go fishing, as both properties, in Pulau Tikus and in Tanjong Bungah, were located by the sea. The students started fishing as early as 18 December 1941. Unfortunately, the Japanese authorities prohibited them from fishing at Mariophile, and it was only in 1945, when the College General was back in Pulau Tikus, that seafood became an important part of their diet, with an average of ten *katis* a day of fishes, crabs and shrimps. They stopped fishing in September when the British Army started to provide them with free fish. Sometimes, a welcome relief from the day-to-day menu came from hunting wild boar, trapping monkeys and squirrels, or going to the bees to 'bring back a good quantity of honey'.

So many issues at hand

Apart from food, everyday concerns included communications and transport, as well as the state of public safety and healthcare. Father Rouhan tells us about the rather new General Hospital, the control of epidemics and vaccinations, and how the health situation worsened during the occupation with the lack of food and medicine, especially quinine. Beriberi, cholera, dysentery, leprosy, smallpox, tuberculosis, typhoid and malaria are all mentioned in the Diary but fortunately none became epidemic. On 10 March 1942, one student died of typhoid at the General Hospital. He was the only member of the College General the Community had to mourn over during the war. All together, the College General had a case of tuberculous laryngitis and eight cases of typhoid in 1944. By the following year, the health situation among the population had become critical. People were weakened by the lack of food. Malaria and dysentery were common. Legs and feet were covered with ulcers. Beriberi was everywhere. In the report he sent in October 1945 to the General Superior in Paris, Father Rouhan wrote 'the population of the Malay village living on our property in Mariophile, estimated at 1,600 people before the war, is reduced by half.'

Father Rouhan also wrote about the modes of transport: bicycle, car, handcart, motorcycle, and plane. George Town's railway station was unique, as one had to board a ferry to cross the channel before boarding the railway on the mainland. Father Rouhan mentions the free travel made possible with the complicity of the local staff. The cycle rickshaw, introduced in 1936, became very popular during the war, increasing from barely 100 when the Japanese forces arrived, to around 2,500 in 1943. The old electric trams had already been replaced by electric trolley buses, running every 30 minutes in July 1945. In December 1945, free bus services were provided. Only one thing had not changed – it still took one and half hours to walk about 8 km from Tanjung Bungah to the city centre.

Father Rouhan regularly reported on the weather, the monsoon system and the rain pattern – all crucial information for farming.

The author touches on the news, and the lack thereof, and how information was transmitted. For example, the local Japanese paper written in English was heavily censored in order to omit, or at least to delay, the bad news. The use of the radio receiver set was a constant preoccupation for the Japanese authorities, and a prohibition was imposed on short wave reception. Towards the end of the war, when the Allied Forces were positioned within closer range and long waves were good enough to receive their broadcast, all sets were confiscated. The College General decided early on to surrender their three receiver sets, as they renounced the use of electricity in Mariophile. The most important information was transmitted by word of mouth, through the telephone or via travelers, through the closely-knit networks of the Catholics, the French and the Missionaries.

Due to the lack of information, any gossip was grist for the rumour mill. The Diary has countless entries of false news:

- Evacuation of the coastal area (1942)
- Arrest of Brothers and Sisters (1942)
- Total occupation of the College General (1942)
- End of the rice ration (1943)
- Allied landing in France (8 January 1944)
- Allied landing in Sumatra (24 January 1945)
- Warnings of impending arrest (27 March 1945)
- Mariophile's chapel is full of rice (8 April 1945)

Rumour-mongering didn't stop in August 1945. By September, rumour had it that the College General would certainly move to Mariophile. By January 1946, British soldiers were said to be renting out their revolvers at night to rich and fearful people. By February, it was war against Russia.

Father Rouhan tells us about the leisure activities of Catholic seminarists. Outdoor activities would include ball games like soccer and *sepak takraw*, swimming and leisure walking. Students were also gardening and taking care of farm animals. Before and after the war, picnics were held at Balik Pulau, Telok Bahang, or even further afield in Taiping. The College General had already sold their bungalow on Penang Hill to the Brothers, but they bought another one in Telok Bahang, on the north-western side of the Hill.

During the war, it was a novelty for the Malayan students to go home to their parents for the holidays. Indoor activities included not only billiards, chess and reading, but also comedy plays, annual concerts, listening to the radio and records, and watching movies (but not in Mariophile, which went without electricity). Manual occupations were printing, bookbinding, and cabinetmaking.

The directors had their own billiard table and library. When necessary, they were able to go to their rest house in Cameron Highlands and, before or after the war, even further to the Nilgiris, in India.

The author gives us a vivid image of the state of security (or rather insecurity) of the College General during the Japanese occupation and after. Thefts were very common during the war. It was almost a daily occurrence in Mariophile, to the point that the College General had to organise patrol squads. The thefts mostly involved food. Some villagers were living on the property, and most of the area was unfenced, creating easy and evident targets. Every other night the students and the Fathers would be chasing away thieves, who came sometimes alone, sometimes in groups, to steal tubers of tapioca and wood for cooking or for shelter. The chase never went beyond some cat-and-mouse game. Later on, the garden of the College General in Pulau Tikus likewise was not spared.

The burglaries were committed out of hunger, desperation and necessity. More serious thefts than that were exceptional. Twice, the Pulau Tikus kitchen was broken into (28 February and 2 March 1945), but not much was stolen. The low crime rate was most probably the consequence of Japanese policies – all weapons had been collected (or hidden) and the brutal force of the Kempeitei had spread fear to all and sundry. It must be noted that armed resistance to the Japanese occupation was almost absent on the island. As a result, the level of public safety was likely quite high.

After the Japanese surrender, the situation worsened even though the BMA also was a military occupation. Terror had disappeared and rule of law had supposedly come back, but the new freedom permitted illegal activities to develop more freely. It was a period of great social unrest, a time to settle the score for wartime enmities. Soon after the return of the British, piracy on the sea was mentioned for the first time by Father Rouhan:

(8 October 1945)…on the East coast, piracy is at its maximum

(26 December 1945)…news that the seas are infested with pirates north of Pulau Langkawi

(31 December 1945) Pirates infest the north of Langkawi and the junks do not dare to go looking for supplies

(10 January 1946)…there are pirates in Langkawi.

Father Rouhan recorded further incidents of crime, not just simple thefts and robberies, but also actions perpetrated by armed gangs:

(20 October 1945)…bold thefts multiply

(27 October 1945)…many daring robberies

(2 November 1945) The robberies by armed gangs around the College are on the increase

(8 November 1945)…series of murders in daylight and gang robberies

(12 November 1945)…the series of armed robbery continues

(16 November 1945)…armed robberies continue

(14 December 1945)…robberies are multiplying… a victim, among others, is Father Baloche at Pulau Tikus, thieves enter his house at night forcing a window bar and take some small things.

(16 January 1946)…armed robbery in College Square at 16:00, in a house. Things are going too far

(22 January 1946)…robbery by a gang, just opposite the main Police station in Penang Road. There is no limit to insolence!

(16 February 1946)…the thefts and murders continue in a worrying way. Despite the death penalty against those who possess weapons

(25 February 1946)…the crime wave that had become alarming in Penang seems to be diminishing.

(21 April 1946) It is in the harbour that looting is the most prevalent. It is said that half of the goods are stolen.

The wave of theft and crime rises again. In broad daylight, at noon, in Macalister Road, passersby are accosted and relieved of all their precious things, including their bicycles. In remote corners, Batu Itam for example, it is the same; people armed with revolvers are looting isolated houses. And when the honest people ask for hunting guns to defend themselves, they are refused. (17 June 1946)

Besides illegal activities, political activities and social agitation were on the rise. While Father Rouhan had made a note of the communist raids south of Ipoh on 21 June 1945, he first mentioned it happening on Penang Island on 16 October 1945: 'Communists put up posters everywhere,' and again on 20 November, 'the communists unscrew the bolts of the railway'. The scarcity of food, jobs and money created a fertile ground for social disturbance. Father Rouhan noted the deadly riots in Taiping on 17 October, and remarked on 30 January 1946, that the 'General strike in Malaya, following the arrest of a communist leader' was disrupting the trolley-bus service in Penang.

Not to forget the people

Besides the French people, the Diary mentions other Europeans living in Penang under Japanese occupation. The German, Hungarian and Italian nationals were living freely as 'Friends of the Axis powers', while the Danish, Irish and Swiss nationals found their movements restricted as 'Neutrals with the Axis powers'. The nationals of 'Enemies at war against the Axis powers', such as the Belgians and the British, were all eventually arrested.

The relations between the Missionaries and the Japanese were far from homogenous. Even among the authorities, an occupational stratification and diversity could be discerned. Although the Fathers' relations with the police were rather tense, the College General's relations with the Education Department were usually friendlier. Among the Japanese were those who were Catholic in faith: a Japanese seminarist educated in Canada, a soldier who spoke French, an officer from Nagasaki, and a professor from Tokyo University. Sharing the same faith as the French Fathers, and sometimes acquainted with the same people, a special bond was established between them.

It was most probably a blessing for Penang to be occupied by the Navy and not by the Army. In his Diary, Father Rouhan wrote on 16 June 1945, 'These Navy people are well disciplined and very decent. On the other hand, soldiers are like soldiers everywhere'. And two days later (at the time when the Okinawa battle was raging), it was noted that, 'Two Japanese soldiers, apparently coming over from the workshop set up in the Novitiate annex school, help us to pick the mangosteens. Nothing exaggerated.' Nothing more, nothing less.

It would be impossible not to mention ethnicity in the Malayan context; of course, Father Rouhan's writing gives us some insight into this matter. It should be noted that, while the College General staff are mentioned by name, other foreigners such as the British (and also English), French, German, Italian, Japanese, and Swiss, are identified by their country of origin. The students are identified by their Mission of origin: Bangkok, Malacca, Mandalay, Rangoon, Saigon, Sarawak, and Swatow. They are also known by their country of origin: Annamite (Vietnam), Burmese (Myanmar), and Thai (Thailand).

The local people are identified by their occupation: coolie, doctor, farmer, police, shopkeeper, teacher. They are also referred to by their religion: Catholics, Protestants, 'Mahometan' (Muslim). Most of the time, however, local people are viewed through the prism of ethnicity: Chinese, Eurasian, Indian and Malay. It is important to remember that the development of the Catholic parishes was mostly ethnically-based: Immaculate Conception for the Eurasians of Pulau Tikus, Holy Name of Jesus for the Chinese of Balik Pulau, Saint Francis Xavier for the Indians, Our Lady of Seven Sorrows for the Chinese of George Town. Only Christian religious leaders are mentioned in the Diary (Catholic, Anglican and Protestant), and not those of other religions (Buddhist, Hindu or Muslim).

In Father Rouhan's writings at least, the relationships which the Japanese had with the locals did not appear to be drawn along ethnic lines. The locals known to be working with the Kempeitai included those of Chinese, Eurasian as well as Indian ethnicities. In Taiping, the Brothers were denounced by a Malay to the Japanese for helping a communist, while in Penang, a Malay testified on behalf of Father Rouhan, allowing the Superior to escape arrest.

The notion of 'Penangites' – as people living on the same island or belonging to the same Straits Settlement – was apparently absent. Likewise, the notion of 'Malayan' was hardly anywhere to be seen. It was only in 1945 that the term 'Malayans' was applied to seminarians from the Malacca mission (Malaya). This was mentioned on 12 February, 2 October, and 8 December 1945, and again on 9 August 1946. Heralding the beginning of a new era, the term was endorsed by the announcement in British Parliament, made on 10 October 1945, of the creation of the Malayan Union.

After almost four years of war, the differences between Chinese, Eurasians, Indians and Malays paled in comparison with their common human condition of exhaustion and hunger. 'Semua orang lapar', noted Father Rouhan in July 1945.

Education and Religion

As an institution that was both educational and religious, the College General was in a unique position to observe the Japanese administration's intentions on educational and religious matters, and the evolution of their policy during the occupation.

The studies at the Seminary were never interrupted, apart from the normal holiday breaks. The main difference was that only part-time study was possible, as half of the Community's time was devoted to agricultural activities.

It is important to note that throughout the duration of war, religious practice never ceased in the Seminary, whether at Mariophile or Pulau Tikus. Daily masses were never interrupted. Even when Penang was being bombed, the liturgical calendar was strictly observed; only the scale of the celebration was sometimes affected. Even Ordinations were celebrated. The Fathers were never short of flour and wine to celebrate the Holy Mysteries during mass.

After the departure of the Community to Mariophile in early December 1941, the College General in Pulau Tikus was left empty. It was not possible for such a building to stay vacant for long. The first ones to make use of it were the Infant Jesus Sisters, back from Singapore. As their Convent buildings had been requisitioned by the Japanese Navy, the Sisters started to utilise the College General's ground floor classrooms as a warehouse. They were soon joined by the Lasallian Brothers, as the St Xavier's Institution premises had been similarly occupied. By June, the Infant Jesus Sisters started to hold some classes in the College General. Taking advantage of the situation, the Japanese soon arranged for the government girl's school to move into the premises.

In June 1942, the Japanese authorities held an 'ecclesiastical conference' with all Christian denominations (Catholics as well as Protestants), to set out the rules for the religious observances. It was compulsory to raise the Japanese flag in front of the church upon request. Sermons would have to be submitted in advance. The authorities would always send a representative to attend the services. Under these conditions, the Missionaries were permitted to carry on.

A few months later, in September, Father Rouhan noted the teaching difficulties encountered by the Brothers and Sisters in Perak. They were not allowed to teach as they used to or wear religious dress in government school. They were required to become secular teachers. The premises of the Ipoh Convent school were taken over by a military school. Interestingly, Father Rouhan observed that Japanese policies towards the schools in the South (KL) and the North (Perak and Penang) appeared rather different, and surmised that the implementation in each case reflected the preferences of the individual officer in charge.

In October, the Catholics became seriously worried to discover the cement crosses at the Assumption Church and at the Light Street Convent shattered by the Japanese occupiers. In early 1943, the Community's policy of 'religion first' in Catholic education was abandoned. The Sisters were not allowed to teach catechism anymore, nor were the Brothers allowed to teach in Latin. By April, the Sisters and Brothers had to take Japanese language exams, and those who failed were replaced by secular teachers. The conflict peaked when the Japanese tried to take over the College General by dislodging the Sisters. Brothers, Fathers and Sisters united to oppose the move by threatening to appeal to the Pope in Rome. The proposal was eventually abandoned, but Brother Paul and Sister Rose were replaced as directors with a Chinese Methodist headmaster, who was relatively well disposed towards them. The Japanese consequently increased the number of government school classes in the College General.

In May, the Japanese for the first time requested a detailed report on the College General. Later, they met with the heads of all the religious training institutions. In August, boys were admitted to the government school. With 1,000 students, it became one of the four biggest schools in Penang.

Then, it was the Seminary's turn to be in trouble. On 5 January 1944, the College General received a visit from the Japanese Head of Education. He highlighted three complaints: the students did not speak enough Japanese, local time was still used, and the Indian students had not yet enlisted in the Indian National Army. The Fathers were asked to cooperate even if they preferred to be apolitical. The Head of Education reasoned that, as politics had now assumed a different meaning, the Fathers should cooperate for the sake of 'world peace'. He further proposed that, henceforth, Japanese officers should give lessons on the meaning of the 'Great Asian War', Japanese language classes should be held for two hours per week, and that outside speakers should be received from time to time. The Fathers adopted Tokyo time and generally agreed to these three proposals. They started teaching Japanese for 15 minutes a day, but this was discontinued well before the end of war. The two other demands were never implemented.

In February 1945, Japanese pressure became more urgent. They asked for a new report on the Seminary. A few days later, they requested the use of more classrooms for the government school in Pulau Tikus, which was indeed unnecessary because the number of students had fallen from 1,000 to 500, and then to 300 in March. At times, no more than 50 children attended classes. Finally, on 11 February, Mariophile had to be totally evacuated as the Navy wanted to occupy the Tanjung

Bungah site. The Community moved back to Pulau Tikus. The College General then accommodated three schools in one: a Sister's Convent school, a government school and a Catholic Seminary.

The following month, the situation eased up. Brothers and Sisters were teaching alongside lay teachers and school mistresses. The 500 students of the government school were mostly occupied with activities such as singing, physical exercise, and gardening. On 23 June, the Japanese war administration's Department for Religion and Education organised a meeting with the Catholics and Protestants at the College General to better understand the various beliefs. It turned out to be essentially a courtesy call limited to the visit of the chapel instead of a genuine exchange of views.

Things seemed to get worse till the end of 1944, before getting better afterwards. The College General in Pulau Tikus sheltered a government school for most of the war, and for three years the Seminary had to operate elsewhere. But as the Fathers maintained good relations – on the one side with the Brothers and the Sisters, and on the other side with the Japanese administration – the MEP never lost total control over the use of the College General premises.

The Danger and the Piety

Ever since their arrival in Siam, the French missionaries were expected not to interfere with local politics. Before the war, the Bishop of Malacca Monseigneur Devals had rolled out the road map for the Priests: 'Don't forget that we are not politicians but missionaries: we are not working for one nation or another, but for the King in Heaven.'

Yet it was difficult for the Missionaries to hide their sentiments. Father Rouhan, who was an officer during WWI, used the term 'Boche' – a derogatory French word for a German person – in the Diary. In a letter dated early 1941, Father Ouillon, in charge of the Procure in Singapore, wrote to Father Rouhan: 'We place our hope in the English victory… What will happen to us if Hitler is victorious?'

By staying behind and continuing to operate the Seminary under Japanese occupation, did the French Fathers thus become collaborators? Collaboration with the occupying force, instead of resistance, could be considered traitorous. Indeed, the line between passive resistance and passive collaboration can be rather thin. Any assessment of the morality of the collaborative action has to take into account the situation and timing. Having a cup of coffee with a Japanese officer might be construed as warming up to the enemy, but not if the motive is to ensure the survival of one's young charges. In order to avoid harassment, it was necessary to nurture good relations with the Catholic Japanese visitors, who were often high-ranking officers. It was necessary to pay courtesy visits to the Education Department as well as the Police for the sake of safeguarding the Institution. Maintaining good relations with Captain S. Hidaka, who lived next door to the Novitiate, was probably the best 'investment' made by the Fathers. After all, he was the Chief of Staff to the Penang Admiral of the Imperial Japanese Navy.

The situation was complicated for French nationals, who were merely 'guests' in Malaya. They had never considered Malaya their homeland. Furthermore, they had no sympathy for the Germans who occupied their country. They depended on the 'French State', headed by Marshal Pétain who let the Japanese station their troops in Indochina before the invasion of Malaya. By the end of the war, the 'French State' was a puppet controlled by Germany, while Indochina had been taken over by the Japanese. By mid-1944, the emergence of the Provisional Government of the French Republic headed by General de Gaulle further complicated the matter of their allegiance.

For the sake of sanity, the missionaries often resorted to resistance. This often took passive forms, like forgetting to learn Japanese or not following Tokyo time, and finally stopping Japanese language classes in early 1945. Fathers, Brothers and Sisters also engaged in active resistance in April 1943 when, faced with the prospect of losing the College General, they opposed the Japanese decision to take over the College General and threatened to appeal to the Pope. The Japanese finally backed off.

Once the Japanese occupation ended, the pressure was off. Neither the British, nor the Communists ever came to bother the College General, which goes to prove that the behaviour of the French Fathers was never compromised. On 23 June 1946, the *Sunday Gazette* carried an article on the Fathers who had stayed on throughout the occupation, helping to uphold social morality and public morale.

As the Diary shows, religious practice never ceased at the College General, in spite of the difficulties and obstacles put forth by the Japanese authorities. With a strong body of belief and a precise liturgical calendar embedded in their way of life, the Fathers and their students found the strength to carry on in their religious faith. At the end of his report to Paris, dated 15 October 1945, Father Rouhan wrote: 'Danger was an impetus to piety, and the obvious necessity to implore succour from above helped to sustain fervour.'

By 1943, the 'religion first' policy became more and more difficult to practice. Yet the Fathers persevered in practicing all elements of their religion and persisted in training future priests – these acts in themselves could be understood as forms of resistance.

The times, they are a-changin'

The Japanese occupation would bring changes within as well as outside the Community, in Malaya and also in the world at large.

The arrival of the Sisters at first, then the Brothers, and finally the requisitioning of the building by the Japanese, would alter the way of life within the College General. For most of the duration of the war, the sanctity of the Seminary was preserved within the confines of Mariophile, but the situation changed once the Community moved back to Pulau Tikus in February 1945. When the College General became a Japanese government school, the premises were encroached upon by lay teachers and children from all walks of life. Once the College General was concurrently used as a convent, a school and a seminary, it was no longer possible to avoid encounters between Catholics and lay persons. The building layout allowed students and directors to live separately, but light screens, serving as temporary partitions, were too thin to stop the noise. 'The commotion and cries of these schoolchildren while we conduct our classes are quite tiresome,' wrote Father Rouhan on 18 April 1945.

The most important novelty for the College General was the gender mix. For the first time, women were allowed into the College General. They were the Infant Jesus Sisters who were not only teaching, but also living and cooking in the College General. It was noted in the Diary entry of 8 April:

> The Sisters are bolder and move more freely in the ground floor of our quarters than before, even after dinner in the evening, although they were asked to leave this area after the end of the student's Prayer, immediately after supper... Fortunately, the war is progressing fast and we can expect a close end to the abnormal situation in which we find ourselves in the College. Without this perspective, it would be necessary to react against this promiscuity at dusk. Students are always instructed not to go into the courtyard at all, especially in the evenings.

One way in which the Sisters brought change to the College General, and for the better, was through their cooking. First, they cooked for the Fathers, then they cooked for the Brothers as well. The Fathers then asked them to come back to cook after the war, while awaiting the return of a Chinese chef.

Besides the Sisters, Father Rouhan also mentioned the girls in the Sisters' charge:

> The girls at the Convent were instructed not to come into the kitchen area after the students' supper. For Easter, they were allowed to come and help the Sisters who are doing the clearing up after the end of our meal. So, they came over and continued to do so for several days until the Reverend Mother called them to order.

Young female students of the government school were performing their Swedish gymnastic movements in the courtyard every morning. Father Rouhan lamented: 'Our students, who are, at this time, taking a break (between end of lunch and beginning of work in the garden) enjoy watching this from the verandah of the fourth dormitory.' And a few days later: In the courtyard, many girls, who are already twenty years old, are doing choreographic exercises which may not be of very high quality, but do not leave our seminarists indifferent'. Father Rouhan summarised the problem, not only for the seminarists, but perhaps for the directors as well:

> During the class, the pupils of the school go up and down almost continually by the staircase of the *locutorium*, from which the location of our class is separated only by a series of screens. And the laughter, the calls of all these young girls, the sweet smells of schoolgirls, penetrate our atmosphere and constitute a very unusual atmosphere for our Theology lessons.

The war also brought another adjustment to the College General's traditions, with regards to the holidays. During each break, Seminarists and directors used to go out together to Mariophile, the country house. As the Community was now staying in Mariophile, there was nowhere to go for holidays and, anyhow, they could not abandon their husbandry. For the first time in the seminary's history, the College General allowed the Malayan students to go home during the holidays.

Another change in store for the College General in particular, and for the Catholic church in general, was the removal of the expatriate leadership. However, this statement needs to be qualified. All the other Christian denominations had their leadership removed after the arrival of the Japanese, as their clergy were sent to Changi for the duration of the war. This was not the case for the Catholic church, which was mainly under French leadership. For the period of the war, all seven directors of the College General were European (one Belgian and six French). On Penang Island, out of five Parishes, only one, the Chinese parish of Our Lady of Seven Sorrows on Macalister Road, had a local priest (Father Koh). The College General requested Monseigneur Devals to send a local priest to take over the direction of the Seminary, in case all the foreign directors were arrested. The arrival of Father Aloysius was a sign that it was time to prepare local priests for a leadership succession. In 1954, the MEP enumerated 60 foreign priests, as compared to 44 locals, to serve in the new Ecclesiastical Province (Singapore–Malaya). The upheaval experienced by the College General during the war was an indication of the times to come.

'A wind of independence is sweeping through the empire,' wrote Father Rouhan on 23 February 1946. As early as January 1946, after the December break, life at the College General had returned to normal. On the surface, it appeared as if nothing had happened. But nobody would ever forget that the 'White Man' had been defeated and had betrayed the people. In Malaya, as well in the rest of the world, new powers were at play. The winds of change were blowing, whispers were growing stronger, and new concepts like nationalism and communism were emerging. Things would never be the same again.

'Father Denarié remains at the Assumption Church in the midst of the falling bombs and composes poems in his shelter while waiting.'

– Father Rouhan, 13 January 1945.

The Diary

September 1938 – September 1946

During most of the war, the College General relocated to their country house in Tanjung Bungah. Their property in Pulau Tikus was occupied by the Infant Jesus Sisters' Convent and by a Government girls' school. In 1945, as the Japanese Navy took over Mariophile to build their defences, the College General, an all-male institution, came back to Pulau Tikus and shared the premises.

The Diary

1938

September 29
An agreement that must remain secret is signed between the College and the Government through Mr Regester of the firm Hogan & Allan, which takes care of our interests. By this verbal covenant, it is agreed upon that the Government can, without further notice, make temporary installations, as would be necessary for the defence of the island, on our land at Mariophile by the seaside, near the *Tokong* and in all the space between the *Tokong*, the two houses built in 1938, the road and the sea. It is understood that these are only temporary installations and, without a new agreement, permanent installations cannot be made. The Government will reimburse the damage done to the coconut trees.

1939

April 10
Departure of the Community to Mariophile for the holidays. In Mariophile, under the terrace in front of the Chapel, a trench is made to see if the construction of a bomb shelter would be possible in case of war.

August 12
Departure of the Community to Mariophile.

September 3
Declaration of war. Nobody moves until the orders arrive.

September 9
The Community returns to the College.

September 10
Return of Mg Htun Lin from Mandalay – he was on medical leave since December 12, 1936. He returned to 2nd year of Theology, and will have to stay two terms after those of his year (August 1942).

September 11
Departure of Tshoa Thaddeus from Swatow, he leaves at his own request. Tonsured, 4th year of Theology. The money for his return to Swatow is given to him.

September 13
Medical examination of the College Fathers who may be called to join the armed forces. The Doctor declares unfit Fathers Monjean, Piffaut and Meissonnier. Father Paroissin is declared fit.

September 17
Ordination by Monseigneur Devals: four Sub-deacons, fourteen Minored, twelve Tonsured.

September 18
Ordination by Monseigneur Devals: two Deacons.

September 19
Departure of Joseph Vong, Layman, 1st year of Philosophy, from Malacca, withdrawing himself, he leaves his books behind.

September 23
Priestly Ordination of Denys Tsin in Lanlung.

October 1
A typhoid epidemic causes us to vaccinate the Community.

October 9
The French Consul of Singapore announces that all the Missionaries are provisionally exempted from conscription.

October 11
Second injection against typhoid.

Mid-October
The renovation of the College's roofs (central building and two wings, except the Chapel, already renovated in 1933–1934) is completed.

October 21–25
Visit to the College by Father Gérard, representative of the Missions of Korea and Manchuria.

November 28

The Georgetown *Municipal Commissioners' Meeting* accepts the Surrender by the College Trustees of the land required for the construction of North Beach Road on the beach in front of the College, and of the land on which is the access road from Kelawei Road to the College, and undertakes to maintain this road in the same condition as the neighbouring roads. The College has an authentic copy of the minutes of this meeting.

December 4

Ordination by Monseigneur Devals of two Priests (Francis Chan and Innocent Fernandez), two Deacons, four Acolytes, one Reader and one Tonsured.

December 5

Departure of Franciscus [*sic*] Chan and Innocent Fernandez, Priests.

December 7

Departure of De Rozario, Acolyte from Malacca, leaving on probation, his studies completed; of Austin, 1st year of Theology, Layman from Malacca, withdrawing himself for an indefinite length of time, for health reasons, he takes his books away.

December 8

Departure of Bunthan from Laos, Acolyte, leaving on probation, his studies completed; of Tekyung from Bangkok, Layman, leaving on probation, his studies completed.

December 9

Departure of Paul Tien from Saigon, Acolyte, his studies completed; of Mascarenhas and Sequeira, from Rangoon, Deacons; of Pereira, from Rangoon, Layman, on probation, his studies completed; of Laurentius, Layman from Toungoo, going on a year's medical leave, he will enter Special Theology on his return.

December 11

Departure of the Community to Mariophile. The Chinese students (six from Swatow and two from Nanning) whose courses are completed, cannot return to their missions (Swatow and Nanning are occupied by the Japanese, no one can embark from Hong Kong to Swatow, and the battle is raging in the vicinity of Nanning with the Chinese trying to recapture the town). These students come with the Community to Mariophile, waiting for instructions from their Missions.

December 21

Ordination in Rangoon of four Priests: Mascarenhas, Sequeira, Remyius and Raphael.

1940

January 10
Return to the College.

January 16
Arrival of three students from Thanh Hoa: Nghia Paulus, Thien, and Ton.
We begin the renovation of the floor in the second dormitory in Mariophile.

January 18
Arrival of Monseigneur Perros and Father Ferlay, who came for the preparatory meeting of the General Assembly.

January 26
Arrival of a Seminarist from Saigon, Nam.

February 11
Departure of Ambrosius from Rangoon, Layman, Philosophy, at his request.

March 1
End of the renovation of the floor in the second dormitory at Mariophile. Renovation of the roof begins in the third dormitory.

March 23
Departure of Kwang Tsi, from Swatow, Layman, 1st year of Theology, takes his books with him, expelled for moral misconduct.

March 24
Departure of Ly Dominicus, from Kontum, 2nd year of Philosophy, Layman, he leaves his books behind, expelled for moral misconduct.

March
Following a verbal agreement concluded with the Municipality in February 1939, whereby the *Trustees surrender* the land necessary for the establishment of the road (North Beach Road) along the sea, land delimited by *pegs* placed on the ground; and the Municipality agrees not to take more land for the construction of the road (even if the sea advanced before the completion of the road) as it is so demarcated; the Trustees of the College have signed the plans for the construction of this road to approve them.

[inserted noted] (see also November 28, 1939 and July 3, 1940)

At the same time, the *Trustees* have the assurance from the Municipality that the part of College Lane between Kelawei Road and the entrance to the College (two columns in front of the Procure) will become public road, and as such will be maintained by the Municipality as the neighbouring roads. Papers have been signed for this purpose.

April 7
Departure of Toan, Acolyte from Kontum.

April 8
The Community goes to Mariophile.

April
The *Land Office*, for the compulsory acquisition of part of the village of Tanjong Tokong, at the junction of the road that goes to the Police Station, granted 10,000 dollars to the College through our lawyer, Mr Conaghan. But at the moment, nothing has been signed, the money has not been paid, and everything is still unresolved.

May 4
The Community comes back to the College.

Departure of Arthur Paul, Layman from Mandalay, 2nd year of Theology, withdrawing himself. Not to be readmitted because of his intellectual insufficiency. He leaves his books behind.

End of the very exceptional drought that lasted almost without interruption since the month of December.

It is decided that Father Piffaut, depressed as a result of a flu with sinusitis and bronchitis, will go to rest, first in Cameron Highlands and then to the Nilgiris until September.

May 20
Renovation completed, of the roof in the third dormitory at Mariophile. Transformation begins of the third dormitory into a *lavarium* and *fabrica* downstairs, and upstairs, a bookbinding studio, a drying room and a store.

May 22
Father Piffaut embarks for Madras, en route to the Nilgiris.

May 25
Departure of Joannes Mg Nyunt, from South Burma, Layman, 2nd year of Philosophy, returned to his family with the agreement of the Apostolic Vicar, due to the illegitimate and insufficient reasons given to justify irregularity.

May
The Municipality begins the construction work of a sea wall in front of the College to stop the advance of the sea.

[inserted note] (see above, March 1940).

June
The Government, which had for several months signified its intention to buy the land we were previously renting to it near the Tanjong Tokong Malay School, says it doesn't want to buy it anymore.

June 25
Armistice.

June 27
Departure of Peter, Layman from Malacca, Theology, eliminated in agreement with Monseigneur Devals, for insufficiency in his studies and inaptitude of character. He leaves his books behind.

July 3
The Municipality decides, because of the war, to postpone the construction of the seaside road in front of the College and to build, for the time being, the *sea wall* intended to stop the advance of the sea. Works have already started for this wall.

[inserted note] (see above, March 1940)

July
The Resident summons Father Michel to request that the College agree to an arrangement with the Chinese Swimming Club, to sell the land where the C.S.C. currently stands, to allow the construction of better facilities. Father Michel says that there is little hope of being able to sell land at this place, but perhaps another place could be considered. Nothing is decided, but the Resident says that he will send a Chinese from the C.S.C to see Father Michel. [Inserted note] Up to September, no one has come yet.

August 2
Departure of two students from Saigon, Loc, Reader, 4th year of Theology, recalled by his mission because of the external situation; Nohm, Layman, 1st year of Theology, sent back to his Mission for a long rest because of tuberculosis, he takes his books away.

The washroom, the drying room, the carpentry and bookbinding workshops in the building where the third dormitory used to be (closed because of the decline in the number of students) are put into service.

August 8
Departure of Wong Joannes from Malacca, giving up his studies, 1st year of Philosophy, Layman, leaves his books behind.

September 15
Ordination by Monseigneur Devals, two Sub-deacons, fifteen Minored, four Tonsured.

September 16
Ordination by Monseigneur Devals, one Deacon.

September 24
Departure of Mg Chit Suve, Layman from Mandalay, 2nd year of Philosophy, giving up his studies, leaves his books behind.

October 11
Departure of Seng Li, Layman from Swatow, 2nd year of Philosophy, withdrawing at the request of his Bishop because of his insufficiency in studies (takes his books away).

October 17
Departure of Godeuho, Layman from Mandalay, 1st year of Philosophy, withdrawing himself, leaves his books behind.

October 31
Date of *endorsement*, based on the College *Trust* Act, of a *compulsory acquisition* by the Government, for 10,000 dollars of land located in Tanjong Tokong, between the main road, the road of the Police Station and the former high-tide limit in the bay reclaimed by the Government in 1939 and 1940. This land becomes *Crown Land* and is intended primarily for the establishment of a road connecting the old main road to the reclaimed land. The land area is 2 acres, 0 roods and 21 poles.

End of October–November
The Municipality works on the road linking the College to Kelawei Road (Extended College Lane), in execution of the agreement mentioned in February 1939 and March 1940 above.

November 8
Father Piffaut returns from the Nilgiris.

November 13
Departure of Goh from Malacca on medical leave for two months.

November 19
Departure of Albanus, 1st year of Philosophy, from Rangoon, takes his books away.

He has leprosy.

December 3
Ordination of one Priest, De Rozario from Malacca, one Deacon and one Tonsured. Reconstruction works, of the sacristy behind the altar in the College chapel, starts.

December 5
Departure of five students from Rangoon: Anselmus, Deacon, he carries his books away; Ko Min, Leo, Robertus and Romanus Laymen, 1st year of Philosophy, returning to their mission, *ad tempus*, to perfect their preparation, they take their books away, and must bring them back when they return. They have left their mosquito nets with their names attached (with the Procureur). When they come back, we shall see if it is necessary to make them restart their 1st year of Philosophy, at which they were practically hopeless, except for Ko Min who was better than the other three.

December 6
Departure of a student from Sarawak, Acolyte, his studies finished, he takes his books away, and of two students from Malacca, Lek and Tan Antonius, Laymen, going on probation, their studies finished, they take their books away.

December 8
Departure of Joseph from Malacca, Tonsured, giving up studies, he leaves his books behind.

December 9
The Community goes to Mariophile. End of the renovation work in Mariophile, of the lower part of the second dormitory.
Departure of Tai from Pakhoi, Acolyte, his studies finished, he takes his books away.

December 10
Departure of Nghu Antonius from Kontum, Layman, his studies finished, takes his books away.

December 14
Departure of Scriven, Acolyte, his studies finished, and of Camillus, Layman, his studies finished, both of Mandalay. They take their books away.

December 16
Departure of Nicolaus from Malacca, Tonsured, leaving the Seminary and the Mission, seeking to be admitted in another Mission. He takes his books away.

End of December
Installation of the new marble altar in the College Chapel.

December 21
Ordination of Anselmus, in Rangoon.

1941

January
Following the death of the old seamstress, Josephine, R.I.P., a servant is installed as a tailor in the College. The Fathers continue to pay for the making and repair of their clothes, although the tailor is paid monthly and not by the piece. The tailor is installed in a room next to the laundry room.

Following the retirement of Ah Kong, old cook and factotum who gave some 40 years of service to the College, a new system is introduced. A servant (Hin Voon) is the chief, responsible for all the servants; he has another servant as number two; one or the other must always be there. They are the only ones qualified to make purchases, place and receive orders. A system of *chits* with a counterfoil book is introduced under the control of the Procureur. Our supplier in Pulau Tikus is committed to deliver to us at the market price all that he currently has in stock. Deliveries of meat and fish will be made to the College by the suppliers. We do not go anymore to town every morning, like Ah Kong used to do, but from time to time one of the two *Kapalas* goes to town in the morning to see the prices and make special purchases. The College's *car* does not go anymore to town in the morning – when a servant goes there, he uses the trolley bus and he comes back with a rickshaw.

Pension arrangement with Ah Kong, he had to choose between two proposals. He opted for the following arrangement. As long as Ah Kong lives, he will receive a pension of 30 dollars a month. He continues to live in the house of the College that he occupied at the end of his services, for a nominal fee of $0.05 per month. He cannot sublet this house. In addition, as long as he has children going to school, he receives a temporary allowance of $5 (five dollars) per month.

January 6
Arrival of six students (including five from Toungoo). Laurentius, coming back after one year of medical leave, with four new, Gabriel, Martinus, Romanus and Vincentus from Mandalay.

January 8
The Community returns to the College.

Arrival of Goh from Malacca returning after two months of medical leave, of Lambert and Paschal, new Seminarians from Malacca.

Late January
Reverend Father Mc Carthy, co-founder and Visitor of the Maynooth Society for China, on his way to Bhamo, visits the Mission. He stays at the Novitiate and comes to visit the College.

January 22
Priestly Ordination in Quinhou of Toan (Dominicus) from Kontum.

Beginning of February
The international political situation seems to have become dangerous for Malaya. All institutions are invited to prepare for passive defence against air raids. As a result, groups of students are being trained in the fight against fires and incendiary bombs; works to build shelters began at Mariophile (shelters under large rocks on the Hill, trenches between the house and the students' water spring on the slope below the kitchen). We prepare ourselves for a sudden relocation to Mariophile, and maybe even to St Jean, if the circumstances require it.

February 8
Ordination in Swatow of six priests: Bak Khue, Kiang Lip, Neng Tsoang, Te Yong Joseph and Yong Thaddeus.

March 9
Departure of Pascheparambil from Mandalay, Tonsured, 3rd year of Theology, sent back for serious disciplinary infraction. He leaves his books behind and remains, temporally at least, in Malaya.

March 19
Priestly Ordination of Joseph Liao in Nanning.

April 12
News from Laos suggests that one of the Seminarians there on probation (Khan? Bunthan? Yandi?) was killed, out of hatred for the faith, after refusing to apostatise. Some Siamese Priests could also be imprisoned.

April 13
Departure of Augustinus from Mandalay, sent back for lack of intellectual ability (Layman, 1st year of Theology, he leaves his books behind). He remains (temporally at least) in Malaya.

April 14
The Community goes for holidays to Mariophile.
During the holidays, we continue the work on passive defence in Mariophile. The town and the surrounding areas are full of European and Indian soldiers. Military cars and *lorries* are constantly driving around.

And the works which began over a year ago to fortify the outskirts of the town (defence line with barbed wires and *pill-boxes* in the Chinese cemetery between Bagan Jermal and Tanjong Tokong, along the entire length of the beach, and also on top of Mount Erskine and in many parts of the island) continue actively for the realisation of the Penang Fortress.

The price of rice has risen considerably. We no longer have rice from Siam. Petrol for cars is rationed.

The general blackout drills are repeated several times for the entire population. We fear a Japanese attack through Thailand and by sea at the same time.

May 10

The Community returns to the College. Classes normally resume on the 11th.

End of the reconstruction work of the small sacristy of the College Chapel, behind the altar, with two small side chapels and two new altars.

June 29

Priestly Ordination of Longimus Tai in Pakhoi.

July

Beginning of sermons in the refectory during the 11:30 meal.

August 8

Departure to Mariophile.

August 17

Father Meissonnier, suffering from malaria, leaves for Cameron Highlands on medical leave for three months.

August–September

The preparatory works for shelters in case of air raid continue during the holidays.

September 1

Change of legal time, advanced 10 minutes.

September 6

Back to College. As the recent advance of standard time (10 minutes) added to the advance of 20 minutes made in 1933, brings – in relation to the daylight – an advance of half-hour, we again shift the entire schedule by half-hour, and the life of the Community is back in the same position, relative to the day and the night, as in 1933.

September 14

Great Ordination.

September 15
Ordination to the Diaconate.

October 5
Departure of Joseph Trong from Bui Chu, Deacon, returning to his Mission before the end of the year because of the external situation.

October 27
Departure of five students from Burma, Joseph Fernandez, Sub-deacon, Stephanus, Acolyte, Felix, Layman, Hieronymus from Toungoo and Eustachius from Mandalay. All five returning to their Missions after completing their studies, a little before the end of the year, because of fears of hostilities at short notice in the region.

November 21
Priestly Ordination of Joseph Fernandez in Rangoon.

A letter from Father Lobez, prisoner of war in Germany, arrives unexpectedly. The Father is fine, in a camp in Bonn.

December 2
Ordination of four Deacons.

December 3
Ordination of five Priests, Lek and Tan from Malacca, Sien, Kimhang and Ra from Bangkok and eleven Tonsured.

Departure of Norris, Acolyte from Malacca, his studies finished.

December 4
Departure of Lambert (brother of the former), Layman, 1st year of Philosophy, withdrawing himself (he leaves his books behind).

December 5
Abrupt departure of the Community to Mariophile because of the imminent danger of hostilities with Japan. A *State of Emergency* was declared a few days ago, with general mobilization.

Departure of four students from Bangkok, Kimhang, Ra and Sien, all three Priests, and Juang, Layman, 2nd year of Philosophy, withdrawing himself, he leaves his books behind, and one student from Laos (temporarily under the jurisdiction of Monseigneur Pasotte, Apostolic Vicar of Rajaburi), as well as Inthi, Deacon, his studies completed, and one from Malacca, Wee, Acolyte, his studies completed. In fact, these students took the last train from Penang to Siam.

December 6
The war with Japan appearing imminent, everything has been prepared in Mariophile for this eventuality.

December 7
Around 22:00, the batteries of the island have discharged a few rounds of gunfire. There was no blackout that night in Penang.

December 8
At the beginning of the Community Mass, we hear the Japanese air raid on Sungei Petani, where we see a thick smoke rising. We say, this time it is for real. A few small attacks follow one another, on Butterworth and the Bayan Lepas Airfield. We reach for the shelters during the alert. From this day onwards, blackout every night.

December 9 and 10
Repeated alerts, fighting between Japs and English fighters, over Butterworth, four Japanese shot down. In town, nobody cares [about danger], the people gather on the Esplanade to see the dogfights between planes.

The life in Mariophile continues as usual, the races to the shelters during the alerts, the work and the blackout. We get up at the usual time, we sup at 18:00, followed by rosary and evening prayer at 19:30, then bed *ad libitum* (obligatory at 21:30). A watch is organised, the students share the night between three groups of three. In addition, there is always a team *contra incendium* on standby. At the College, we dug a shelter nearby the toilets, where Fathers Michel and Piffaut are staying.

December 11
Black Day for Malaya. English naval disaster on the East coast. (Prince of Wales and Repulse sunk).

A little after 9:00, the city of Penang is seriously bombarded by air. Father Michel in town, at this moment, takes refuge in the shelter of the presbytery of the Assumption Church; bombs fall on Love Lane, the Brothers' St Xavier's Institution *padang*, near the Convent, among other places. The Japs machine-gun the streets. The Mercantile Bank is hit by a bomb. The stained-glass windows of the Assumption Church are shattered. The priest's house (Father Dérédec in the absence of Father Souhait resting in Cameron Highlands) is terribly rattled and becomes dangerous to inhabit. Around 9:30, Father Koh brings to Mariophile the Blessed Sacrament and three orphans; at the end of the raid, he goes back to see the wounded. Father Michel at this point does not find his *car* at the place where he left it, but the *driver* is safe and has run away. The *car* is not damaged although a bomb fell very close to it. After taking the *car* back to the College in the afternoon, the *driver* disappeared. He was severely concussed.

Other alerts at the beginning of the afternoon. The market (Chowrasta) has been hit, as well as the houses on stilts in the port, and we are talking about two hundred killed. In the evening, from Mariophile we see big fires in the city. Six hundred European women and children are evacuated from Penang.

December 12
No more bread, bakery employees having fled.

Between 9:00 and 12:30, successive raids, a plane is shot between the College and the town. No bombs at Pulau Tikus. The defence, with anti-aircraft batteries, almost absent at the beginning, starts to be organised and starts to fire back, joined by the English fighters.

December 13
Several raids during the day. It is said that five Japanese planes were shot down. Less damage this time.

A Christian died on the *estate*, no way to transport him to the cemetery, he is buried near the Malay cemetery.

December 14
Sunday, everything is quiet until the end of lunch at 12:30. At this moment, a big Japanese formation appears, greeted with cannon shots. We go to the shelters. The formation turns to another direction.

In town, we are just starting to get organised but, up till now, there is the looting, [which is] allowed for food. In Tanjong Tokong, the police have disappeared, and the inhabitants stop the vehicles coming from town and take all the goods they can find.

The Sisters are all leaving for Balik Pulau. Low Mass early morning and blessing at 15:30. Father Koh takes refuge in Mariophile.

December 15
Monday, the shooting gets closer, in Kedah.

The Brothers, who were up in the hills,[1] are ordered to come down because we fear an attack by paratroopers, and we do not want them to get stranded.

We are talking about bringing all Europeans together.

In the morning, several alerts. In the evening, the island's guns shoot at the Japanese who are already closing in.

Father Paroissin comes back to the Community.

December 16
The Japanese are said to be in the south of Kedah (infiltrations). The island's guns frequently fire towards the Province [Province Wellesley]. Besides that, it is the beginning of a quiet day, no air raid alert. In the evening, it is said that Penang was

---

1   This refers to the Hermitage on Penang Hill, owned by the MEP. It was bought over by De La Salle Brothers, who named it 'Mount Sacred Heart'. They extended it and turned it into a retreat house, known as the 'Christian Brothers' Bungalow', and built a large dormitory with a chapel on the upper floor.

declared an Open City by the English; likewise, Hong Kong. Everywhere we hear explosions from the destruction which the English are carrying out before leaving. No more electric power.

The students use a handcart to move some of the things from the College, to bring them to Mariophile.

The *Penang Gazette*[2] publisher, Mr Saravanamuttu, takes charge, waiting for the arrival of the Japanese. Catholic Eurasian Jockey Ivan Allan and two Japanese civilians, formerly interned but since released, leave by boat for Sungei Petani to contact the Japanese command.

December 17

In the morning, many people return to town, believing the danger to be over. The students try to go fishing.

Around 11:30, a strong Japanese air force bombards the Chulia Street area. Many are killed, including the boy and the gardener of Father Souhait, in the latter's *car*, which is burned. Two Christians are also killed. Again, the exodus of those who had returned to town.

In the evening, the students make a new trip to the College to bring a few things back to Mariophile.

It is said that the Japanese bombed again because the British flag had not been replaced by a white flag at the signal mast, or because of the gathering of English troops in town, getting ready to leave the island. In the evening, it is said that Japanese delegates are in town and ordered a curfew from 18:00.

December 18

The looting in town continued today.

Good fishing by the students in the evening.

The supply of food is not bad.

Japanese troops are expected to arrive in town from one moment to the next. But around 10:30, a Japanese air raid is conducted on the city (Lorong Slamat district).

Around noon, the planes throw leaflets. Some land at Mariophile.

Since yesterday, Father Piffaut has decided to sleep at Mariophile, and Father Michel at Pulau Tikus with Fathers Souhait and Baloche. The College remains deserted at night. There is not much left to take anyway. Father Michel has brought a lot of things here after several trips with his car.

During the midday rest, the planes come around again but it is a false alert. Some, however, have run to the shelters.

---

2   The *Penang Gazette* was first published in 1838 as *Pinang Gazette*. It was bought over in 1939, (together with Ipoh's *Times of Malaya*, started in 1904) by the *Straits Echo*. (established in 1903). The *Straits Echo* (known later as *The National Echo*) became the biggest newspaper in North Malaya. Years before it closed in 1986, it was eclipsed by *The Star*, started in 1971.

Guards were formed by the Government Committee[3] to stop the looting. Father Dérédec, sick, takes refuge in the College.

[Hand-written note added in the top right corner of the page] The Pinang Gazette will mention several thousands of deaths which were caused by bombing during these days

Notice [4]

1. The Japanese Armed Forces wishes to share the well-beings with the officials and peoples of the native land.

   Wait the arrivals of the Japanese troops with confidence and ease. Regardless of the nationality, no one is necessary to flee.

2. Making resistance or taking the hostile actions against the Japanese Armed Forces, in any manner, leads the whole native land in ashes. Therefore, everyone should come under the protection of the Japanese Armed Forces without seeing even one drop of blood, and should continue daily business as usual.

3. Anyone who falls under the any of the followings will be considered as the interfering of the well-beings of the native people, and therefore be subject to the death penalty. Be aware of not committing any of said crimes.

   (1) Those who show hostility against the Japanese Armed Forces.

   (2) Those who jeopardize or break any existing means in politics, economics, industry, transportation, communication, financials, and etc.

   (3) Those who disturb the thoughts of the officials and peoples.

   (4) Any actions disturbing the economic and financial status.

   Those who report to the Japanese Forces of any flagrant offense or preventing of any said crime will be rewarded by the Japanese Armed Forces.

Commander-in-Chief

The Japanese Armed Forces

---

3 The Penang Service Committee was formed on 17 December by a group of civil leaders who met at no. 10, Scott Road. It was composed of three representants of the four different communities (Chinese, Eurasian, Indian, and Malay) and headed by Mr. Saravanamuttu, editor of the Straits Echo. They released the Japanese civilians who were jailed and used the radio station to ask the Japanese to stop bombing Penang. They also formed a Volunteer Police with the Penang Volunteer Corps to maintain order.

4 Printed notice dropped by plane on 18 December, in original English, inserted in the Diary. A hand note points out there are three other versions, most probably in three other languages.

December 19

Passes are required to transport possessions from the town to the countryside. In Bagan Jermal, luggage is stopped and belongings of those who do not have a pass are searched.

In the morning, two Fathers and twelve students, according to our previous agreement with Doctor Baboo in charge of the hospital, go there to treat the wounded. But upon arrival, a counterorder was given, some of the doctors disagreed and we returned to Mariophile. The students go fishing and, in the evening, bring a load of goods from the College.

Robberies continue all around Mariophile. The Penang Swimming Club, Dr McKern's house, the New Springtide are looted. We enter the house of Mr Hansen, our tenant by the seaside, and we remove several things. At the request of Mr Hansen, we will keep watch until he instates a *jaga*.

In the evening, it is said that the Japanese arrived in town, 300 or 500 soldiers. In the morning, only the planes came and bombarded the other side of the channel.

December 20

Saturday, quiet morning. The students go fishing. At 10:30, confessions.

In the evening, we go with Mr Hansen to try to get a bit of flour. Our baker sends a bag to the College. He promises to send two to St Nicholas' Home, which Mr and Mrs Hansen are taking care of. These Danes sometimes come to Mariophile and share our meals.

A printed sheet of the Penang Service Committee described the fall of Hong Kong and gives us some news of the world. The battle zone in Malaya should be on the Krian River in the south of the Province.

December 21

Sunday. Order to Europeans not to leave their home. The Japanese authorities will see them at home.

No singing of Mass, only Blessing in the evening.

December 22

Monday, the students go fishing. We work in the vegetable garden under the direction of Father Denarié.

December 23

Tuesday, we buy chickens and we start a henhouse. Good fishing in the morning. Supply is sufficient.

The interdiction made to Europeans not to leave their homes is renewed. But Mr and Mrs Hansen get an armband each to move around.

Our servants are faithful at their job (there is food at home). To note that Koh Nhien and especially En Voon are doing to us the greatest services and will be rewarded when it is possible to do so.

The College's car is requisitioned, guns and daggers must be delivered before the 25th, subject to death penalty.

December 24
Wednesday, Christmas Eve. We do some preparations (the Crib) for Christmas. We continue the work in the garden and for the henhouse.

Eurasians must be registered.

Afternoon, singing class. In the evening at 17:30, procession of the Crib, a bit like what we used to do after supper on Christmas Eve. Nothing at night.

December 25
Thursday, Christmas, about thirty Christians, almost all Chinese from the neighbourhood, come to the Mass and approach the Sacraments.

Sung Mass at 8:30. Morning is quiet. We know nothing about what is happening on the Peninsula or in the rest of the world. Father Souhait was informed that in a few days we would be able to move around. Life is only slowly returning to town where dirt and stench prevailed before.

Masses are only held in Pulau Tikus and Ayer Hitam, to where Father Riboud of the Indian Church went, following the majority of his Christian refugees.

It is regrettable that the Sisters were forced to evacuate with the other Europeans.

We bought five goats and three kids for $120 to start rearing goats. Supply is enough. We have flour and we make *matefains* to replace the bread.

We learn that English prisoners are cleaning the town and repairing telephone communications. It is said that about 1,500 people were killed in Penang during the bombings. We can find bread again in town, the Danes bring us some.

December 26
Friday, quiet day. The works continue. Since there is no more electric power, the day begins at 6:10. We learn that two European Sisters remained in Balik Pulau with the children after the European Sisters were evacuated with the other Europeans.

December 27
Works continuation (hen house, goat barn, firewood) during the calm.

The Council considers the measures to be taken for the resumption of classes on January 8th. It is decided to cancel the basic course, and to do classes (two) in the morning or in the evening only, the other part of the day being occupied by various works, fishing etc. Dogma and Moral, alternately, and Philosophy every day (except Sundays) are the subjects of the main class. As for secondary subjects, only Sacred Scripture (three classes a week), Canon Law (one class), Liturgy (one class) and Singing (one class) are included. Sunday remains the day of rest (sung services and confession).

The supply remains very sufficient.

1942 (2602 Japanese era)

> [Handwritten note in English inserted in the Diary,
> about a conference of Major General Manaki
> on 2 January 1942 at Asdang House.]
>
> 4. Regarding former European houses and properties, a decision will be made later.
>
> 8. If you do not help the Nipponese, you may go to jail, property confiscated.
>
> 13. All houses and properties rented to Europeans or Government should be reported.
>
> 14. All properties entrusted by Europeans to anyone must be reported.
>
> 17. Any transaction in land or property before December 8, 1941 will be recognized but anything after the 8 December will not be recognized.

January 5

We buy from a Chinese *towkay* (son of Hen Say in Tanjung Bungah), who sells rice with permission and approval from the Japanese authority, ten bags of rice at $12.50.

January 8

Classes start again. We are very quiet in Mariophile. So far, the Japanese have not visited our house, but have come over two or three times by car by mistake, turning around at the top end of our cement road. Several servants spontaneously speak to us about planting vegetables.

Departure of Aemilius Fernandez, Acolyte from Malacca, leaving for probation after finishing his studies. Because of the events, he couldn't return to Sungei Petani in December.

January 13

The Japanese bomb and machine-gun the Penang hills, Bel Retiro, the Sacred Heart Convent, where a bomb sinks deeply near the Chapel without exploding, and the Sisters' country house in Ayer Hitam, where the Indian Priest is staying with his orphans.

A so-called Japanese soldier, in fact, an armed Chinese, came with some Malays and 'requisitioned' Father Monjean's motorcycle. They carried out a battue on the hill to find out if there were any hidden English soldiers.

January 17
Ordination in Singapore of two priests from Malacca, Norris and Wee.

January 18
A squad of Japanese soldiers carried out a battue again around the house for the same purpose.

January 20
Great event, Father Michel and Father Souhait get a pass from the Japanese authorities.

For the period since January 8, the supply is sufficient, but curry is missing from the menu! Rice is bought in sufficient quantity to maintain our provision.

Classes carry on according to the programme that was decided.

January 21
Great joy, visit of Father Michel who, with his pass, can now walk to Mariophile. He didn't come for a month or so. His pass is a rectangular paper, hung around his neck by a rope, with a red circle and a half-Chinese, half-Japanese inscription.

February 15
Fall of Singapore, there are no more free English except those who hide in the jungle.

March
Although Tokyo time is imposed as standard time (1:30 ahead of Singapore time), we keep the old time and follow the sun.

The Sisters, whose Convent is occupied in town by the Navy, come to the College to store some materials.[5] Several classes on the ground floor are filled with it.

March 5
Ordination of Hieronymus in Toungoo [inserted in pencil] (known only after the war).

March 10
Death of student Paul Tôn of Thanh Hoa, from typhoid fever, treated at the hospital since a week.

April 10
Father Meissonnier came back to the College. He went to Cameron Highlands for a rest on August 17, 1941, and was delayed in his return by the events. He is

---

5   On 14 December, the Diary mentions that the IJS are all leaving for Balik Pulau. On 25 and 26 December 1941, we learn that the European Sisters (except two) were 'forced' to evacuate earlier with the Europeans. However, in March, it is noted that 'the Sisters, whose Convent is occupied in town by the Navy, come to the College to store some material', meaning that they decided to come back to Penang after the fall of Singapore.

wearing a pass and an armband from the Japanese authorities. That's two of us at this point who have passes.

April 18

Oral exams and the end of the first trimester. The Community takes three weeks of vacation on site. Fathers start to risk going to the College from time to time. We are still uncertain if a pass is required for us. Impossible to know for sure.

Malaya resumes postal relations with foreign countries.

May 1

Death of Ah Kong, cook and factotum of the College, retired since the end of 1940.

We are able to receive some money from our agent in charge of collecting rental from our houses in Pulau Tikus, Tanjung Tokong and Tanjung Bungah.

May 10

We resume the trimester schedule and the classes start again on Monday, May 11. Father Michel continues to remain at the College. He stays in the Novitiate at night, and has breakfast there after celebrating Mass. At noon, he dines with Fathers Baloche and Souhait at Pulau Tikus, except on Mondays and Thursdays. He does not eat in the evening. Twice a week, he comes on bicycle to spend from 10:00 to 14:15 in Mariophile, and has lunch with us. Father Dérédec, who is taking care of the Assumption Church, lives at the Indian church with Father Riboud in charge of Saint Francis Xavier's Church. Father Koh, in charge of the Chinese, is living alone in the Seven Sorrows. From time to time, we have a visit from Father Vendargon (Sungei Petani) and the Seminarist Emile Fernandez on probation at the same post, of Father Vong posted at Machang Buboh, and of Father Teng, posted at Bukit Mertajam. Except Father Koh, who came several times, the Penang Fathers have not paid us a visit since the beginning of the hostilities. Father Selier of Balik Pulau made one or two appearances at first, then, no longer having a car, does not show up anymore.

On several occasions, some jokers try to 'requisition' Father Piffaut's motorcycle, as others had done with Father Monjean's, shortly after the arrival of the Japanese, but we do not let ourselves be fooled after that first time. The College's car, which had been delivered to the Japanese on the general order of requisition, is returned to us.

The new rice of the Province is hiked to $15. We get it without difficulty, we are entitled to 9 bags per month (4 *gantangs* per head). The entire supply remains good. We can easily find pork, poultry, eggs, not too expensive. Our garden starts to provide us with vegetables (5 meals a week).

May 14

Arrival of two new students from Malacca, Danker and Dorett.

May 27

Through Father Ouillon, some news from the Procure of Saigon, informing us of the death of Father Louis Boulanger – the first news from France.

June 3
Monseigneur Devals arrived two days ago in Penang during a quick visit to the Diocese, he comes in rickshaw to dinner at Mariophile. He is in good health, lively and very practical. Father Selier also comes that day. The Bishop says he was able to send a message through radio to Paris via Saigon, and to Rome directly.

June 4
Corpus Christi Feast. Procession as usual. Around the house of the Fathers, a short itinerary had been decorated with greenery and banners. The Altar of Repose was held under the portico.

June 5
Monseigneur Devals leaves for Sungei Petani, and from there he must return to the South. He takes with him a new student for the Minor Seminary (Reutens). The rice goes up (new rice at $20 a bag). It seems that it reaches $40 to $50 in Singapore. On the contrary, in Kedah, it is cheap ($4.50 a bag), but no means of transport, and taxes are imposed for crossing the state border.

Everything is quiet in the region, the bellicose noise that began on December 8 has gradually disappeared. Barely any noise, except from time to time an airplane passes, or one hears a round of artillery. We are already well outside the theater of hostilities. We are planting, always planting, vegetables, banana, pineapple etc.

Mid-June
Electricity is restored up till Mariophile, but we disconnect to save money. The metres are removed by the administration.

We receive some money from Singapore's Procure.

June 20
The Fathers of the town are summoned for an *Ecclesiastical Conference* with representatives of other Christian churches. They undergo a series of interrogations. They must agree to submit their sermons before preaching them. They are warned that representatives of the Authority will inspect their offices. They must hoist the flag on the prescribed days at the front of the church.

Around this time, the French in Singapore are either put into concentration camp (eleven individuals) or invited to leave for Indochina, Missionaries included. Monseigneur [Bishop Devals] who was at Tanah Rata is urgently recalled to Syonan. He manages to get the Missionaries to stay.

The College has a new appearance these days. In the morning, the Sisters are working with their girls to put in order the material that they have gathered in several rooms of the ground floor. In the afternoon, the Brothers of the Novitiate (there are also the Brothers from town since their school, Saint Xavier Institution, like the Convent, is occupied by the Navy) bring their *boarders* there for recreation, to collect *Achatina* for the ducks they raise, and even to grow vegetables on our land. In the evening, the cows of the herd belonging to a *Kling* graze in the courtyard, below the classes.

At this point of time, Father Michel begins to sleep, at least from time to time, at the College (instead of the Novitiate). If the house has not been looted so far, it is due to his presence, there or nearby.

Boats were sunk near Penang. It is said that Sungei Petani was raided. The British with a few planes tried to bomb the *airfield* around 15:00, but local *fighters* prevented them. The British threw their bombs up-country behind Bedong Hospital [Kedah] and slipped away. The blackout that had been removed (replaced by brownout maintained from midnight to 4h00 Tokyo Time) is reinstated with severity, and the precautions in case of raid inculcated. Emotions in town, exodus of people to the countryside despite the opposition of the Authorities.

Two families come to stay in Mariophile in the *rubber* estate houses.[6]

June 23

Our tenant of bungalow no. 516 by the seaside, the Dane Mr Hansen, does a moonlight dash. For a long while, he no longer lived there, but kept a *jaga* which was very useful for keeping watch on the place. He lived in Saint Nicholas Home and took care of it with his wife. There, he had spent more than a thousand dollars on the little blind children. On his return from Sumatra, where he had been looking for his children, he was ordered to leave St Nicholas and the island in three days. For the last point, he got a reprieve. He went on to settle with another Dane, Mr Long, at Macalister Road.

June 24

Rice rations reduced from 4 to 3 *gantangs* per adult per month. Price: $14.80 in Penang for a bag of rice from the previous harvest. Profiteers who sold it at $20 are punished. In town, retail bread goes up (8 cents for ordinary bread). We still enjoy the old price (4½ cents) and consume 31 loaves a day – 25½ for the students and 5½ for the Fathers. It is said that flour will be unavailable soon.

June 30

Arrangement is made between the Brothers, the Sisters and the Authorities to open schools in Pulau Tikus. So far, all such permission has been refused. As a consequence, the Sisters, whose school at Pulau Tikus was cluttered with materials, came to bring some more to the College (where they had already stored a lot since March), and settled here themselves. They occupy almost the whole ground floor, except the servants' rooms, the Procure, the students' library, the Superior's office, the nook under the staircase near the clock, the *fabrica,* and the *capsarium.* On the first floor, they occupy the infirmary, half the dispensary, the fourth dormitory, the guest rooms and the room between the second guest room and the next room (Father Piffaut), the second and the first dormitory, the room between these two dormitories. They

---

6 Part of the land in Mariophile has been converted into a rubber plantation.

intend to put the Novitiate in the first dormitory. They wanted to put the orphanage in the second hut, as the orphanage has been put under the direction of people who don't belong to the Community of the Dames of Saint Maur, we refused. An agreement is signed on June 30th between the Reverend Mother Tarciscius and the Superior, a copy of which is attached to the Council's notebook. Soon the Sisters are conducting classes in their Pulau Tikus school, as well as having some classes in the College. The Japanese are quick to include this in their School System, and so the College becomes the Japanese School without prejudice of the occupation by us and by the Sisters. It is, at the beginning, exclusively a girls' school.

July 1
Thirty French residents in Syonan (Singapore) are sent by rail to Indochina, 'at the request of the government of Indochina.' Originally, the Missionaries should have gone with them. In Penang, there are no more French except for the Fathers, Brothers and Sisters. All remain. As for other Europeans, there are two Danes (Hansen and his family, wife, one son and one daughter, and Mr Long, Danish consul, from the Eastern Asiatic Company). Reverend Scott, the Englishman who was in charge of Butterworth until the arrival of the Nippons, stayed, got a pass from the beginning, then settled in Saint Nicholas as if he was in charge (just like Hansen and his wife), then had his pass cancelled and was interned at Saint Nicholas.

Major Harvey of the Salvation Army is in prison. The hospital's Chief Medical Officer Dr Evans is interned at the hospital (or at his house next to the hospital) and continues to work at the hospital – but no longer as the Chief Medical Officer (who is now a Japanese doctor), only as auxiliary; he found his loneliness too heavy to bear and asked to be sent to a concentration camp in Singapore. There are still some old Europeans, old Englishmen, like a certain Mr Wills who lives in a hut in Tanjung Tokong. Our tenant in Tanjung Bungah, Mr Cumming, would be home in Ipoh. The manager of 'Fun' in Tanjung Bungah, a Swiss, is there. Also living near 'Fun' are a Hungarian and his wife, belonging to the orchestra of a local hotel before the arrival of the Japanese, and nearby, a European, married (?) to a Chinese.

July 6
Received by a messenger (Abd el Kader, *O res mirabilis*) from Bangkok a letter from Monseigneur Perros, first communication from Thailand since December '41. The three Priests who left in December arrived safely, on the very day of the declaration of war.

The Sisters' Orphanage, which was transferred to Balik Pulau in December and taken over by the Japanese, is brought by them to Poh Leung Kok (Vermont Road). The *inmates* of Poh Leung Kok have all been taken to St Nicholas' Home with the little blind children. Both institutions are under the direction of two Eurasian Catholics, Miss D'Oliviero and Miss D'Mello respectively. The Sisters (six natives) are with the orphans (a hundred).

July 7
A bamboo (yellow) is selling for a dollar!

July 11
Agreement with Crawford for the care of the two bungalows, 514 and 516.

July 14
The Fathers, the Annamites, Thai and Burmese students go to the Police Station, near the Main Post Office, to register and have their papers stamped. It is compulsory for all those belonging to a power of third category (Third Nation).[7] The first category are the powers of the Axis, the second category the powers at war with the Axis or having broken diplomatic relations. So, we get up at 5h00, at 6h30 we leave (thirty-four students) for Bagan Jermah [*sic*]. From there, some go by trolley, the others on foot. We arrive, some at 7h30 and the others at 8h00. Around 9h00, the operations begin. The Brothers are there too, the Reverend Mother, many Thais, a Swiss lady, etc. Around 11h30, it's over for us. We were inscribed in a special register and the Third Country rules are copied on our passport. No clubs, no companies, no communication with enemy subjects, prisoners of war, or guardians of prisoners of war. Prior authorization before change of address or travel. We can move freely around the island without permission, but we must have authorisation to spend the night in a place other than our own address. The exercise and administration of religion is permitted, if it does not hinder the military administration. Finally, we shall be given a *badge* to be worn on the left arm, white, red and white fabric band. They are kind to us and even considerate.

Four hundred banana trees are planted since our installation in Mariophile.

The Taiping Brothers who had been interned were sent south, to an unknown destination. Their arrest had taken place after the baptism at the hospital of a young Chinese Communist who was converted. They were denounced by a Malay, who accused them of relations with the Communists. We later learn that they are in prison in Kuala Lumpur.

July 20
Departure of Victor from Malacca, on medical leave, to return to his family.

July 27
Explosions are heard from here, forcefully, several times in the evening, from Sungei Petani and Padang Serai. Bombs? We do not know, nor do we know about the explosions in the following days. The Japanese announce the destruction, by a seabed mine, of two enemy submarines in the *Straits* of Malacca.

---

7   The first countries are the Friends of the Axis Powers (Germany, Hungary, Italy, Japan, Thailand…), the second countries are the Enemies at war against the Axis Powers (Australia, Belgium, Canada, China, Netherlands, New Zealand, Poland, the United Kingdom, the United States…) and the third countries are the Neutrals with the Axis Powers (Burma, Denmark, France, Indochina, Ireland, Portugal, Switzerland…).

August 14
The French and Annamites (with the Irish and some others) are invited to go to the Keimubu to personally receive *badges*, a rectangular strip of white, red and white cloth, to wear pinned to the sleeve, with our name in Katakana script, a registration number and the seal of the Penang Police. We are told that the French and Annamites are entitled to it as *Axis partners*. The Thais are from an *Axis Nation* and do not need it. The police can arrest any European who is not wearing his *badge*.

Father Michel, although he had his passport *endorsed* on July 13th, becomes the first European not to receive a *badge* since Belgium has broken off diplomatic relations with Japan. Father Michel is ordered to stay at home and not move. So, he cannot come to Mariophile anymore, and he does not even dare to go eat with the Fathers at Pulau Tikus. At most, he takes a risk by going to the Novitiate. The Taiping Brothers are released and treated very well by the Authorities.

August 21
The Agricultural Department sends us four farmers to plant vegetables on our land at Mariophile. They all pay a small monthly rent.

August 30
Taking of the Habit and Profession of Faith in the College Chapel. Father Souhait officiates. Present are Fathers Michel, Riboud, Koh, Piffaut, and Rouhan. A Japanese Naval Non-Commissioned Officer (calling himself a Catholic), whose mission is to supervise the schools of the Brothers and Sisters at Pulau Tikus and to direct the teaching of Japanese in their classes, attends the whole ceremony from the tribune.

September 1
Bungalow no. 516 is rented out ($22.50) to Jockey Ivan Allan, who took a boat for Sungei Petani, with two Japanese residents of Penang, to inform the Japanese army that Penang was an Open City; this was in December 1941.

September 7
Classes start again.

September 11 and 12
Ordination to the Sub-diaconate and Diaconate of Emile Fernandez.

September 13
Major Ordination in the Chapel of Mariophile. One Priest (Emile Fernandez), twenty-six Minored and four Tonsured. Monseigneur Devals stayed with us from Thursday evening to Sunday afternoon. Then he went to Pulau Tikus to administer the Sacrament of Confirmation to one hundred and forty children.

The same day, Father Piffaut returned from the College by bicycle; swerving to avoid a child, he fell into a drain and broke his arm. Admitted to the hospital the same day.

The Japanese forbid Radio Receiver Sets using shortwaves. In fact, the news does not look good for them and, probably, the course of the war is beginning to change.

September 18

We stop buying bread. The baker has no more flour, but the Sisters get some and provide enough for the Fathers. The students who until now had half a loaf every day for breakfast, stop having it and instead eat either some porridge of *nasi krinh*, or some tapioca. We still have three bags of flour for making *matefaims* and bottled flour for making hosts.

Father Piffaut leaves the hospital but will still have to endure arm immobility for about four weeks.

The houses by the seaside, from the city to Birch Road, are evacuated by civilians by order of the Japanese who move in.

September 19

Now rationed and can only be bought with the rice card: rice, sugar, salt, and matches.

September 20

The *caretaker* of bungalow no. 514 by the seaside (Mr Crawford) leaves the house. The next day, the military administration asks to rent the house. This is to put up a Chinese man who is in the pay of the Intelligence Service.

September 22

The situation of schools in Perak is very difficult. Brothers and Sisters cannot teach. (They are only allowed to teach as individual *teachers*, without religious dress, in any government school as if they were secular *teachers*, without attachment to a Community.) The Sisters manage to keep a foothold in their Ipoh Convent which is taken over as a military school. Father François is always confined to the church *kampung*, but he can go to the Convent.

September 23

The Japanese round up the bicycles in town, they give 10 to 15 dollars in compensation.

September 26

We surrender our three Radio Receiver Sets. Nothing is given to us.

There is a rumor that the whole coast area must be evacuated by those who are living there. Also, that we will be confined to the house again... or gathered elsewhere.

Adventure of Father Piffaut who had been to the hospital to have his broken arm treated. He has to wait in a room with a Japanese soldier. He greets him 'O Hayo!' The soldier doesn't answer, takes a piece of paper, writes a few words, puts it on the table and leaves. The Father reads what is written: '*Foolish Gentleman! Good morning.*'

September 28
The Keimubu refuses to grant Father Meissonnier permission to go and stay in Balik Pulau. It is said that for the moment it is useless to reiterate this request. No reason is given for this refusal.

September 29
Alert. A rumor says that the European Brothers and Sisters will be put into a concentration camp. Nothing about the Fathers, but will we be spared? We prepare ourselves for any eventuality.

September 30
Impossible to get our ration of rice for September in full. We only have 3 bags instead of 7½.

October 1
Restoration of postal communications with Burma, Hong Kong, China (sector occupied by the Japanese), Java, Borneo, and Japan. But you have to write in Japanese (Katakana or Romanised) or Romanised Malay. Nothing yet with Thailand and Indochina. But in fact, this is only for the Japanese, no letters are circulating for the public.

October 4
Sunday, the Japanese break the cement cross above the porch of the Assumption Church, and break a cross on the Convent building. Father Dérédec who is in charge of the Assumption and resides at the parish house is worried...

October 5
Monday, it is announced unofficially that the ration of rice per adult, which at the start of rationing was 4 *gantangs*, and then reduced to 3 *gantangs*, will in the future be 2 *gantangs* and 1 *chupok* only.

Great aerial activity, a squadron of 27 planes, flying often in formation over the island.

October 8
Thursday, we start to eat rice only once a day (at noon). In the evening, we eat *sagu* cooked with coconut and salt. The students have nothing else at first, but soon vegetables from the garden are added, and we hardly buy outside vegetables anymore, only on special occasions.

Serious sickness of Father Souhait after multiple stings by hornets which attacked him as he was leaving the College.

October 12
In the evening, for the meal, we alternate *sagu* and maize.

October 14

Interdiction to go to the mountains, to everybody, but especially to Europeans.

Father Souhait received Extreme Unction at the hospital from Father Koh. Septicemia and pneumonia.

October 15

Barrage of soldiers at all entry junctions to town (Bagan Jermal, Burmah Road, etc.). It is difficult to get out of town and impossible to enter even for government employees. It is said that the Post Office in town is closed. We do not really know what is happening in town, no new details. We are talking about numerous arrests.

October 16

Like the 15th. It is said that on the 17th, there will be arrests on our side.

October 17

The morning at 6:00, many arrests in Tanjong Tokong. Many people flee to the mountain. Almost all those arrested are released before 10:00. Only two or three arrests were maintained. The Bagan Jermal roadblock is removed. News from the arrests in town on the 15th. Everyone – so to speak – had to appear for police investigation. People were taken out of the houses and gathered together in public buildings, schools, etc. and kept from dawn to 17:00. It was permitted to leave one guardian behind, per house, usually an old woman. It seems that they were looking for Communists, who came in secret from the Peninsula, and Radio Transmitter Sets. At the College, at the Novitiate, at the Parsonage of Pulau Tikus, everyone was left absolutely quiet. On the 16th, the roundup took place in Balik Pulau.

Around 11:30, a Japanese officer of the *Military Police* comes by car to Mariophile and goes up to the Fathers' floor (first time since the arrival of the Japanese that one of them is going so far). He speaks amiably, and so does the Chinese police inspector accompanying him. A lot of questions (how many Fathers, students, nationalities, if among the servants there were newcomers, if we went out after the curfew, if we went to town and why, at whose place, what was our daily schedule, if we got married). The officer opens the door of Father Michel's room, glances and withdraws. Returning to his car, he admires the garden and asks if we have enough to eat.

Rumour has it that the many planes that were noticed these past few days were being evacuated from the Andaman Islands where the bombing was making the situation unbearable.

Father Souhait is better.

The 17th was declared a *public holiday*, because of the *Harvest Thanksgiving Festival* (*Kanname-sai*) of Japan.

October 25 to 31

Agricultural Week. Taking advantage of an opportunity to have tapioca and sweet potato plants in abundance, we give predominance to the garden work during the week. One day, even the classes are completely suspended. Enthusiasm, admirable dedication of all. Emulation leading to rivalry... We plant thousands of sweet potatoes and tapioca.

Mid-November
We stop having bread. We replace it with tapioca cakes or pancakes, then with *ragi* (millet) flour cakes. We are returned the Radio Receiver Sets, modified in order to disable shortwave reception. We declare that we do not want to use them and so dismantle them.

TURNING OF THE TIDE. [In capital letters in the Diary]

End of November
Sister Saint Charles, Superior of the Penang Community, hardly two months (since the departure to Singapore of Reverend Mother Sister Tarciscius) after she went to Singapore as Superior, is replaced at the College by Sister Saint Louis.
Bangkok is bombed.
We plant another thousand (or more) sweet potatoes. And some tapioca every day.

November 29
Bungalow no. 514 in Tanjung Bunga[h] is rented to the manager of the *Nissan Jidosha*, Japanese company of *car* construction and reparation.

End of November
Three births of kids.

December 1
The power plant becomes a *private concern.*
A large Tokyo firm is buying (compulsorily) all *lorries* and buses in Malaya.
Toulon is occupied by the *Boches*, the French fleet prefers to self-scuttle rather than to fall into the hands of the *Boches*.

December 3
The St Francis Xavier Feast is celebrated with services, as during the most beautiful days. We implore his intercession to avert the threat, apparently a very serious one, as reported, of the total occupation of the College by the authorities who intend to make a school with a thousand students (boys and girls), where the Brothers and Sisters would teach English.

That same day, in addition to good fishing, the students catch a big boar that had gone astray in our tapioca field. The owner does not want it anymore (it seems that the boar would become a *tokong*).[8] We decide, after having duly informed the owner and the police, to kill it and eat it. The meat lasts for four days!

December 6

The Community makes a wish to St Joseph to get the College buildings in Pulau Tikus to remain at our disposal as they are now. We shall observe the month of Saint Joseph, and on March 18th we shall fast, and on March 19th we shall have Mass and Solemn Salut, with adoration of the Blessed Sacrament, and to observe this vow for five years.

December 8

Anniversary of the 'Greater Asia War', triumphal arches throughout the town. Houses, trolley buses... Great procession (Chingay), posters in Malay and Chinese characters announcing 'Pendirian Timor Asia Raya', with a Japanese flag standing out on a map of the Far East. The English newspaper *Penang Daily News* takes the title of *Penang Shimbun* (press), though it is still written in English.

December 9

Further damages were committed in Saint Jean by wrongdoers who broke into the house.

December 10

The broken arm of Father Piffaut gives him concern. It does not seem to work anymore. He will move to Pulau Tikus to be closer to the hospital and get massage therapy. He comes here from time to time, for his classes and for students' confessions. Besides, the holidays are approaching.

December 19

Exams end. Holidays start. Eight students from Malacca will spend their holidays at home. Three students from Burma who have finished their studies (these are the only ones in this case) will stay with us for an indefinite period. When will we be able to send them to their Missions?

Arrival of Michael Then [*sic*] from Sarawak who had studied at the Lower Seminary of Serangoon.

December 25

At midnight, three low Masses, strictly private, without the faithful from outside, then Midnight supper, largely prepared by the students themselves. At 6:30 and 7:00, masses for the faithful. Students get up at 7:30. At 7:50, breakfast. At 8:30, Grand Mass during which some Japanese enter the chapel, out of curiosity, it seems.

---

8   The owner believes that the boar was possessed or would turn into a spirit and was therefore superstitious about keeping it or eating it.

December 31
Between prayer and rosary, traditional compliments of the year's end. The Dean's speech is so long that we need to get him a candle to finish reading.

1943 (2603)

There is no *Ordo* for 1943. We manage with the *Ordo* of 1937, and the English calendar edited by the Mission for the Diocese of Malacca.

Supplies are sufficient. Rice, 3 *gantangs* per head and per month, at the end of the year. On occasion, we have a bit of bread, some good Sumatran potatoes, not too expensive. The garden provides us with the bulk of the required vegetables.

You can drive around in town (and even in Malaya) with the authorities' permission. We sometimes sleep over at Balik Pulau, and at the Brothers' bungalow on the mountain. No permission is required to go to Saint Jean, or even to stay there for several days.

The street names are unchanged, but Japanese signage appears everywhere with the Japanese characters Katakana, and it is the same for all the inscriptions that the government has made for the public. The inscriptions in Latin characters have disappeared. This does not apply to private inscriptions, but it will come.

The whiskey reaches the price of $60 a bottle. For us, we are happy to have a small glass of claret at each of our meals. The supply of claret that remains with us apparently does not keep well (especially because of the poor quality of the corks used), we prefer to enjoy it rather than taking the risk of seeing it spoilt.

At the beginning of January, there is a rumour that the ration of rice is going to be further reduced, and that sago will be distributed to supplement the difference between January's ration and that of December. In Singapore, the situation is worse, the chicken eggs that were worth 7 to 8 cents here are priced at 20 cents and more there. Food supply, without being rarer, is more expensive. As for the Mass intentions, we are abundantly provided by the Fathers of the Mission and the Sisters. The latter, in recognition of the facilities of the College made available to them, have repeatedly made important donations, in kind and in cash, to us.

January 4
Agreement with the coolies of the Health Department to allow them to grow vegetables near the *kongsi*.

January 9
We buy Hermitage no. 505 in Tanjung Bungah from Mr Lim Cheng Lau for $500. We do not currently sign a *Deed of Sale*, but receive a simple receipt with indication of the sale of the house.

Arrival of Joseph Poo from Malacca.

January 10
Arrival of three Seminarians from Malacca: Jee Gregorius, Benedict Fair, and Yim Simon.

The Seminarists from Malacca, eight of them, come back from vacation. One of them brings from Singapore some letters from Burma, the first for more than a year (a letter from Monseigneur Perros dated December 9 and two from Father Mascarenhas).

January 11
Classes start again, the schedule is similar to that of 1942, with fifty-six students.

Father Michel is summoned by the Police to answer a number of questions and fill out two sheets of information about those under arrest. They told him that he will soon be summoned to take an oath, and that a residence will be assigned to him. The price of sweet potatoes, which rose to nearly 20 cents for one *kati*, comes down to 14 cents. We plant everywhere.

January 17
The *Military Police* conducts searches, looking for unauthorised radio sets. At the College, the Police stops at the door, reads the Japanese inscription (school no.), and although the Reverend Mother invites them to enter, they leave. At Mariophile, an officer who is accompanied by armed soldiers comes by car and asks in Malay if we have radio sets, we answer in the negative, and after having persistently asked the same question, he withdraws without search.

January 20
Fruitful squirrel hunts. By trapping them, we catch enough to cook some excellent curries etc.

January 25
All the Neutrals (Europeans, Arabs, French, Indians, and Annamites) are summoned to Keimubu for an admonition: We are not happy with them; they have not been grateful for the favored treatment accorded to them. Some positively helped the enemy. In any case, there is not the kind of cooperation that was expected from them. As a result, the special protection granted to them will be withdrawn in the future. In addition, they should pay attention to four points to be observed:

1. Obey military orders concerning neutrals.

2. Observe laws of international morality.

3. Sever all relations with nationals of countries at war with Nippon.

4. Refrain from all acts contrary to Japan or helpful to it enemies.

This is first read out in Japanese, by the Japanese Keimubu's chief, then translated into English by a Chinese policeman (Inspector Chin). Then the names of those present are taken, and it's over.

January 30

Father Michel, who had already been summoned by the Police the day before, appears again and is released on parole, after having sworn that he will observe a certain number of proscriptions (no correspondence with anyone, do not leave after 19:00, do not leave his residence without permission, even for one night, etc.), but he can travel by day in Penang. He receives a small booklet with his picture and his written commitment to comply with the said proscriptions. His status is defined as an *alien enemy* subject, allowed to stay outside a prisoners' camp. He will receive a distinctive *badge* and should always wear it when he goes out.

That same morning, Reverend Scott of the Church of England who was in the same circumstances as Father Michel, confined to Saint Nicholas Home, was arrested at 4:00 am and taken to Butterworth with other Europeans (the Reverend of the Seventh Day Adventists,[9] among others) and from there, some say, to Singapore; others say, to Kedah.

The same evening, just after dark, lightning strikes the coconut trees in Mariophile, in the immediate vicinity of the infirmary. The coconut trees are blazing. The fire spread to the *attap* roof of the infirmary. A patient who was there runs away. Students climb and extinguish the fire. Damage: some *attaps* burnt, a shutter of the infirmary ripped off, the electrical installations of the infirmary vanished, the boxes of the fusible leads burst – same thing in our house above – some broken glasses in the dispensary (bottles, glasses), three students, more or less strongly, concussed.

The Christmas breeze that had continued till now seems to have been replaced with storms, without interruption.

February

Supplies are still adequate, although the rice ration is low. The price of rice goes up from 0.52 to 0.60. The sugar ration goes up from 8 *tahils* to 12 *tahils* per person, the price decreases from 0.20 to 0.18 per *kati*. Green vegetables are relatively cheap in this dry season. Our garden produces less than our consumption now and we have to buy vegetables several times a week.

February 8

Father Michel's first reappearance at Mariophile since August 14 of the previous year.

---

9 The Seventh-day Adventist Church is a Protestant Christian denomination which is distinguished by its observance of Sabbath on Saturday, the seventh day of the week in Christian and Jewish calendars. It was formally established in the United States in 1863. On December 1924, J. Earl Gardner opened the Adventist Mission Clinic on Muntri Street, then expanded to Burmah Road. In 1942, the Japanese took over the hospital and renamed it 'The Love Hospital'. Two years later, the left wing, also known as 'The Japanese Wing', was built. Today, Penang Adventist Hospital and the Seventh-Day Adventist Church are both located on Burmah Road.

February 18
People are nervous, especially as a result of news about the Rangoon bombings by the British. Those who live in town or by the seaside are concerned about finding a shelter further inland or in the countryside.

February 20
The yield of sweet potatoes planted in November–December is rather low. However, it is an additional source.

February 22
Compulsory registration of Eurasians.

February 25
The Japanese come to inspect the Brothers' Novitiate and also the Sisters at the College. They withdraw the permission, previously granted, to teach the Catechism. They declare that they cannot accept the formula 'Religion first'. They forbid all teaching in Latin for the Brothers.

Father Michel receives an *armband badge* with the distinguishing mark of enemy subjects on parole (white star on a red background), and also a small plank, bearing in Chinese and Japanese characters, the words: 'here lives an enemy subject free under oath'. This plank must be prominently displayed outside his residence.

March
In fulfillment of the vow issued by the Community, we observe the month of Saint Joseph (as the month of May is to Mary).

March 8
The rain appears after an absolute dryness for almost a month. The students who built a large monkey trap capture five of them in one go. Great feast of monkey curry as a result of this happy occasion.

A decree appears, according to which, from April, the income of the houses etc. will be 50% (instead of 30% so far) of the old tariff. This will put our revenues on a more advantageous footing.

This month the ration of rice (3 *gantangs*) is reduced to 60%, but the sugar is quite abundant. Salt is measured at 4 *tahils* per person per month at the official stores where we buy only by showing the rice card, the price is very reasonable (9 cents for a *kati*). We can have more salt by paying the full price. Oil at 14 cents a *kati*, a *kati* per person per month, we can have more, by paying the full price. Our garden gives us some disappointment over the sweet potatoes, yields are low, nothing comparable with tapioca.

April
This month we will have 70% of the rice ration.
In early April, major Japanese language exams for all government employees.

April 6–7

New and serious alert about the College. The Department of Education wants to merge the four schools currently operating in Pulau Tikus into one co-educational school here, in order to dislodge the Sisters – who should go occupy their school in Pulau Tikus (which had become vacant after the move). The Sisters refuse on April 7 to evacuate the College. As has happened previously, on account of the Japanese language tests and other excuses, the Sisters (and a few Brothers, too) have been partly eliminated, replaced by secular teachers. The government's intention to do without them becomes more and more obvious. The Number Two of the Department of Education, a Japanese Mahometan, seems resentful of the Sisters. The same day, April 7th, we all agree (College, Brothers, and Sisters) to adopt the following position: Objection to the co-educational school. The Sisters will leave the College only under duress. We shall appeal to the Pope through the bishop if the government wants to proceed further. The Number Two, in view of this position, declares, after a stormy session at the College, that he will refer to the Number One. At the same time, we take our measures to evacuate as many things as possible from the College to the Novitiate, to Pulau Tikus, and to Mariophile. At this point of time, the Mission, including the posts south of Kuala Lumpur, are carrying on without difficulties and the administration is, all in all, favorable. The Religious personnel are teaching, Catechism can be done without obstruction. But Ipoh, the North, and Penang are struggling with opposition to matters that seem to arise because of personalities.

For three days, going to the seaside and fishing were prohibited. The beach is guarded. We are talking about the wreckage of a sunken ship thrown back by the sea.

April 12

Easing. The four schools of Pulau Tikus (two near the Church, the Brothers and the Sisters), the annex school of the Novitiate and the College (presently occupied by the Sisters) remain where they are. But Brother Paul and Sister Sainte Rose, till now the directors of these schools, have been replaced by a Methodist Chinese (well disposed towards us) who is in charge of the whole. The Sisters stay in the College (at least for the moment). *Deo Gratias et Sancto Josepho.*

April 13

The Japanese have another try and ask for thirty classes at the College. The Sisters and we are all expected to evacuate to meet this demand, but nothing is said directly about this. Counter-proposal, twenty classes only, we should gather together, at the College, the students from the two schools near the Pulau Tikus Church; the status quo would remain at the Novitiate annex school.

April 14

Yesterday's counterproposal is accepted. At the College, the Brothers help us to clear out the rooms, especially the dormitories that will be made available for education.

April 16

'Nicodemus Style'[10] visit by Inspector Chin. He gives a warning on the attitude to be observed in future because of the march of events:

1. New circumstances require great caution.
2. Better stay at home (i.e. near the house, not where you can be seen from the main road).
3. Absolutely not by the seaside, under any pretext whatsoever.
4. In the town, rarely.
5. The fact that Mariophile commands a view of the sea may cause difficulties.
6. It's good that we do not have electricity.

April 20

The town is crowded with soldiers.

At the College, dormitories were cleared and partitions were made to arrive at the number of classrooms required. As a caution, statues, crucifixes, etc. are removed. The BMV statue at the main entrance is parked in my office.

At Mariophile, we are preparing a large plantation of durians and *janggus*. Our long stay there will have been, we hope, the starting point of the transformation of the property into an orchard. The banana and pineapple plantations are already very prosperous and soon we will have these fruits in abundance. The season has been very wet since the beginning of April. And that gives a magnificent vigour to the vegetation. The breeze has not stopped since Christmas and the weather is remarkably pleasant. Easter is April 25th. It would have been a complication under normal circumstances but, being permanently based here, it is not inconvenient at all. As our exams ended on the 18th, the holidays started. Holy Week[11] will be the first of our three weeks of vacation. The students do not like this very much, because it takes a lot of freedom out of that week. But this only happens once in the century, and it is war...

April 22

Order, all radio sets not licensed (such is the case with our sets which have been disassembled) must now be accompanied by licence or given to the government. We sell our sets.

April 23

The Governor of Penang and P.W. (Lieutenant-General Shotaro Katayama) is transferred to Selangor (he had been in office here for a little more than a year) and the

---

10 Nicodemus, a Pharisee, came to see Jesus 'at night' to discuss Jesus's teachings (John 3:1–21). The term 'Nicodemus Style' usually refers to a person who dissimulates and conceals his true beliefs, or is used to describe someone foolish because his questions are considered naïve from a Christian perspective.

11 Holy Week in Christianity is the week just before Easter.

Governor of Johore comes to take his place here (Major-General Masakichi Itami).

We sell the College's big billiard table.

May

A Jap Seminarist, educated in Canada until war broke out between Japan and the Americans, is in Penang. He comes to Communion in the churches when he is free and also comes to the College.

The Japs announce (but not in their newspaper) the capture of an English submarine near here. Some people say that members of the crew are interned in the prison.[12]

Rations, the same as the previous month, 70% of the full ration of rice, half a *kati* of coconut oil, 12 *tahils* of sugar, 4 *tahils* of salt per person (the latter cannot be found outside the official rations), a matchbox per house.

Some cases of malaria among students, although the government continues to spray oil (using *rubber* oil).

Almost no more boats passing through are to be seen. For months there was traffic but, by the end of last year, it slowed down and it is rare to see anything passing through now. A hospital ship once. Some submarines. Some transports or freighters now and then. Other than that, some small boats (*tankers*).

May 12

Visit to Mariophile by Johannes Hirata Sadane (the Japanese seminarist mentioned above). He spends the day with us. He speaks French well and manages a little bit in Latin. He comes from Fukuoka and, having spent several years at the Tokyo Seminary, he knows many Fathers from our Missions. He makes a very good impression.

May 13

Communication of a government circular (Bureau of Religions) asking for complete details on missionary schools, seminaries, novitiates, churches.

May 15

The organisational work of the College to accommodate twenty classes has not yet started. The authorities who, until now, had left the Saint Joseph's orphanage in peace, are beginning to eye it as accommodation for all kinds of vagrants. Upon encountering resistance, they propose the transfer of the orphanage to Saint Nicholas' Home. Native Brothers are still teaching at the Brothers' School, and at the Sisters' School, there are even European Sisters who continue to teach. The Jap Seminarist comes back to visit us.

---

12 They are most probably the 22 crew members of US (and not English) submarine *Grenadier*, captured in the Straits of Malacca in April 1943. Kept in the Convent, they were tortured before being transferred to Singapore in August. Their names are still visible on the wall of the school.

May 25
Meeting at the Education Department (Bunkyoka) with the representatives of the Christian churches. The Brothers, the Sisters, and the College were also invited to send representatives. Address by the Bunkyo Kacho, Mr Mori. Similar meetings will be held from time to time. The College Superior is designated as a representative of the *Training Institutions.*

May 31
The dormitory division work begins at the College to set up classes there. This is done inexpensively and with bad wood.

Penang has run out of quinine. There is no more in pharmacies. It is not sold in the hospital. Incidentally, we have a few cases of malaria in Mariophile. Fortunately, we have a supply of quinine.

June 28
The difficulties concerning Saint Joseph's orphanage are ironed out and the aid granted so far by the Authorities will continue. The institution remains under the control of the priest of the Indian Church. Likewise, Catechism continues to be taught to the children of the Indian school, either in church or at school.
Visit to Mariophile of an ex-Catechist soldier from Fukuoka, speaking quite good French, very amiable.

News arrives that five Brothers from K.L. were arrested and sent to Singapore.

The season is very wet, the vegetables are growing well, the garden produces enough for the Community.

Father Riboud received a letter from his home through the Red Cross and the Vatican Apostolic Delegate.

A lot of Germans in town. We encounter them in groups in the streets, dressed in civilian clothes. They would be technicians who come to work here in the torpedo workshops.

The Mariners who until now had been seconded as liaison officers between the schools and the authorities are recalled. Henceforth, the Department of Education deals with schools alone. The Sisters' house at Tanjung Bungah is occupied by the Navy (coast guards).

The price of food continues to increase.

It is said that an anti-Axis aircraft flew over Penang at high altitude.

Our goats give us an appreciable amount of milk. We have 14 of them, also 5 cows or calves. Rabbits thrive quite well. We have tapioca in abundance. With that we stuff our bellies.

June 30
First anniversary of the installation of the Sisters in the College.

July 14
So-called alert in town. Siren twice. We do not know exactly what happened.

July 16
Upon waking, a Japanese patrol arrives at the house, goes to the door of the Chapel and then turns back to park for half an hour in front of the refectory, facing the Grotto of Lourdes. Then, the patrol withdraws.

Sometimes in the morning, an Indian inspector of the Secret Police comes to ask to see us. He wants to know if we are here, all the Europeans of the College. He asks for some information and then withdraws.

July 18
We have yet to receive rice this month. Fortunately, we still have a little advance, fifteen bags.

July
Regrettable cases compromising some Eurasians, and even Eurasians in general. There is a spate of arrests; most of the people arrested are freed. The result is a certain suspicion against the Catholics. The Pulau Tikus Church is closely watched.

July
Monseigneur Devals reaches Penang, at the end of a tour of Confirmations in the Peninsula. He shares his fears about the near future and asks that the Ordination of his priests, previously fixed in December, be advanced to September. A council is held and calls are made. The students of last year, who may receive the Orders, will be called to the Sub-diaconate, the Diaconate, and two Malayans will be called to the Priesthood.

At that time, the office of the Superior at the College is destined to be occupied by the Chinese director of the government school, who is being instated at the College. The furniture is transported to the student library and the books of this library are brought to the library of the Fathers.

It is also the moment of Mussolini's fall and his replacement by Badoglio.

August 8
The reorganisation of the College dormitory into classrooms is finished, and classes begin. From now on there will be, in addition to the girls, some little boys, all together around one thousand students in the College; the Sisters and the Brothers will teach, with a Director and Mistresses.

August
Some students arrive from Bangkok.

The College's car is sold for $1,700 to the authorities. No way to refuse.

Our holidays start on August 14th for three weeks. The Malayans go to their homes and will not be allowed to choose holidays other than those taken to visit their family.

Prices go up. A ribbon of *typewriter*, $45. A nice bicycle, $1,000. The government wants to put the brake on the rise and we must, like everyone else, declare all that we have, such as thread, material, new clothes, tires, bicycle. Then comes the declaration of cars, motorcycles, production equipment, engines, scrap metal, nails. We declare the electric motor of the Mariophile water pump.

Visit of a Catholic Japanese officer from Osaka, a Christian sent by Father Deyrat.

August 27
As the telegraphic relations with Saigon resumed, we telegraph to Monseigneur Cassaigne for having the *dimissionales* of Dominique, a seminarist here. The answer arrives on September 4th.

September 4
Visit of a Catholic Japanese paymaster officer, Michael Imamura, from Nagasaki. His brother, a former student of Propaganda, is Father Paul Imamura, from Goto.

September 5
Back to school. The Governor comes to visit the Sisters at the College.

September 10
Visit of Dr Kanabe, Catholic, Professor at the University of Tokyo and Embassy Attaché in Bangkok. He promises to take care of the return of our Thais (five) who are finishing their studies.

Unconditional surrender of Italy.

The College is closely monitored at Pulau Tikus. The reason is not known with certainty. The arrest in Tanjung Tokong of *Towkay* Thye Choon Yew, carrying ten thousand dollars which belonged to him, and which he came to recover in Mariophile, perhaps has something to do with it.

September 9, 10, 11
Ordinations.

September 12
In addition to the two priests of Malacca, there are two priests from Rangoon who are summoned by Monseigneur Devals to work in the diocese of Malacca. So, we have on that day, priestly Ordination of Dominicus Saminathri and Ly Georgius from Malacca, and Celestinus Hton Kin and Georgius Ng Kiaw from Rangoon.

That day, the Italians Sisters were arrested and spent one night in jail, then a day and a night at Poh Leung Kok.

September 13
The Governor General of Penang visits the Sisters and allow them to return to the Convent (6 Sisters). In the future, they will be treated as enemy subjects and equipped with the same armband as Father Michel.

Health is good, but almost all are emaciated. Tapioca is the base of our diet and sometimes the only item on the menu, boiled tubers with a little bit of salt. Some are very sensitive to the poison contained in tapioca and are suffering a lot.

September 16
A boat explodes and sinks in the harbor.

September 17
Departure of Father Celestinus Hton Kin (from Rangoon) to Singapore, where Monseigneur Devals named him Vicar at the Cathedral.

End of September
Warning given by the authorities about the danger of air raids. Organisation of passive defence, digging of shelters. Light minimization, three sets of regulations have been determined. *Preparatory control*, which comes into effect from 22 September and is expected to last until the end of hostilities, consists of the suppression of any external lighting. Interior lighting is permitted without restriction or *shading* until midnight, Tokyo Time (22:30 local time). From midnight, everything should be turned off; however, if light is necessary (birth, death, illness or the like) lighting should be reduced to a strict minimum. The rules concerning, secondly, *on guard control*, and thirdly, *air raid control*, will be effective only during periods of pronounced danger or air raid.

September 25
The defence preparation of digging shelters being officially lifted, everywhere teams are at work in town to organise themselves. We are talking about the closure of all schools. Meanwhile, the students leave aside their Nippon-go to practice *air raid emergency drills*. We, too, in Mariophile, go back to the preparation of our passive defence, dividing students into three groups: shelters, access to shelters and [unreadable].

September 27
It is said that guns were taken up to Penang Hills.
Few arrests in our neighborhood.

September 30
A Catholic *dresser* and bacteriologist from the hospital comes with the *traveling dispensary* and vaccinates almost all of us against typhoid and cholera.

October 1
Great aviation activity, 3 squadrons of 27 planes are mobilised. It is unofficially announced that in case of raids, road blocks will prevent the exit of the town, and those who are not provided with passes but try to flee will be shot. People who now want to change homes and get out of town are prevented from doing so, or will have to lose their rice cards, it is said. It is certain that the *government servants* are

forbidden from changing their place of residence. However, women, children, and men, very young or old, can go elsewhere.

A chicken egg costs $0.25 in Penang and $0.18 in Prai, a duck egg, $0.22, and a coconut, $0.25.

Everywhere in town, shelters against air-raids are established.

October 10
The health of the Community is excellent.

As we have three priests and five deacons, there is solemn Mass every Sunday and on holidays.

October 14
We celebrate the annual feast with concert and lottery. It's a little bit simplified, during the daytime only, of course, since we don't have lighting at night, except for some oil lamps, but it's still cheerful.

October 15
Statutory site visit, the *Military Police* comes around 9:00 by bus. The *matamatas,* with their rifles, guard the entrances of the stairs leading to student dormitories. The Japanese officer goes to visit Fathers' rooms with a Eurasian inspector, while a Japanese Non-Commissioned Officer and other local inspectors inspect the dormitories and search the students' luggage, tables, desks etc. They came especially for the French and the Annamites, but everybody had to go through it, more or less. Anger upon discovering in the pulpit of Paschal (Malayalee), an empty matchbox with a Chinese soldier on the box, with a Chinese patriotic inscription (trademark of these matches). They take the name of the owner and the box is taken away as an exhibit. A map of Burma found in a Father's room is confiscated. The room of one of the Fathers is not examined at all. After that, we offer as much drink and bananas as they like, to all the team, and they leave, in fact, quite good friends. They had already been to the College before coming here and had been ordered to search all the Neutrals' houses (Third Nation) by the seaside.

Great aerial activity.

A naval division stays a few days with a transport convoy.

In town, the sentries are protected by walls of bags filled with soil, which gives an appearance of war to Penang.

October 20
Every Sunday we have a Solemn Mass, where the students in the Major Orders perform all functions, including that of celebrant. Directors no longer work at all. Prices are still rising. 1 *kati* of cabbage $0.22, pig $2.2, goats $2.50, shrimp not at all beautiful, $1.00, *groundnuts* $1.10. We find a kind of bread made with corn flour and soya at 15 cents a roll and in limited quantity. Our tapioca plantation serves us well. Sweet potatoes give us only 4 or 5 meals a month, but tapioca almost

every day and abundantly. We ended up having plants of the best species of tapioca giving in five months abundant tubers, only slightly poisonous, really pleasant to eat simply boiled with salt. Maize has been abandoned as a crop, yielding too little, but the *sengkuang* are doing very well.

The states of Perlis, Kedah, Kelantan, and Terengganu become Siamese territory.[13] The border is the Muda [River]. Rice even more rationed in Kedah than here (we still touched 2 *gantangs* per person this month); in Kedah, 1¼ *gantang* only.

The Navy comes to examine the positions of Mount Erskine.

We receive notice that all Third Nation and all Enemy subjects must leave the seaside (between the sea and Burmah Road / Mount Erskine Road). The Novitiate, the College, Mariophile, are affected by the measure. Each French Father (six) and Annamite student (five) receives a notice to relocate before November 18th and to submit an indication of his new residence as soon as possible to the police. Immediately, we are looking for suitable homes.

October 21

A War Council is held. Balik Pulau seems appropriate for the students and some of the Fathers. It is easy to reach an understanding, after inspection of the site, with Father Selier in Balik Pulau. Three Fathers and the students will find ample lodging, it might even be possible to bring the whole Community there and to allow them to continue their studies. But we want to occupy Mariophile as much as possible to avoid the loss of our belongings and the ruin of our facilities there. The European Sisters and Brothers must also leave the College and the Novitiate, so Father Dérédec must leave the presbytery of the Assumption Church. Father Reboud has not received anything yet. Fathers Baloche and Souhait remain in the Pulau Tikus church, although it is in the prohibited zone.

As a result of agreements between the Anglo-Americans and Portugal over the Azores, the Portuguese Fathers of Singapore and Malacca are interned.[14]

November 4

The days since October 20 were feverishly busy, first drawing plans for the execution of the order and searching for locations for Fathers and students, either scattered or

---

13 An alliance between Thailand and Japan was formally signed on 21 December 1941. On 25 January 1942, the Thai government declared war on the United States and the United Kingdom. Japan agreed to return to Thailand the four British Malayan provinces of Kedah, Perlis, Kelantan, and Terengganu, which had been ceded to the British under the Anglo–Siamese Treaty signed in Bangkok in 1909. On 18 October 1943, the four Malay states were transferred to Thailand. The Japanese authorities, however, retained a great degree of control. After being occupied by the British military, the former Thai-occupied states joined the Malayan Union on 1 April 1946.

14 On 18 August 1943, the British and the Portuguese sign an agreement, granting Great Britain naval facilities at the port of Horta and air rights at Lagens Field on Terceira. The British are allowed to occupy these Azores facilities on 8 October. In return, the British promise to withdraw all troops upon the cessation of hostilities and to guarantee the Portuguese sovereignty over all their colonies.

together, even thinking about the transport for the whole Community. However, in principle, those who are not directly targeted by the order must cling to Mariophile as long as possible, then seek a request for exemption from the order to relocate. Successful application on the Feast day of Saint Charles of Borromeo, Protector of the College, *Deo Gratias!* Brothers and Sisters are also exempted. The second-in-command of the Police came with two officers and a secretary to Mariophile and inspected everything. They were very kind and promised to send one or two instructors to teach Japanese. They permitted us to remain where we are until further notice, but we must keep our outings to a minimum. The Superior must answer for the others. The detailed list of Japanese alumni must be provided as soon as possible. This is then conveyed to Father Dérédec who was also supposed to leave the Assumption Church.

November 10

The ration of rice remains at 2 *gantangs* per person. Passive defence drills, blackouts for several days. Houses that do not dig shelters should expect to have their rice ration cancelled.

The town takes on a new appearance with all the shelters made by covering the street drains with planks, earth, and turf. But these shelters would be unfit in the case of heavy rain.

November 18

Brother James and the Superior of the College go to thank the Police chief for his kindness and promise to express their gratitude for having been allowed to stay where they are, with all the cooperation within their powers. The Keimubu-cho responds by saying that it is a privilege given to the Fathers, Brothers, and Sisters (except the six Italians Sisters who must go to Balik Pulau the next day), but that at any time an order may come to go elsewhere and even to evacuate the buildings. We must look for a new place to stay. He asks us to exert an influence of obedience and good order around us, especially necessary in this coastal region. He asks us to restrict our movements and our correspondence as much as possible. The Superior gives him the list of Japanese alumni of the College, then he requests that of the Koreans too. The secretary of the Police, a Methodist Chinese, reads to the Keimubu-cho a passage of Saint Paul recommending to the Christians the submission to official authorities. The Chief of Police is happy and asks for a second reading of the passage. He is very courteous and benevolent.

November 22

Departure for Kuala Lumpur (via Cameron Highlands) of Father Meissonnier, feverish, tired, coughing, suffering from prolonged insomnia and obviously needing a good rest. The permission to go to Camerons and to come back was not granted, he made a change of residence to Kuala Lumpur and from there, he will go where he will be useful, if the Police refuse to let him come back to Penang when he gets better.

In town, more Germans. It seems that two hundred more just arrived, they are technicians. They march in uniform, singing, through the streets. You can see them everywhere, even in the countryside, on foot or bicycle. Some are staying at the Elysee Hotel or at Hutchings School next to the presbytery of the Assumption Church. Some come to mass on Sunday.

We still have some bottles of red wine that we are finishing up, on occasion. The bread (no wheat of course, but corn, soya etc.) is not bad when it is fresh. $0.15 a small roll. People are eagerly looking for it, and in Tanjong Tokong as well as in town, there are endless queues every morning to get one.

We have just finished our supply of butter but we still have some tins of margarine. Father Riboud receives a postcard directly from Switzerland through the Catholic Red Cross Committee, giving some family news.

November 25–26

Large passive defence exercises, with simulated attack by hydroplanes launching flares with parachutes.

The control of coconuts (sales and prices), of vegetables, of fish (price only) will badly affect the supply. Not a coconut or a sweet potato on the market. People are flustered. Secretly, a coconut sells for $0.60 and more. At the official price, we can only buy… fish heads. An order is issued ordering everyone to plant vegetables. Several Chinese come over to make a deal with us to cultivate our land at Mariophile.

On dark nights, even if there is no blackout, because of our lack of lighting (we still do not want to resume the use of electricity for many reasons) the Community life takes special aspects. The fathers have oil lamps in their rooms. In the main room, a small oil night light. The lamp of the Blessed Sacrament is extinguished at nightfall. The students make their own lighting oil with coconuts gathered here and there in the plantation (we can make lighting oil with *rubber* seeds but we have not done it yet; however, with the restrictions on coconuts, it will undoubtedly be necessary to do so). There are candles here and there in the dormitories or at the oratory. Sometimes, one person or another would be circumambulating with his little lantern in which a photographic plate is used as glass. Electric batteries are out of the question, but there are some of the old stock, reserved for extraordinary occasions and used from time to time. Circulating in the darkness between the end of the rosary (19:45) and the curfew (21:00), the students, in the beginning, used the sound of their baton hitting the ground. The fashion has passed and we make noises with the tongue or hum a nursery rhyme. The Senateurs repeat aloud the formula of absolution to memorise it. But when the rain is too strong, the sounds of the rain cover the other noises and it is necessary to advance with the greatest precaution in order not to collide.

A band of wild pigs appears on our *estate – tujuh ekor*. The theft of wood is more frequent on the hill and some students who have completed their courses occasionally serve as guards.

November 29

We receive a letter from the Police confirming our momentary exemption from the order to evacuate the coastal area, but insisting that the order remains and that we must maintain a place to stay outside this area should the order to leave be given. Apart from that, the letter assures us of the benevolent feelings of the authorities.

The faithful come quite infrequently to the chapel on Sundays. Some Sundays, there are many confessions and communions.

Thanks to our goats, we have enough milk for the sick.

For a fortnight, we don't go to see Father Michel. Neither does he come to see us, because there are arrests everywhere and it is better to stay at home, according to police advice.

Our system of water pipes in the hill is giving us trouble; some old pipes burst, most are clogged with rust and internal deposits. Not enough water comes through, at least in the kitchen.

One of our cows is calving. We hope the result will be better than the calf bought a year ago with his mother in Ayer Terjun and the one born here, six months ago, from the cow bought in Kepala Batas. So far, we have five cattle.

A naval squadron – the biggest we have seen in months – stays in the harbour for a while. As for merchant ships, they no longer come.

December 3

We celebrate St Francis Xavier's Feast with Solemn Mass and Vespers. Our Patron Saint has protected us well so far! The same day, a search is conducted amiably by two policemen, including a Japanese, looking for an escapee. In fact, this escapee visited us a fortnight ago, in the evening, asking to be received and to stay among us, to which we refused. Happy to have tracked down the passage of the escapee, the Police officers withdraw by thanking us for the indications given.

The rice ration for December remains the same for adult men in Penang (2 *gantangs*), reduced to 1½ *gantang* for women, and 1 *gantang* (instead of 2½) for children. In Balik Pulau and Province Wellesley, the ration becomes half that of Penang, for the reason that in these places everyone can have land to cultivate, which is not possible in town.

We receive 1½ bottles of oil per rice card. Our rabbits finally seem to thrive and multiply well. Guinea pigs and ducks are not doing so well. The hens are giving satisfaction. Firewood sells for $18 to $20 a handcart. Following the advice given by the Authorities, we hardly go out anymore.

We see Father Michel here every two weeks.

December 8

Second anniversary of the beginning of hostilities in our region. Solemn Mass of Thanksgiving for our preservation.

December 16

Departure of five students (four from Bangkok – Hong, Kit, Sanit, Savat – their studies completed, deacons; one from Laos, Joseph Inta, minored, his studies completed); after two months of procedures, they obtained passports to go back home.

December 17

Departure of two students from Malacca, Dominicus Saminathan and Lee Georgius, priests.

The ration of rice this month (2 *gantangs*) is collected in its entirety (partly at $0.60 per *gantang*, partly at $0.50 for broken rice). We also received 12 *tahils* of sugar per person and ½ *kati* of salt per person. We begin to receive bread with the food card. Usually, you cannot have more than 3 loaves per card, regardless of the number written on the card. Sometimes, we have been able to have up to 7, because the distribution is done by the heads of thirty families, and the leader of our group is Koi Nian, our *kapala* in Mariophile. In the future, the foodstuffs for which price is controlled will be distributed by the group leaders (*kuchos*, group leaders of three hundred families, *kumichos*, heads of thirty families) instead of being sold in the shops. This is a big blow for the merchants.

December 18

Goh from Malacca leaves for Bukit Mertajam on vacation. You cannot leave your residence, even for one night, without prior authorisation from the Police and you have to report to the Police where you sleep for the night. The students who are leaving have the greatest difficulties. It is necessary for them to present their books, with complete lists in duplicate, eight days in advance to the Propaganda office, and then to obtain from another office a licence to export – another three or four days wait. Everything is done to hinder the movement of people. These days, the permit to move is refused to all those who do not have an absolutely urgent reason to do so. Anthony, from Malacca, posted to Sungei Petani (now Thai Territory) cannot get permission to go there. Neither can the Protestant Tamil pastor who wanted to celebrate Christmas services there.

The families are summoned by the government to plant sufficiently for their consumption, even in the neighbour's land, if there is free space. So, a large number of people come to ask us for a piece of ground to cultivate on our land. There are about thirty lots allocated to date, especially near the main road, near the cement road, and towards the seaside.

December 20

Night alert at 1:00, not announced by the newspaper. *Precautionary air raid alarm.* The *all clear* is sounded around 7:00. Exercise? Real alarm? The newspaper relating the fact does not give any explanation. But that night, there was a very big raid on Bangkok.

December 22 to 27
Major PAR exercises, which from December 25th will be for the whole of Malaya.

December 25
Nothing during Christmas Night, because of the strict darkness which had to be observed. It was the same in the parishes. The traditional procession of the previous evening was carried out after dinner, before dark. The terrace in front of the Grotto had been previously decorated by planting a multitude of shrubs, like a small forest at man height. At night, Christmas carols until 21:00. In the morning, getting up at 6:10, prayer and private meditation, at 6:30, three Low Masses, the rest of the programme as during holidays. At the High Mass, we did not have Japanese soldiers like last year, but only a Eurasian *matamata* of the Tanjung Tokong police (who came for Communion). The assembly of the faithful was all the greater as the road traffic was interrupted. There were more than 40 Communions from outside people.

The morning newspaper announces a big raid on Bangkok, Thursday, the evening after the supposed arrival of our 5 students, who left from here December 16th. Very quiet day. The weather is beautiful, the Christmas breeze did not miss the rendezvous.

December 28
Arrest and internment at the Penang prison of Father Michel, around 10:00, because of his nationality (*Enemy Alien*). He does not have time to inform us in Mariophile, and after his departure from College, Brother James sends us an express to inform us. A Japanese policeman, a Chinese man, and six Indians or Sikhs take him in a Police car. At the same time, English or American women with their children, as well as Jews and Arabs, were also interned. We do not have direct communication with him.

December 29
Father George Mg Kiaw (Georgius from Rangoon) is leaving for the Penang Indian Church, waiting for the opportunity to return to Rangoon. He will temporarily lodge at the Brothers' Novitiate in Pulau Tikus to conduct the daily Mass service there, and also for the Sisters of the College. By day, he will work at the Indian church.

December 30
We learn that Father Michel is still in Penang and he says he is well. He requests whatever is necessary to celebrate Mass.

December 31
We send to Father Michel what he is asking for.
The wishes of the 31st evening are exchanged with the Community at Mariophile, as usual.

1944 (2604)

January 1

Departure of Anthony, acolyte from Malacca, his studies completed. As he cannot reach the place of his probation (Sungei Petani, now in Siamese territory), Monseigneur Devals told him to stay home and look for work as a Catechist or otherwise. This is not a proper dismissal, but it is not much better. We learn that Father Vendargon from Sungei Petani expects to be expelled from one moment to the next.

Father Michel is still in Penang Prison and we are taking steps to get him released. The Police are very well disposed.

All our neo-mystes having gone abroad, the directors begin officiating the sung Mass again, which they have not done since the month of September.

No news from Father Michel. An English lady having been released, there is hope for him. Brothers, Sisters, as well as the College, are praying for his release through the intercession of Saint Peter in Heaven.

During these holidays, students work morning and evening in the garden. Indeed, we are warned that as food supply diminishes, the people will be able to eat only what they have planted. The large yams are in favour, with one tuber we replace the rice ration of three people. But it takes a year for them to mature.

Some news from Father Meissonnier, already installed in Kuala Lumpur, brought to us by one of the two new seminarists arriving from Serangoon to enter the College. He is much better after his stay in Cameron Highlands and awaits the orders of Monseigneur Devals.

We are preparing a dismantlable cottage so that one of the Fathers can settle near Mariophile just outside the boundary of the coastal area, if we are evicted.[15]

January 2

Sunday evening, Father Michel is taken with a hundred other internees to Syonan (Singapore), presumably to the Changi concentration camp. We will be sure of that only two days later. Other internees from Siam were on their way when Father Michel was interned in Penang Prison, between December 28 and January 2. When they arrived at Prai, the Penang internees went to join them. All our attempts to secure Father Michel's release were unsuccessful. When will we meet again? It seems that the internment of Jews and Arabs born in Malaya will be imminent.

Here, January 2, the Ordination to Priesthood of the students from Bangkok (Hong, Kit, Sanit, and Savat) will be registered.

---

15 If the Community is evicted and moves to Balik Pulau, one of the Fathers (that is, one of the five missionaries) will be able to stay near Mariophile to keep an eye on it.

January 5

Unexpectedly, during the preparatory singing class for Epiphany, the Head of Education Mori-san arrives at Mariophile. First of all, he asks us to continue the class, then interrupts and speaks to the students through an interpreter. He asks questions about the daily schedule. He is not happy because the students do not speak much Japanese and because we use local time. He blames the Indian students for not joining the Indian National Army.[16] He goes up to the quarters of the Fathers and, for more than an hour, he addresses us, taking refreshments. He says he will come back the next day. The next day he apologizes by letter, postponing his visit to January 7.

January 7

Mori-san returns, escorted by another Japanese officer and an interpreter. He visits the second dormitory, *le lavaruim*, etc. and the chapel. Then he goes up to the Fathers and, for two hours, asks questions about the Church, its constitution, our position in the Church, our dependence on the Ecclesiastical Authorities, our resources and expenses. He explains to us the guiding principles of Japanese politics (universal peace, felicity of the peoples of Asia, to make all Asians true citizens of the Greater Asia). We must cooperate with this programme and when we tell him that we do not get involved in politics, he reiterates that now the word politics has taken on a new meaning and that, surely, we would want to work for world peace. He makes three proposals:

1) We shall let them explain to the students the meaning of the Great Asian War (*Dai Toa Senso*).

2) Students will study Nippon-go for 2 hours per week.

3) Occasionally, we shall let outside speakers give lectures on various topics.

    We say that we do not mind, and that it is good for students to know more Nippon-go. These gentlemen then retire at dinner time. We adjust our schedule, without delay, to Tokyo time. Which makes us wake up at 7:40.

January 8

The next day, (false) news that the invasion of our country has started. We fear the consequences for ourselves and we prepare ourselves for an immediate departure, although still uncertain.

January 9

The students are informed, and at High Mass, the harmonist plays the *Chant du*

---

16 The Indian National Army or INA was an armed force formed by Indian nationalist Rash Behari Bose in 1942. Its aim was to secure Indian independence from British rule. This first INA collapsed and was disbanded in December that year after differences arose between the INA leadership and the Japanese military over its role. It was revived under the leadership of Subhash Chandra Bose in 1943. In Penang, INA used the new Penang Free School as its headquarters and training ground.

départ. For when will it be? We shall still try to start the new term and we shall live from day to day...

Arrival of new students from Malacca, Lourdesamy and Gregorius Yong. Goh, who had gone home on vacation, is back from Malacca.

[This notebook is packed away at the College for safety reasons
and the Diary is continued on loose sheets which will be inserted here.]

January 10
The Diary is continued on loose sheets because the notebook has been placed in relative safety. We start writing again today. The 13 Supersénateurs will follow the full courses and will have 'Eloquence' and 'Pastoral' as minor lessons. On this day, too, we start Nippon-go (Japanese) classes, ¼ hour every day after the *prandium*. A Eurasian from Penang, V. de Souza, is the tutor, pending the arrival of the teacher announced by the Director of Education. Great aerial activity, day and night, we have superb moonlight, a good night for raids, and the planes fly around with their lights on, over the airfield of Mata Kuching. Even from so far away, the powerful and continuous whirring becomes tiring and annoying.

January 11
Obvious nervousness. The order comes to appoint a man from each house, armed with what he can, if the gong rings.

January 12
In the clear night, with the splendid moon, the planes patrol without interruption. Detailed reports must be provided on everything that we grow.

January 14
A Workers' Service for Public Works is started.

January 15
We learn that Father Michel was seen in K.L. – happy, but hungry and thirsty – and some provisions were brought to him.

January 19
Father Michel would be on Saint John's Island, near Singapore.

Salt is scarce this month – no distribution for animals, human rations are halved. Rice cards are transformed into ration cards; they bear all the names of those who are included. Unimaginable precautions are taken to prevent fraud.

January 21
We ask our agents to make payment directly to Father Koh, without going through the bank where we have an account. We do not leave more than $19 in our bank account.

The belongings that Father Michel had parked with the priest of Pulau Tikus are all removed.

January 22
The planes that so far made so much noise every night seem to have gone elsewhere.

We are preparing for the Chinese New Year. The *kueh bakul* is $3.20 per *kati*!

The Service for Public Works resulted in the formation of a Labour Corps. Men aged 16 to 40 are designated by the Authorities for the Auxiliary Police Force (Self-Defence Corps or Jikeidan). There are obviously some disagreements, everyone tries to slip away. Workers receive $1 a day and a meal; if they have to stay several days away from home, they have 3 meals a day.

January 29
The season remains splendid, the Christmas breeze is still blowing, but a little bit hot and dry, more than it should be for the gardens.

February 1
As for the two previous years, no blessing of the Candles. The Brothers were levied, 20 men (out of the 60 who are in the Novitiate), for the Labour Corps. The affair was happily arranged afterwards. The greatest difficulty was the supplies, following the formation of the official Trusts for vegetables and fish, which have become scarce in the market as soon as these Trusts were created, as they are only agencies of the military commissariat.

February 5
It starts to rain a little and this is very good for agriculture.

February 7
Nothing yet about the requisition of our staff for Public Works. The Chinese and Eurasian Catholics from Syonan are taken in groups to the Catholic Agricultural Settlement of Bahau (N.S.).[17] Monseigneur Devals makes frequent visits there. Father Becheras also established himself there, joining Father Berthold who was there from the beginning.

Father Ouillon sent us a list of 34 deceased confrères (including several dead in France). The list came through Saigon, it seems. He reported, he himself was fine. No news of Father Michel, neither by Father Ouillon nor by Monseigneur Devals.

February 18
We are graciously exempted from participating in the Labour Corps.

---

17 The Japanese administration established a Catholic Agricultural Settlement in Bahau, Negeri Sembilan, for the Eurasian and Chinese Catholics of Singapore, with the first arrivals from December 1943. The settlers experienced great hardship, suffering from harsh conditions, malnutrition, disease, and lack of medical facilities. See Places mentioned in the Diary.

February 24
We receive 2 *gantangs* of rice per person for this month. Our supplies of rice are exhausted and we must use the dried rice we found on the market at fantastic prices ($230 per *picul*), to continue providing a meal of rice each day as before. So, we cancel the rice given for breakfast to students every other day, and we give green peas or beans instead. We also begin to really feel the restrictions. But it is motivation to intensify the agriculture. We obtain a permit to pluck for our personal use 300 coconuts per month (instead of 50 provided by the regulations).

February 27
Sweet potatoes are hard to find in our neighbourhood, people keep for themselves what they harvest (besides, the yield is generally low). In town, we find enough at a controlled price of $0.24 per *kati*, but they are unsorted and we cannot choose; you have to take the good and the bad in bulk. Sorted potatoes sell for $0.40 (by cheating the regulations) at the *black market*. Soap becomes more abundant (3 pieces per person per month); sugar and salt have diminished in quantity and increased in price (4 *tahils* of salt per person, 8 *tahils* of sugar). Still no news from Father Michel, and we do not know exactly where he is. German sailors, crew members of a submarine, are in town, some are [unreadable] and they say they are survivors of a ship torpedoed by an enemy submarine, not far from here. Passive defence exercises for two nights. Here, at Mariophile, nobody cares about us and we only observe the prescriptions regarding the lights; which is quite easy to do with our meager oil lamps. The Police come occasionally to inquire about us, either directly or by interviewing people in the neighbourhood. Nothing embarrassing.

March 1
Departure of Cherubinus Thottyo, of Toungoo, Secular, dismissed as manifestly unfit for the Priesthood and Father Teng accepts the responsibility of taking care of him and gives him some work at Bukit Mertajam. We remain sixty on the ration card, including five Fathers and forty students.

We learn that two English soldiers and a Bengali soldier who had been hiding for more than two years in the forest towards Balik Pulau have been captured. Those who fed them were taken in as well.

We receive news from the four Thais who left in December; they were ordained priests in January.

Mid-March
Great emotion, Father Teng is arrested upon being denounced.

March 21
The cost of living is still rising. And some things cannot be found in a reasonable quantity, for example, sweet potatoes that each one keeps for his own consumption.

They would be very useful mixed with rice to balance the deficiency of the latter ration, but they are very difficult to find, even paying the full price.

After dinner, a Navy *car* brings a Japanese and a Chinese who ask to see the property to plant fifty acres of medicinal plants for the maritime hospital. They are shown the available land. Around 17:00, the two return with a *dai jin* (an important man) in another *car*, flanked by a Marine officer. He is polite and asks some gentle questions. He confirms that he wants to take fifty acres and says that he will go at once to see the *seicho* (local administration) and will return the next day to give final communication on his projects. Great consternation, for fear that he wants to take the buildings in whole or in part, having visited the house and found that it was very good, and having stated that rather than building barracks he would take existing facilities. In the evening after supper, we hold a War Council on what to do.

March 22
The Navy does not appear that day.

March 23
Nor the next day. We breathe a little bit. Many thanks to Saint Joseph!
We still receive 2 *gantangs* of rice per person for the month of March.
Father Teng is acquitted and released. *Deo Gratias.*

April 5
The Navy returns and conducts the Superior to the Government *Offices* (Agriculture) over the same question of land. Agreement is made on this basis: the Navy rents fifty acres of land (coconut and *rubber*) for six years, will pay $4 per acre per year, will not cut trees, and will respect existing gardens.

April 6
The Navy comes to sign a contract according to what was decided the day before. This is supposedly to plant a medicinal herb garden, but we think the real reason is different, for example, to place ammunition depots.

The thefts of tapioca in our garden are becoming a worry. We will have to keep watch.

Our supply of rice is diminishing seriously. We shall organise serious restrictions.

April 7
Today we start the *cangee* instead of rice every other day. So, we think we can bridge the gap between two deliveries of rice. As a surplus, in case of delivery shortfall, we have 3 bags of rice and a bag of *nasi krinh* (rice dried after cooking) plus ten bags of *padi* which are equivalent to five bags of husked rice. Our regular is as follows, for everyone: one day, tapioca in the morning with banana; rice, fish or meat, vegetables from our garden at noon; in the evening *sagu*; the next day, beans boiled in the morning, with banana; at noon, *cangee* with fish (either fresh or dry), vegetables from the garden; in the evening, tapioca. Sometimes, students make small supplements

by themselves, or there are two bananas in the day. Students have pork once a week, Fathers more often, depending on whether or not fresh fish can be found. The only pork we can find costs five dollars a *kati*. The beans we are eating have gone up to an incredible price. They cost $37 a picul two years ago; these days, nearly $200 per picul. For two bags of beans, we pay almost 800 dollars!

April 15
The Navy comes again to inspect the land just rented. It is found hardly suitable and they ask us if they can give it a try when the seeds arrive from Tokyo, to see how things go. Then, it will be decided whether to pursue the idea or not. The same day, oral exams and the beginning of our three weeks of vacation.

April 22
Departure of Laurentius, from Toungoo, withdrawing himself and being accepted at Bukit Mertajam by Father Teng until the return to Burma becomes possible.

We work in the garden morning and evening during the holiday period. Prices are rising day by day. The pork is $8 per *kati*, and sweet potatoes sell under the counter for up to 60 cents per *kati*. It is also the price of an egg.

April 23
Departure of Joseph Poo, Seminarist from Malacca, Secular, 2nd year of Philosophy, withdrawing himself. Leaves his books.

From April to June
Several attempts by the Authorities to take over the College completely, even by displacing the Government school which occupies it partly. St Joseph did not abandon us.

The price of food increases. The cheapest is tapioca, costing up to 0.50 per pound. A European-made *changkul* $180. A pair of shoes, $200.

The Government, in early June, announced that rations currently distributed (rice etc.) could not be confirmed for next year and that we must plant now what we shall eat then. So, we adopt a work schedule that further reduces classes and gives more importance to the garden, where all are put to work, alternately, 4 hours per day, two hours every other day. The Navy does not seem to follow up on the plantation project here. We get permission to cut some *rubber* trees near the football field to plant vegetables. All in all, we are left quite alone, but we are always in expectation of some intrusion. At the outbreak of the Anglo–American invasion of France, we are made to clarify our status and provide a declaration of our property.

June 28
Departure of Victor, Malacca Seminarist, Reader 3rd year of Theology, withdrawing himself. He takes away some of his books.

Father Meissonnier, who had gone from KL to the Agricultural Settlement in

Bahau (N.S.) to take care of the young seminarists who had been transferred there from Serangoon, had fever again and had to go to the Seremban hospital to get treatment. He then returned to Bahau, but as Father Berthold has taken over the direction of the Minor Seminary, Father Meissonnier was employed as an assistant in one of the farm divisions.

July 16

The news comes to us about the death of Father Pagès, former Superior of the College. A telegram from the Vicar General, Father Olçomendy, tells us that Father Pagès is suffering from pneumonia, in serious condition. On that same day, July 16, Father Pagès passed away at the Singapore Hospital, as a second telegram informed us the next day. A service was held for the repose of his soul in our chapel at Mariophile. He had been Superior of the Minor Seminary until the beginning of this year; when the Minor Seminary was transferred to Bahau (Agricultural Colony of Singapore in Negri Sembilan), he retired to the Procure of Singapore where he kept company with Father Ouillon, Procureur. He died at the age of 79.

August 4

Father Aloysius arrives at Mariophile from the Malacca mission. Monseigneur Devals, at the request of the College, is kind enough to second him to us to face any eventuality. He learns the ropes.

August 12

Thirteen students from Malacca go back to spend their holidays with their families. It is the day of the oral exams and the beginning of the holidays after the second term, which will last three weeks. That same day, a true alert was sounded around midnight. It turned out, apparently, to be a raid on Palembang. Earlier, we had an alert because of an attack on Sabang at the northern tip of Sumatra. Some time ago, an American submarine had attacked Siamese boats in front of Phuket.

Pepper is becoming more and more scarce. The *kumiai* of fish (official organisation for its sale) distributes about once a week only, when it has some. As contraband, we can have it more often, starting from two dollars per *kati* in our neighborhood, in town it goes up to 15 dollars. And the pig up to 19 dollars per *kati*, a *coconut* 50 cents, a cup of coffee in a *coffee shop* also 50 cents. Each rice card holder must pay at least $3 per month to the savings bank.[18] He must also pay his share (at least $4) towards the salary of the worker chosen by his kumi for carrying out public works.

August 27

The levy of a contribution is announced, 500,000 dollars for the Eurasians' share, 2 million for the Malays, 10 million for the Indians, 20 million for the Chinese. A

---

18 To promote savings, it was compulsory to make a monthly deposit of at least 1 dollar for every *gantang* of rice received.

new governor has just arrived, Lieutenant General Seiichiro Shinohara, replacing Lieutenant General Masakichi Itami, who had been very reasonable.

August 29
We learn about the capture of Paris by the Allies and the arrival of de Gaulle with his Liberation Committee in the capital. We wonder if there will be consequences for us. A few days ago, we learned that French Indochina had received the status of an independent state with Admiral Decoux as supreme leader, invested with dictatorial powers. Shall we be bound to connect to it? The French government of Marshal Pétain left Vichy to take refuge further east. Will we be sworn to obey this government?

The ration of salt (4 *tahils* per person per month) being insufficient, the students make salt by boiling sea water.

September 3
Alert, with air raid signal but without prior precautionary warning. Some townspeople flee the city.

September 4
Classes resume for the beginning of the third term. The retreat for this year is postponed until December, when it will coincide with the Ordination retreat. The students returning from their Singapore holidays are delayed by the difficulty of the trip.

September 20
Governor General Lieutenant Shinohara Seiichiro comes to visit the Sisters at the College and is very well disposed, shaking hands with each and every one. Same at the Novitiate of the Brothers. Our work in clearing the *rubber* forest near the football field is progressing and we have about one free acre where we plant *ragi* and sorghum.

Buglary at the College, unknown persons open the lock on the door of the *fabrica*, take away this lock and a ladder that was in there, along with a basin.

In Mariophile, a lot of damage is caused to the forest near the Swimming Club for the value of the wood, which is difficult to stop. There are gangs of thieves...

Eggs cost $1 each. *Black market* fish, at least $3 per *kati*. We still make some provisions (6 piculs of *broken rice* at $120 or $220 per picul; 7 picul of *sagu* at $90 per picul; 1 picul of *mee* (*Bee Foon*) at $450 per picul).

Some internees in Singapore send news via postcard. Nothing of Father Michel, though. Father Meissonnier is still at the Agricultural Colony of Bahau near Seremban, employed as chief of agriculture of Lot Six. It is Monseigneur Devals who is governor of the settlement.

It appears that, following the denunciations, we would be suspected of feeding enemy soldiers hidden in our forest. An officer comes, inspecting this corner, but says nothing.

September 30
A letter from the new Apostolic Vicar of Kontum, Bishop Zion, arrives through the care of the Military Administration. It is dated January 24, 1944. The letter asks us to send to Indochina a seminarist of Kontum.

October 1
The football field, transformed into a banana plantation in its farther half from the house, and a pineapple plantation in the nearer half, with sweet potatoes between the banana lines, begins to look like a flourishing garden despite the poorness of the ground.

October 2
Feast of the S.S. Angels. Holidays, offices. Pork meat at noon, and in the evening.

October 3
Towards evening, after having celebrated Saint Thérèse Feast with sung Masses, a constable of the *Marine Police* comes, picks up our tailor, and takes him to the Police Station, supposedly to do an investigation. He comes back, 3 hours later, beaten, full of bruises and scratches. He had been accused of feeding Englishmen hidden in our forest. Always the same foolish story, repeated so many times since the beginning.

October 4
Two officers and a soldier of the Marines come to make a reconnaissance of our hill over the morning.

October 5
We are still not interned, despite the fact that the French troops openly fight against the Germans, already with a French territory almost entirely liberated. This is due to the transfer of Marshal Pétain and his government to southern Germany; the Germans and Japanese profess to consider this government as the only true French government and proclaim it a friend of the Axis. Moreover, the government of French Indochina has been declared independent and here, we can hope to be assimilated with the Indochinese French.

About a hundred iron bars that we declared last year to the government are requisitioned. We receive a compensation for this.

The price of food continues to increase. An empty brandy bottle is worth $3; a *gunny bag* $5. Fortunately, our garden provides us with plenty of vegetables; and with our 500 banana trees and more, we have a profusion of bananas at our disposal. The harvest exceeds all that we had gotten so far. We have picked thirty bunches, which are waiting in our fruit store-room for the moment to be consumed.

At the College, the Sisters set up a water point in front of the window of the Superior's office.

The rice ration continues to be provided regularly, 2 *gantangs* per head.

Father Meissonnier is still at Bahau *Catholic Agricultural Settlement*, with Monseigneur Devals, Father Bécheras, Father Berthold, and the Minor Seminary. He is *Settlement Chief* of Lot Six.

The steps to obtain the authorisation to send back two Indochinese seminarists (one from Kontum, courses completed, summoned back by his bishop, one deacon from Bui-chu) to their homeland have been taken; meanwhile, the request for passports has been forwarded by the Police, with goodwill, to the Military Authority. We only have to await their response.

We still do not dare to go up to Saint Jean, nor to send the students there because of the suspicions that this could provoke. The Chinese living right below informs us that new thefts of equipment have been committed there, and that white ants are active. We send him Rangoon oil to try to stop the termites.

We find some acquaintances to provide us with enough fish, especially some ray, at $2.50 per *kati*. The Community therefore has fresh fish at least once a week (twice when there is an official distribution of fresh fish), 4 *tahils* per person about every fortnight; pork once a week, too; now and then some poultry; the rest of the time, dry fish for the Community, and for the Fathers there is often about a *kati* of fresh fish for lunch or for the evening meal.

October 11
Annual concert, quite well done. During the session, an M.P. comes and takes a chair. Sensational! But he was just a skillfully dressed student. At the end, he reads an address in Japanese, translated by an interpreter. Ends with the singing of Kimigayo.

October 17
Precautionary alert in mid-morning. It lasted till nightfall. And there was no signal to end the alert; apparently, this has become the routine, when there is only the precautionary alert. Besides, activities and traffic continue normally in this case.

The town takes on an increasingly warlike appearance, with the erection of watchtowers rigged out with A.A. machine guns, and the installation of anti-aircraft guns in the midst of dwellings.

October 18
On the evening of the 18th, the alert continues.

October 19
It is only on the 19th that the blue-white flags erected by the roadside – which at various points indicate the state of *precautionary alarm*, disappear. Some say there was action in the Andaman.

October 20
Several times these days, officers from the Marines come to conduct a reconnaissance of the land near the house. Distributions of fish ration are more frequent (one every

three days, ¼ of *kati* per person, price 1.50 per *kati*).

Case of flu in the community (four or five) of a rather strong type, fever 105 degrees during three or four days, with recurring bouts of fever, vomiting, shivering, violent migraines, bone pain, even a case of delirium. This is the first time since the war that such serious cases have come up successively. Overall, health is remarkably good. We still have a Swatow student who is likely to have TB laryngitis and is spitting blood frequently since the beginning of this year. He is rather better now.

We rent tamarind trees (21 trees) for $350!

The news arrives about the invasion of the Philippines by the Americans. The paper also says that operations must be expected in the Indian Ocean.

Explanation of the two previous days' alerts appears to be in the announcement of a prominent attack on the Nicobar (Andamans) on the 17th or the 18th.

October 23

Japanese soldiers are undertaking defence works above the main road facing the sea; three works above the village of Tanjong Tokong, one, extensive, above the New Spring Tide; and in connection with these works, they have cut a lot of our *rubber* and coconut trees.

October 27

After dark, the immediate danger alert. We do not move, and two hours later, the signal is given for the end of the alert.

Everywhere along the main road between Bagan Jermal and Tanjong Tokong, the soldiers are carrying out defence works, laying barbed wire. Feverish activity. A lot of coconut trees are cut by them.

The contract with the Navy serves us, repelling several other distraint attempts on our lands. Besides, the Navy itself does not do anything.

All the iron wires, barbed or not, from enclosures are collected by the government.

One of our cows falls into debility, from old age it seems. We are taking steps to obtain permission to kill her on the spot, but the procedure is dragging on.

Coastal monitoring is becoming more and more stringent, and it is becoming more difficult to buy fish. Fortunately, the distribution of fish rations has improved slightly these days.

Relapse of the flu, one new case, very strong, with delirium. Six cases in all. Dorett, from Malacca, got a fever record (107 degrees minus 1 point), unheard of.

November 4

Saint Charles of Borromeo. Breaking with the custom, we do not sing the Mass that day, but the Community Mass is said for the Feast.

The newspaper announces the reduction of the rice ration from 2 *gantangs* to 2/3 *gantang* for adult males living outside town limits (from 12 *katis* to 4 *katis*). Women have 3 *katis*, children, two. In town, the ration is a bit more than double. The blood of our seven feverish patients, taken to the hospital and examined, gives negative results for malaria.

November 5
Sunday. Alert is sounded during the Community Mass, preparatory alert and almost immediately after the end of the Mass, raid alert. Nothing has changed in our programme. We sing the High Mass during which the end-of-alert signal is given. But an hour later, the raid alert sounds again. For an hour or so nothing happens, but before lunch the air defence goes into action (especially machine guns, not many pieces of A.A. and even then, of low calibre) against a plane that flies high and passes over the town as coming from the Province and going west. There was a short fight with a defence plane apparently without result. It lasts about five minutes, during which a floating mine explodes at sea in the vicinity of a small steamship (was it not a bomb dropped by this plane?). Then everything is calm again for five minutes. Then we hear the air defence of the Bayan Lepas airfield go into action for a few moments. Calm again, then the end-of-alert signal just before the beginning of lunch. This is the first visit of enemy planes we have seen in almost three years.

All our patients have returned to normal temperature.

November 6
According to the fishermen of Tanjong Tokong, a small boat was sunk by a series of bombs launched by one of the planes on November 5. A large patch of oil is still visible on the sea. Today's newspaper announces that two enemy aircrafts flew over Penang territory at 9:10 and three others at 12:15. They were beaten off by an interception unit.

November 8
Precautionary alert, then raid alert around mid-morning, end of alert during lunch. No enemy planes visible, no defence reaction. In the evening newspaper, it is said that the air forces [unreadable], but could not fly over northern Malaya.

November 10
Telegram from Monseigneur Devals, no Ordination in December; he summons five final-year Malacca Seminarists from Penang – to where Monseigneur Devals will not be coming – to proceed to Seremban for their Ordination (or maybe probation).

Malays, Chinese, etc. from Tanjong Tokong take the construction of shelters seriously, and quite a few of our coconut trees are sacrificed for the occasion. A lot of our rubber trees are also cut down during the works to fortify the area, which continue to be carried out on our land by the Japanese.

The price of food continues to rise. Green peas (*kachang hijau, look teou*) sell for $540 a picul, *bee foon* $10 a *kati*. The pork from 19 to 21 dollars per *kati*. A small fish as long as the hand, a dollar; a cup of coffee at the *kedai*, 80 cents. But provisions remain abundant. We buy 6 sacks of rice flour (1 picul each) at 264 dollars each, 6 bags of green peas at $500 (wholesale price). Pork is easily found.

Received letter from Monseigneur Perros. Catholic schools are opening up there again. The Minor Seminary has about twenty students, not to mention ten who study with the Salesians, including three in Philosophy. Alerts and bullets are not lacking at this time of early November. Churches demolished during the persecution are slowly rebuilt. The students wrote to him two months ago and he received the letter informing him about our seven patients with fever.

November 12

News arrives (via Father Arokianathes and Father Georgius) that the student from Toungoo, Cherubinus, expelled from here, received by Father Teng at Bukit Mertajam, had disappeared without leaving an address. The Police investigate. Some friends came to pick him up by *car*.

During lunch, senior officers of the Marines come to inspect the position of Mariophile, with plans in hand; they go up and walk to the end of the first dormitory, from where we have a beautiful view, and examine the defence works which now adorn the slopes of the mountain above the Chinese cemetery, and are clearly visible. Then they come near the refectory, next to the bell, and inspect the Straits; finally, they leave as they came, in three big *cars* with flags.

Dr Oon, summoned to see our patients, declares without hesitation that our seven feverish students have typhoid. Complete isolation prescribed, severe measures of prophylaxis and disinfection, boiled water for the whole Community, no more use of human fertiliser or urine in the garden until further notice. It is strange that the seven cases broke out less than a year after anti-typhoid vaccination (November 1943) but as the blood test done on November 4th at the Hospital is negative for malaria, and fever continues, he sees nothing but typhoid.

November 13

Two of the patients have a little fever in the evening; the others are normal.

Investigations are being made by the Military Police regarding the flight of some people out of town due to air raids these days; the reason being that stores have closed in some places, and a growing number of children are missing from schools.

We begin to see again, in the journal, *air-raid shelter* plans and practical tips to build them. The Tanjong Tokong Malays are finally starting to build covered *shelters*.

We, ourselves, make one near the infirmary, in front of the garage on the slope of the Grotto of Lourdes for the sick who cannot easily reach the shelters.

November 14

We summon a *dresser* from the Hospital to revaccinate us against typhoid. He arrives at once and deters us from being revaccinated, since we were vaccinated just a year ago. We can contract the disease, but it will not be serious; and a new vaccination could be harmful on weak bodies. Importantly, he assures us that we cannot rely on the results given by the hospital's bacteriologists who are doing the routine analyses. They throw the *slides* into the basket and put any results on their report. He then retook the blood from the seven patients to test for malaria and, in addition, took some blood test tubes from the two most feverish patients for the typhoid agglutination test. He assures us that there is a lot of malaria around us. As the two patients continue to have fever in the evening, we anxiously wait for the result of the examination promised for the 15th at noon; one of the two patients in question is one of the five students summoned to Seremban immediately for Ordination and Dr Oon absolutely refuses to allow him to travel because of his typhoid. The other four are having trouble getting their passports; it is always postponed to 'tomorrow'.

November 15
Departure of four students from Malacca, Chew Aloysius, Chin Thomas, Anthony Michel, and Anthony Khaw, called to Seremban by Monseigneur Devals. They will be acolytes, except Anthony Michel, who is an Exorcist. They were about to finish their studies.

Results of the second blood test of our seven patients suspected to have typhoid. Two have some sort of malaria. One of these two has, in the opinion of the doctor, some sort of typhoid. Another also, Saul (from Bangkok), the most severely affected, would have typhoid only. He receives Extreme Unction.

November 16
Patients have no fever except for the two most seriously affected.

November 17
No patient has fever in the morning; in the evening, the fever comes back for three patients. The state of Saul's health remains worrying.

The Governor issues an urgent appeal to the people, inviting them to build solid shelters, and makes the danger sound imminent (see today's newspaper).

The Japanese established on the slope above [where] Kikie[19] [stays], and almost to the ravine where our pump is, a beautiful trench with flanking elements.

Monseigneur Devals sends a telegram informing us that he will make the Ordinations at Seremban on the 24th, 25th and 26th of November.

November 19
The newspaper announces the Enemy bombing of Mergui and Labuan.

November 21
Student Saul sees his typhoid becoming complicated with breathing problems. The doctor fears pneumonia. The other patients are fine. One of our servants, who had been taken away for a month to do corvée labour for the Japanese, comes back to spend two days here. He is making bomb shelters at the Bayan Lepas aerodrome. To redeem oneself from the obligation to work a month, one has to pay $500. So far, no student has been mobilised to do corvée labour.

---

19 Kikie is likely an animal that was managed by one of the servants. As the College General owns a bullock cart, it could be either an ox, a cow or a bull.

November 22

The newspaper mentions several raids on Singapore during the previous days. It seems proven that Seletar was bombed.

Our patients are better. We build an *air raid shelter* near the infirmary for their use. A new case of fever occurs and we follow it closely.

November 26

Sunday, 21:00, precautionary alert; then after ¼ hour, raid alert; ¾ hour later, *all clear*. Nothing happens.

Priestly Ordination at Seremban by Monseigneur Devals, for four priests from Malacca, Chew Aloysius, Anthony Khaw, Chin Thomas and Anthony Michael. This is the first time that there are four priests in a single Ordination for Malacca.

November 27

11:00, precautionary alert that endures, without raid alert, until evening. The defences are occupied by their garrisons. The newspaper says that during the alert of the 26th evening, three B-29 planes approached but could not reach – in fact, there was a strong thunderstorm.

November 30

Our patients are better. Patient no. 8 does not seem to have the same illness as the seven so-called typhoid sufferers who react very favorably to quinine. We are a bit reassured. Father Chin Thomas comes back from Seremban where he was ordained Priest with 3 others. It seems impossible to get a passport for Penang. Father Anthony Khaw wanted to come here for a First Fruit Mass[20] but could not obtain a passport, nor could Joseph Reutens, who was to come here as a new student – the only one – for the next school year. Neither could Monseigneur Devals get a passport for Syonan.

We receive our ration of rice for November, a quarter less than in October. As compensation, we are given 1 *kati* of rice flour per person, at 3 dollars a *kati*.

Due to the epidemic that reaches one-fifth of the Community, and the likelihood of some aggression in early December, we decide to have the annual retreat from December 5th to 7th, so that by the 8th – the ultimatum – everything is settled and finished for this year.

December 1

Finally, news of Father Michel, for the first time since he was interned (we had a little bit of news in early January, while he was passing Prai and KL on the way to the internment camp). A Brother, interned with him (there are eleven of them), says in a postcard to the Brother Visitor that Father Michel *sends regards*; they have the facilities to exercise religion, and celebrate Mass every day in the camp chapel. This little information brings us the greatest pleasure.

---

20 The First Fruit Mass is the first Mass of a newly-ordained priest, usually celebrated in his home parish.

December 2
Oral exams are quickly over, with all the sick students, and the Supersénateurs who only sit for the writing paper. We are not on vacation yet because the retreat will take place on the 5th, 6th and 7th.

December 4
Koi Nian, our *kapala* (and *Rimpo hancho* or head of thirty families), is taken by the Police towards the evening, by *car* to the big *Police Station* on Penang Road, along with two Malays. He was in a *kedai kopi* and could not go home to inform anybody.

December 5
We saw Koi Nian at the Police Station. He said he hoped to be released on bail soon. We are starting the annual retreat of the Community.

December 6
Koi Nian has still not reappeared.

The other arrests made at the same time have not been maintained. The thefts of tapioca, vegetables, etc. are more common because of the reduced rice ration. At least a company of *Marines* has settled in the *Convent Bungalow* by the sea, and almost every night they come to manoeuvre around Mariophile. We can get eggs and fish, and pork, abundantly; but the prices are high. However, buying directly at the slaughterhouse, we get bones at $2 a *kati,* which allows us to make good soups every day for the Community. It is also cheaper to buy pork that way, $16 per *kati* (instead of $20).

December 7
Half an hour before the midday meal, precautionary alert, then raid alert. Just before the meal, *all clear.* Nothing happened.

The Malays gang up to come and ask to cut trees for building shelters.

December 8
Anniversary day of the beginning of the war in Malaya. It is going very peacefully, but the celebrations are much less spectacular than in previous years.

Our patients are better, but it seems that there is a new (ninth) case of typhoid.

December 9
The Japanese soldiers stationed in the *Convent bungalow* at Tanjung Bungah cut our *rubber* trees, and give the branches to the people; and then the people start to cut the *rubber* trees on their own authority.

December 10
We must intervene to stop the depredations made in our *rubber* plantation in front of the New Spring Tide. The College staff put to flee around fifty thieves, they pick

up and carry the wood left by the fugitives. Coconut thefts are multiplying too; but people plead extenuating circumstances. The coconut rations are reduced to one per month per family; and in the *black market*, one coconut sells for almost two dollars.

December 11

Departure of Noel Gott, acolyte of Malacca, his studies completed. His illness had prevented him from leaving with the other four already ordained priests on November 26th.

December 12

Koi Nian is back, detained for a week in the main Police Station, to testify in an investigation made about a Chinese shopkeeper in Tanjong Tokong who would have 'talked about the war'. Our patients are better, even the ninth case. The Health Department orders doctors to treat as typhoid any fever with symptoms not apparently foreign to this disease. A Brother of the Novitiate is seriously afflicted, at the hospital.

Received through the Police a communication from Monseigneur Pasotti, Apostolic Vicar of Rajaburi, who received instructions from the Vatican so that we could ordain our seminarists without *dimissionales*. He asks, on behalf of Burma's Bishops, for news of their students here. He says that everything is going well in Thailand's three Missions. The Police invite us to answer, which is done on December 12th.

December 19

We arrive with the greatest quietness at the third anniversary of the entry of Japanese troops in Penang. A modest ceremony in town marks the occasion. But the return of the Americans to the Philippines (Leyte, Mindoro) takes the momentum away from this event.

Our holidays continue peacefully. Our patients are feeling better. *Deo gratias!*

December 20

Great passive defence exercises, on the 21st as well. We buy a *kati* of *pulut* per person at $4 per *kati*. Like the previous month, we also buy a *kati* of broken rice per person at $3.60. Many people come to ask us for land lots to cultivate on the *estate*; the decrease in the rice ration is the cause. Our Japanese tenant by the seaside, who did not pay his rent for October, does not seem willing to pay for November either. He was so punctual at first! Of course, we don't mention anything to him...

December 23

The Japanese remove and take away the cement poles that were part of the fence surrounding our five houses on Kelawei Road. It seems that we have to accept a compensation of $5 per pole. The *hydrants* along the roads are protected by mounds of turf. Sentry boxes are set up at certain intersections, protected in a similar way, for two watchmen. The light signals for traffic on the roads are almost completely obscured.

It is said that considerable supplies were mounted on the *Penang Hills*, with powerful weaponry. More and more pieces of A.A. are installed in town. The Mount Erskine road and all the slopes between the Penang Hills and this road are equipped with strong defences in the most intensive way. On January 5th, there will be a general visit to the shelters that individuals have organised for their families; as a result, the inhabitants of Tanjong Tokong ask for coconut trees and are allowed to cut those which were in the middle of *rubber estates* near the village. The news arrives about a great German counteroffensive towards Belgium and Luxembourg, with penetration of these regions in certain points, but it seems that the shock is short of influencing the course of events. Americans have firmly established themselves in several islands of the Philippines.

December 29

There is a case of *blackwater fever*[21] in Tanjong Tokong. One of our patients at Mariophile had malaria again and passed red urine. This is worrying. The other patients are frankly feeling better.

1945 (2605)

January

Four Malays are buried today in the cemetery near Mariophile. The village is full of feverish people. The dirt of the locality is repulsive.

We have news of Father Michel by a nurse who saw him in Changi (Singapore) smoking his pipe, with a team of Brothers of Christian Schools cultivating a garden.

January 2

The Malays from Telok Bahang, going to the mountain in search of rattan to make their fisheries, have made Saint Jean their headquarters. They asked permission from Heng Kai (who lives below and whom we have appointed as a kind of guardian).

The ration of rice is diminished this month (8 *katis*, instead of 9 *katis*, for adult males, much less for women, and even less for children, this for the town, which we're supposed to be part of. Elsewhere, it's half!) So, all the prices are going up, the pork from $26 to $28 per *kati*. People make a rush for tapioca; the surroundings of Mariophile, where our servants have planted on our land, present a lively spectacle; the buyers of all races thronging to buy as soon as the tubers are lifted, two dollars per *kati*. Some of our servants make about ten thousand dollars from tapioca! One of them, who does not have as much land as the others, goes this month to seek his

---

21 Blackwater fever is a severe form of malaria in which blood cells are rapidly destroyed, resulting in dark urine.

fortune in Kapala Batas; the cook of the students, Loi Fatt, aka Chew Kweh Chin, turned out to be an inveterate pilferer, one not to employ again.

Moreover, he is not replaced, the students often cooking for themselves, and the tailor being ready to cook on occasion, leaving for that day the sewing machine for the stoves.

January 6
An enemy raid on Medan is announced. No alert was sounded here, but at the time of the raid, some activity had been noticed. The Japanese are nervous as a result of this raid.

January 7
Cholera and typhoid vaccination for the whole Community.

The resumption of classes for the beginning of the school year is postponed to Tuesday, January 9th.

January 8
Monday, false alarm around 14:00. Raid alert is sounded then, almost immediately, the end of alert.

January 9
At 2:00, an isolated plane, flying relatively low, approaches the town. At the same time, a battery opens fire. No alert sounded and everything returned to calm. Another mistake, most probably. Resumption of classes today for the beginning of the year. Same routine as last year.

Thirty-nine students all together, no new arrival, because the only seminarist from Malacca who was at the Agricultural Colony in Bahau cannot (being Eurasian) obtain a passport to Penang. It's Joe Reutens, whose family is nonetheless in Penang. Two in Philosophy, twenty-three in Theology and fourteen with studies completed, total thirty-nine; Fathers present, Rouhan, Denarié, Monjean, Piffaut, Paroissin, and Aloysius. Father Michel is interned in Changi and Father Meissonnier is in Bahau (N.S.)

January 10
Preparatory alert around noon. Nothing happens. The newspaper says that on the 9th, very early in the day, an enemy plane flew over, launched *flares* and a few *leaflets*. Very daring tapioca theft on our land at the expense of our boy Lee Chong, sick at the hospital. People steal almost by force and we turn to the civilian Police (Jikeidan).

January 11
Around 9:00 (Tokyo Time), a bomb falls in the harbor, without any warning. The raid alert sounds almost immediately afterwards. Two more bombs next, then another very far away. No firing of anti-aircraft batteries, barely a few machine gun shots.

No indication of air combat. The sound of the falling bomb is heard clearly and for quite a long time, and ends with the explosion of the bomb which, as we can hear it from here, is not very violent (except for the first one, but it is psychologically always like that). End of alert, after about an hour.

Two submarines, which were in port, are leaving, zigzagging, turning, stopping, starting off again, returning towards the port. Then a bomb descends on the port, then another. An interruption, then a third bomb, the smoke we see rising in a column towards the Cape of the town. No alert with the siren this time, but only with a gong, from the Tanjong Tokong Police Station. Father Aloysius, who had tried to go to town at the end of the first alert, was, at the beginning of the second one, already in Tanjong Tokong, where the Jikeidan told him that the phone does not work anymore.

At noon, a series of small aerial fights, very high in the sky, begins. Some anti-aircraft shells, very few. Then two bombs on the harbour, then two more, then one, then one, at intervals of a quarter of an hour or so. One of the submarines disappears, the other is motionless in the Straits in front of Mariophile. Simultaneously in several places, reactions occur which seem to indicate several planes attacking together. At 13:30, signal of the end of alert and immediately afterwards, signal of air raid, and a quarter of an hour later, end of alert.

At 14:30, a signal that an alert is coming soon, and after a quarter of an hour, *all clear*. Meanwhile, we make a thrilling manhunt to chase out coconut thieves near the village.

Three planes would have intercepted the assailants and a Japanese might have been shot down.

Information coming from town, a bomb was dropped on the Convent, which was then refuted – the bomb would have fallen close by, in the sea. The Telegraph would have been hit (several victims at this place), some homes demolished at Bishop Street, the corner of Government Buildings where the Governor's office is located (this is where the Resident had his office) would be destroyed, as well as the Victoria Clock Tower, several bombs on the buildings of the Navy Plane Factory (on the old Esplanade); Butterworth Wharf, Mitchell Pier, and the Power Station in Prai would have been just missed.

The news comes that Monseigneur Devals received the Extreme Unction (malaria and septic ulcer at the foot resulting from a spider bite).

January 13

In the morning, two cannon shots on a plane flying over the town, and we believe a raid is coming, but it is limited to these two white trails of smoke surrounding a plane that continues to circle around in the sky, no warning. In the evening, a strong explosion believed to be a bomb, but nothing precise. The newspaper does not say much about the raid on the 11th. Ten B-29s flew over Penang; other towns in Malaya would have been bombed, especially Seletar in Singapore. The chief of the Military Police exhorts everyone to stay calm and to cooperate.

Moreover, it is known that the number of deaths would be anywhere from 2 to 300 casualties, no Catholic killed, but two Indian Catholics slightly injured. The central building of the Government Offices might have been razed to the ground; there would have been a lot of deaths in the shelters of the *Naval Aircraft Factory* (on the old Esplanade). A submarine was allegedly sunk. Two German pilots and a Japanese man tried to intercept the raiders; the Japanese would have been shot down. Government offices are being relocated and dispersed in various locations.

We can easily find beef at 15 or 16 dollars per *kati* in Ayer Itam, more difficult elsewhere.

The leaflets launched by the plane that came on the 9th contained a few things (in Romanised Malay):

> We have reduced Germany to powerlessness, so we now have time to take care of you. We will come from time to time, but have no fear. Stay away from military objectives. Do not cooperate with the Japanese. You will have to suffer a little, but it will not be for long.

No news from Monseigneur Devals.

It is said that the alerts will no longer be given with the siren.

Father Denarié remains at the Assumption Church in the midst of the falling bombs and composes poems in his shelter while waiting.

January 14

Alert during the High Mass at Mariophile (precautionary only). We continue as if nothing had happened. At 13:30, at the beginning of the meal, raid alert for 20 minutes, but it is not heard at Mariophile. The precautionary alert lasts until quite late in the afternoon.

January 15

At 1:00, precautionary alert, then after 15 minutes, raid alert that lasts 45 minutes. Nothing happens and you cannot even hear a plane. The Community has been quietly sleeping. Father Anthony Michael, ordained in November in Seremban, could come to see his family and he says the Community Mass at Mariophile. In the evening, around 18:00, precautionary alert. For an hour or so. A plane flies very high and some say it's a B-29. People do not worry and traffic in the streets is perfectly normal.

It is reported that Monseigneur Devals had his leg cut off and is better.

January 16

Quiet day. Father Denarié, recounting his impressions, said that the bombing was not frightening; the sound of the fall was more like that of a plane moving laterally, and the explosions seemed weak as if the projectiles were exploding deep into the ground.

Our servants, who are earning thousands of dollars selling their tapioca, offer us a *Makan Besar* (rice, pork at $44 a *kati*, fish).

January 17

Monseigneur Devals dies at the Seremban Hospital at 15:00. The news arrives through the phone around 23:00 in Penang.

January 22

Alert at 2:00, precautionary first, then a plane flies over town and the raid alert is given; the plane leaves without having done anything but observe, and after ¾ hour, end of alert. This is the second time this has occurred on the night of Sunday to Monday.

January 23

A little before midnight, precautionary alert and almost immediately raid alert, a plane passes and circles over, then leaves. We are going to sleep.

January 24

Around 2:00, raid alert, two planes fly along over the town and island. After two hours of alert, the *all clear* is sounded. The Community remains quiet, laying low. In fact, nothing happens.

The Japanese make shelters in the *kampung* of the Assumption Church, between the road, the church, and or Fathers' house.

We cannot find chillies anymore. If we manage to find some, it is 1 dollar a piece (for dried chillies). Four thousand dollars are offered for a *second-hand* bike.

The Japanese dig trenches on our land at Mariophile near the Malay cemetery. News of an Allied landing at Sumatra reaches us.

January 25

Around midnight, between the 24th and the 25th, alert. Allied planes arrive flying very low. They follow the coast of the island and arrive above Tanjong Tokong, then fly towards the opposite coast. We can discern them pretty clearly in the night. They fly away, then come back after a circuit and fly the same route again. A series of muffled sounds are heard. A big explosion shakes the ground and the whole house shakes. A noise is then heard from the direction of Sungei Petani. No Japanese reaction. In the morning, the Japanese blow up the mines in the channel and we assume that the planes which came in the night had launched them.

The day is calm.

January 26

Again, around midnight between the 25th and the 26th, alert, the Allied planes pass, then move away. The *all clear* is sounded, but a quarter of an hour later, a new alert, a plane coming from the South, following the coast of the Peninsula, is flying North. It is greeted by a burst of machine-gunners and *flaming onions* rising to the sky, following a sinuous trajectory. The plane flies away and the *all clear* is sounded again. Around 15:00, a very strong explosion, difficult to locate.

The newspaper announces a big enemy raid on Sumatra.

A telegram dated 23rd announces that Monseigneur Olçomendy has been elected Capitular Vicar of the Mission.

January 27

The night from the 26th to the 27th is quiet in Penang. But Singapore is visited by planes.

Departure of Fair, from Malacca, withdrawing at his own request, by himself.

January 28

Alert in the night from the 27th to the 28th, around midnight. The raid alert sounds ¼ hour after the precautionary alert. After one hour, *all clear*. Besides that, nothing to see or hear.

January 29

Alert in the night from the 28th to the 29th. After one hour, *all clear*. The planes flew past over and over again without any reaction from the defence. At the Hospital, the Head Doctor orders the staff to no longer take notice of nocturnal alerts and to continue to sleep as if nothing happened; we would come to wake them up, if needed, to tend to the wounded. At 14:00, precautionary alert, then nothing else.

January 30

The night between the 29th and the 30th is quiet. Around 9:00, precautionary alert. The battle is raging in Burma around the Mandalay region and elsewhere. At the Hospital, surgical operations are going on smoothly. A Novitiate Brother, who was urgently operated upon for acute appendicitis on the 16th, is standing and walking on the 27th. But it seems that the Japanese doctors occasionally want to intervene to get a hand in the operation. What Doctor Apparajou himself does is very well done.

Around noon, precautionary alert, followed by raid alert. The raider appears, flying at great height. No defence reaction. *All clear*. Marines are patrolling our surroundings day and night. Teams of soldiers and coolies dig trenches at various points of the property. The hill crest that dominates Tanjong Tokong is fortified as an island of resistance with shelters and nests of machine guns. The Superior walking in the rambutan plantation in the evening, to detect tapioca thieves operating at nightfall, was arrested by a patrol, searched, brought to the officer commanding the Tanjong Tokong detachment and, with the assurance of a Malay that he was well known, released without being molested in any way. All night we hear the calls of soldiers from one post to the next. It seems that the authorities fear a landing by air or sea. The Germans stationed in Penang are taken to Singapore and, according to one of them, would be parked in a hotel, then interned in a camp when Germany surrenders; it is only a matter of days, he says.

A Japanese police officer comes to Mariophile to find out if there are any premises available and to ask who we are administratively dependent on.

January 31
At 1:00, precautionary alert, then raid alert, then *all clear* with nothing more. At 8:00, precautionary alert. No more medicine available to the public, everything is requisitioned by the Authorities, and permits that were previously granted are suspended. Quinine distributions to doctors are also suspended. It is only available at the Hospital, and merely in solution. At Mariophile we continue our routine as usual, classes and fieldwork. The alerts do not bother us and the Community remains very calm. A *kumiai* is formed for the pork and almost overnight pork meat disappears from the market. We rather enjoyed it lately, despite the high prices (45 dollars a *kati*). From time to time, we had beef at $20 a *kati*, sheep (or rather goat?) at $28. We buy with licence 1 picul of corn, 1 picul of *ragi*, 1 picul of *green peas* at prices around $500 per picul, which is very cheap at the moment; retailers sell *green peas* at $17 per *kati!* We also have a permanent licence to buy a picul of any commodity available at wholesale-*controlled price*. We also buy 3 baskets (about 3 piculs) of dried *mee* for a thousand dollars a picul (retail price is 14 dollars per *kati!*) Our servants earn around twenty thousand dollars each, selling the tapioca they had planted in the lots of land that we had allocated them (in lieu of salary increase); they have also deposited with us much more money than we have ourselves. Amusing things happen, like this one. On pay-day, Father Aloysius gives a servant his wages for the month (twenty dollars). The servant takes the money, and donates $400 to the Community to buy meat. Our boy, Lee Chong, who was so faithful and devoted throughout the war time, came back from the Hospital where he had spent nearly two months, suffering from tuberculosis. He is resting here now. One day, he offers the Community a *makan besar* of peace time with rice, meat, fish in abundance. He too sold the tapioca that he had planted before falling ill. He and two other servants (Teng Loi and Hin Min) buy a plantation in Balik Pulau for 40,000 dollars. Money no longer has value. A used bicycle, $4,000. A tyre (*locally made*), $240.

A circular of Father Olçomendy, Capitular Vicar, orders the imposed oration *De Spiritu Sancto* for the election of the new bishop, and says that he will announce when circumstances make it possible to vote for the election.

February 1
Precautionary alert during the Community Mass after a quiet night. Raid alert around 7:30, and around 14:15. The bombardment of the town begins with a plane flying very high up. The first bomb apparently falls in the vicinity of the Railways Building, the second, further, perhaps in Prai, the third, on the Municipal Workshops in Sungei Pinang. Reaction of the anti-aircraft defence for a few moments. The bomber plane is perfectly visible despite its great height, against the very clear sky. It moves away, towards Muka Head, then returns. Three bombs, clearly on the right of the Railway Tower. One more round, a direct hit near Sungei Pinang. Other planes arrive. Five bombs land on the town between the Cape and the Railway Tower. The series of four or five bombs follow each other about half an hour apart, while new bombers appear from time to time, coming from various directions. At

the end, a little before noon, two bombs are launched by a bomber chased by a Japanese fighter, they swoop over town, on the Cape; the bomber, still pursued, heads towards Tanjong Tokong, he launches a bomb in the sea, a good distance from the College, then the last one, also in the sea, near Tanjong Tokong – at the end of the sandbank where the students used to fish – and disappears. *All clear* during lunch, the Community having returned to the refectory at noon to dine. With all this, we skipped the morning class. After dinner, two alerts in quick succession, with an airplane passing overhead and a defence response. We return to the shelters, then the third *all clear* of the day is sounded, the spiritual reading takes place at 15:00 as usual, and then work in the garden.

In town, according to the news that we could get the same evening, Father Riboud and the orphans of the church are uninjured, and the church and the presbytery were not hit, but it fell very close to Penang Road and Sri Bahari Road. The Assumption Church was surrounded by bombing, bombs at the Convent and at the Brothers [School] – two houses demolished in Love Lane near the church, others in Muntri Street, a wing of Hutchings School demolished. Father Dérédec, seeing the shaky state of his house, took refuge just behind, in a house in the passageway leading from Love Lane. Neither the presbytery nor the church was hit, but the force of the explosion broke windows and doors. At the Chinese church, Fathers Koh and Thomas Chin are doing well, although a little concussed. A bomb fell on Patani Road and wiped out an outstanding Eurasian family. Another in River Road killed sick people. Most of the victims are still under the debris. A Catholic Indian cowherd is injured and many of his cows were killed. No fires at all in town.

February 2
Quiet night. A brief alert in the morning, without incident.

February 3
Alert in the morning, without incident. Father Dérédec, who had left the Assumption Church on the second morning and spent the night at Pulau Tikus, comes in the evening to stay in the College, in a servant's room near the workshop. Some of the Sisters leave the College, going either to Balik Pulau or Bukit Mertajam. The Superior also intends to go away, but postpones her departure. In any case, she will leave behind four Sisters and twelve girls in the College.

February 4
Precautionary alert in the morning. Yesterday's newspaper announced that the Russians are sixty miles from Berlin and that the Americans have surrounded Manila.

Many people evacuate the town of Penang and go either to the Peninsula or to less exposed corners of the island. The Government is also interested in out-of-town facilities. Already, in addition to the visit mentioned on January 30, a Marines' doctor came to Mariophile to inspect the premises on February 2nd; he came back on the 3rd, with another military doctor. Very amiably, they said, 'This is a holy place, we won't disturb you'. They went first to the Novitiate. They are looking for a building to use as a hospital. On the same day, the Bunkyo Kacho (Head of Education), Hirano-san, arrived impromptu to Mariophile during the class and asked some questions, in a very kind manner. He asked for a report about the house, which the Superior must bring to his *office* within two or three days.

According to the newspaper, on 1 February, there were ten enemy aircraft flying over Penang and ninety over Singapore. Other towns in Malaya were not affected.

February 5
The night is quiet, the morning, too. At the end of dinner, a precautionary alert; no other event.

It has been more than three months since our Japanese tenants, at Bungalow no. 514 by the sea, last paid their rental. At first, they were so punctual! All our other tenants pay very regularly. The report on our staff, Fathers, students, and servants is given to the Bunkyo Kacho.

February 6
Very quiet. The fall of Manila is announced in the newspaper as of February 3.

February 7
The Bunkyo Kacho comes to the College to find room to put soldiers and sailors. The Reverend Mother says that she has no authority to hand over the College. Then the Bunkyo Kacho takes the Sisters' school in Pulau Tikus to put up the sailors. Already, the Kelawai Malay school and nurses' quarters at the Hospital have been taken. No alert that day. The fall of Manila makes a great impression everywhere.

February 8
At the end of the Community Mass, a precautionary alert, nothing more. Permission is given to the inhabitants to leave town.

The ration of rice for the month of February arrived yesterday in full, it is of very good quality.

The Japanese Marines dig, with the help of local requisitioned labour (without taking in the staff of the College), a trench with its flanks in our garden, beginning at the turn of the cement road near a big *janggus*, then running towards the Malay cemetery. At the College, a great moving of materials by the Brothers and Sisters from the Sisters' School at Pulau Tikus which is occupied by the Navy offices. The transport is executed by Navy *lorries* with the help of 200 children, from the Navy school, from the Brothers and their students, and from the Sisters and their children. It is a continual ebb and flow between the two establishments, and very picturesque, with the uniforms of the boys of the Navy school. This transported material is partly housed in the *lusorium*. Also, on that day, the Deputy Director of the Government School in Pulau Tikus, whose house in Penang Road was bombed, to whom the Sisters had given asylum in their school in Pulau Tikus and who, on that day, was dislodged by the Navy, is authorised to settle temporarily in the *fabrica* with his family. The material of the students who were there is partly buried in the two corners facing Bagan Jermal, the middle remaining free. Few things are stored in the store at the end of the *fabrica*, and the ladders that were there are put in the *lavarium*. Mr Hansen, our former Dane tenant of no. 516, Tanjung Bungah, is very tired and it seems his lungs are affected. He settled with his wife and his son in a shack near his River Road factory. Lately, his wife was in Bahau with other Danes. It seems that his daughter is living together with a Dane who stays with them here, since more than a year ago, and whose wife is in Cape Town.

February 9

Precautionary alert during the Community Mass, nothing more. At the College, intervention of the Navy seeking to install accumulators in the store at the end of the *fabrica*, and the Director of Education asking to use some new buildings for the classes because of the occupation of several schools by the Navy. The Navy is pushed aside by the resistance of the school staff and it is decided to give the Science room (occupied by the *barangs* of the Sisters and of the College) to Education if it insists. But in fact, the premises already allocated to teaching are more than sufficient because, out of a theoretical number of more than five hundred students, there are barely fifty who make an act of being present. In Mariophile, nothing alarming, the Marines helped by local workers continue to dig their trench in our tapioca field. On occasion, they come to the house and inspect the dormitories. The Sisters' house by the seaside is inhabited again, but by fewer people.

February 10

Early in the morning, precautionary alert. Again, at the beginning of the afternoon, nothing more. Navy soldiers continue their trenches in our garden. The Military Authority cut many coconut trees between the main road and the sea in Mariophile. No further developments at the College with regard to its occupation by the Navy.

February 11

Sunday, towards the end of the Community Mass, precautionary alert, nothing more. Solemn High Mass of thanksgiving for the recovery of all our sick students. In fact, the infirmary is empty in the morning, all our typhoid and malaria patients were released from their prolonged captivity in the infirmary. All this did not prevent a student, Jackson from Mandalay, from being admitted there with 104 fever in the afternoon.

Shortly after the end of the High Mass, the Bunkyo Kacho, Hirano-san, comes in and tells us that Mariophile must be completely evacuated by us, the nearby private houses, too, because the Navy wants not only the buildings, but the whole position for the defence. We are not even allowed to occupy *sheds* if we were to build them on one end of the property. We can harvest everything that is harvestable, the Navy will compensate us for the rest of our plantations. As our livelihood comes from our garden, in compensation for this loss, the Kacho offers to ask the Navy for an extra *gantang* of rice per month and per person. He proposes two evacuation plans, one to the College, and the other to the Agricultural Colony of Penang located in the Province. The Navy would provide the means of transportation. The Superior asks for 24 hours to reflect, which is granted to him.

February 12

Quiet night and day. For the last 3 days, the rain comes in abundance every afternoon towards the evening. What a shame to leave our garden which is green again after the drought of January! Council is held at noon to deliberate on the response to give to the Bunkyo Kacho. We decide to go to the College where the bulk of the Community will remain, from which two Fathers and the students of Malacca, now ten in number, will be dispatched to Province Wellesley to start a plantation – in case of need, it would be possible to emigrate the rest of the Community there, and which we could liquidate without difficulty by sending the Malayans home if the enterprise does not succeed. The Sisters will remain in the College quarters and the Government School will maintain its position. We ask for compensation for the abandonment of Mariophile, one additional rice *gantang* per person per month, the Navy card to get our rations from Navy Supplies, the use of the Mariophile chapel as a store-house to keep our bulky furniture, and the transportation facilities required for our baggage to the College and the Province. The Superior goes to the Bunkyo Kacho office. His proposals are accepted (that of the Navy Supplies, not without difficulty), that is to say, the Bunkyo Kacho is responsible for presenting them to the Navy, which will decide. Hirano-san is very kind and presents the Superior to the Governor who expresses his regret for the obligation to move us, thanks us for the goodwill we show, for the way we cultivated the property of Mariophile; he promises help if needed for the Community members who will go to the Province, and wishes us good luck in our new facilities. He shakes hands with the Superior, from whom he takes leave. The Bunkyo Kacho will inform us when there is a response from the Navy, which must also indicate the time allowed for evacuation and the area to be evacuated. In the morning, four Marines, including an officer, came to inspect the buildings and were very interested in the Frigidaire; they were told it was not working (which is true because we have no power). At the College, the *modus vivendi* with the Sisters is elaborated without delay and their moving operation, from the Chapel wing to the wing of the study, begins without delay. Already in the morning and afternoon, with the tricycle and the handcart, students bring down some fragile equipment (Sacristy and infirmary). The phone (no. 548) which was at the Pulau Tikus Brothers' school is transported by the Navy to the College and installed in the parlor.

February 13

Precautionary alert in the morning, nothing more. The Bunkyo Kacho comes to Mariophile, says that Sunday, the 18th, is the last day for our stay up there. On the 16th, *lorries* will come, one to move our luggage from Tanjong Tokong to Pulau

Tikus, throughout the day, another to take the group that is going to the Province, to the quay, with another trip for the luggage of the group. A special sixty-tonne *launch* will transport them to Prai, and from Prai, a government *lorry* will take them to Machang Buboh or Matang Tinggi, making as many trips as necessary. The concession of an extra *gantang* of rice is not granted by the Navy, nor is the use of the chapel, nor the use of the Navy card to access the Navy Supplies. The Kacho has with him, as interpreter, the Director of the Penang Teachers' College, Miura-san, who is quite unpleasant in his manner. On this day, we make several trips with luggage from Mariophile to the College with the tricycle and the handcart, and we try to contact Father Lek by telephone, without success, to arrange our resettlement in the Province.

February 14

The Superior is going to meet Hirano and try to obtain more than one *lorry* from the Navy for the transport of luggage. He will also ask for an extra *gantang* of rice for Province Wellesley settlers, as it is given to the Settlers of the Agricultural Settlements, and insist on our determination to stay in the College at all costs, at least a small group of Asians, to safeguard our belongings and the Convent's – a statement motivated by a remark from Hirano-san, saying that we should move to the College with the idea that we might have to leave it to go elsewhere, as well as the Sisters who would be split up and sent, some to Balik Pulau, and others to Bukit Mertajam.

Officers from the Naiseika come to Mariophile to estimate the amount of compensation to be paid us for the occupation of Mariophile by the Navy.

Efforts to establish communication with Father Lek are still fruitless.

Around 10:00 precautionary alert, then raid alert. *All clear* half an hour later, then again raid alert and *all clear* around noon. The enemy planes fly past over and over again, without being disturbed. Later, we learn that a dozen enemy planes had observed the town at leisure.

February 15

Raid alert late in the morning. Just before, Matsuta-san arrived from the Bunkyo Kacho with Mr Chan, the chief *clerk*, to Mariophile to draw up the papers for the police with regard to our departure from here, and also for the rice card, and what will happen to our servants, currently four. They will remain on site as much as the Navy will allow them, and will cultivate tapioca and other vegetables on the *estate*. The rice cook will come to the College every day to cook the rice. During the morning, students bring under the first dormitory supplies, bags and crates, ready to be removed. Shortly after midday, a *lorry*, on loan from Mr David from Balik Pulau, made six trips. The students here load and accompany the *lorry*; at the College, Brothers and Sisters unload the *barangs* and carry them. All are exhausted. What will happen tomorrow when several *lorries* arrive, and our numbers are reduced due to the group of eleven leaving for the Province? The answer arrives from Bukit

Mertajam, where Father Teng is still with Father Lek; it is to Matang Tinggi that the group will go. Miura-san of the Education Office comes to warn us that the Military Police will be strictly examining the baggage of those who cross the channel.

February 16

Great moving day. Fathers Piffaut and Paroissin, along with nine students from Malacca and Sarawak, first leave for the quay and Matang Tinggi. A student from Malacca, de Souza, accompanies them to Prai, comes back, stays at Mariophile, and will follow us to the College. The *lorry* provided by the Education Office arrives around 9h30, leaves, returns, and makes a second trip. In addition to Mr David's *lorry*, two government *lorries*, also arrive, and all day long, there is a constant coming and going between Mariophile and the College; here, the students loading, there, the Brothers and Sisters receiving the *lorries* and unloading the things, and stowing them under the direction of Father Aloysius. The Brothers even come to Mariophile to help with the loading. Meanwhile, our famous tricycle carries the most fragile things. We take the benches, the tables, the beds, the altars, the furniture, except those from the Fathers' house, the billiard table, the large table and the large cupboard, and the large cemented and tiled tables in the refectory, totalling twelve. De Souza, who had accompanied the travelers, returns to bring us news of the trip. All was well, no bombing, no alert, as we already knew, no hitch, until the departure from Prai. The MPs searched the people only, not the luggage on the pier in Penang. No rain here, only late at night, during the last trips of the *lorries*. The *drivers* eat with us, and we give each of them $20. While luggage is being transported, Japanese or local officers from the Education Office, including Mr Siew Tat, brother-in-law of our former seminarist Michael Loh, stay put with us at Mariophile. We are trying to sell our billiard from Mariophile, but we do not succeed because it is a French table, without pockets. In the evening, our new rice cards are made ready, with great speed and graciousness on the part of the Authorities. But a counterorder arrives regarding our servants, they will not be able to plant as they did until now, nor stay in the hut in the middle of their plantation. This is a big disappointment for them, a big loss, too. So far, none of our students have been recruited by the Japanese to dig trenches around Mariophile, but one of our servants was recruited for a week.

February 17

Saturday. The Blessed Sacrament is removed from the chapel of Mariophile after three years and almost three months of continuous presence except during the shelling, when we moved it to the refuge at St Peter's. Mr David's *lorry* comes for a full day again. Mr David's foreman willingly consented to help, because he earns a big profit from buying piculs of tapioca hurriedly extracted here by our servants, and selling them in town for a huge profit margin. The students do not have time to uproot, so, it is our servants who extract and sell ($3.50 per *kati*). By Saturday night, goods worth more than eight thousand dollars have been sold. Precautionary alert, then raid alert in the morning, without bombing and with merely a little defence reaction against enemy planes, as we can clearly see in the sky. After about an hour, the raid alert stops, but the precautionary alert lasts most of the day. At 16:00, the Superior, summoned to the Education Office, is informed that the rental of our buildings is for a period of six months to a year, not more than a year in any case; we are given $3,600 as rental, and compensation of about $18,000 for what we lose as fruits, coconuts, vegetables and so on, in total about $22,000. In the morning, with the first *lorry*, Father Monjean left with five students, settled in the College, and is responsible for repairing the floor of the fourth dormitory, all worm-eaten; that is where we shall pack all the students for the night. Five other students will join them around noon, and only the Superior, Father Denarié, and eighteen students remain in Mariophile. Father Aloysius is still sleeping at Mariophile, but during the day, he spends most of his time at the College.

February 18

Sunday. In the morning, there are three Low Masses, the third one serving as a substitute for the High Mass. There is no longer a single altar, no statue in the chapel. Mass is said on a table, which is slightly elevated. The first Mass is celebrated by Fr. Denarié, the second (Community) by Father Aloysius, the third (replacing the sung Mass) by Father Rouhan. Meanwhile, two trucks (one from the government provided by the Education Office, and the other on loan from a friend living in Balik Pulau, Mr David again) make many trips, the beds are all sent to the College. We also bring tapioca, bananas, papayas... Matsuta-san from the Education Office comes to see if everything is going well. A Marine officer goes around and orders us to clean the house and its surroundings before we leave. We tell him that on Sunday, it is impossible. He insists and gives the order. We tell him, tomorrow; after a little hesitation, he agrees. Towards nightfall, Father Denarié and the students, except five, leave with the last trucks, and Father Rouhan stays to guard the house at night; in fact, the cleaning work begins with the remaining students and continues through the night, interrupted by a meal a little before midnight. Five hundred empty bottles are transported to caretaker Koi Nian's house.

February 19

Before the sun rises, Father Rouhan goes to the College to say Mass and then returns to Mariophile. After breakfast, a dozen students, along with Father Denarié, leave the College to clean up at Mariophile. Mr David's truck was supposed to carry them, but a raid alert early in the morning stopped him. Students set off on foot, on *all clear*; but a new raid alert immobilises them in the vicinity of Tanjong Tokong. Many planes pass by, heading to Kuala Lumpur, and swoop past, dropping some bombs on the Bayan Lepas airfield. The students, in small groups, sneak by along the footpaths and arrive at Mariophile a little before noon. They are given a meal at Koi Nian's home and then they start the cleaning up at Mariophile. The Marine officer, who came on Sunday, makes a brief appearance to see what is happening. Around nightfall, the work is finished, Father Denarié and the students, except three, come back to the College with two handcarts filled with various things. Father Rouhan and the three remaining students spend the night at Mariophile, the former leaving before daybreak for the College to say Mass.

February 20

Tuesday, around 9:00, a Navy detachment appears with brooms, sprayers, etc. and begins cleaning and disinfecting the premises. The officer who had asked for the clean-up compliments us on the way we did it and thanks us. Shortly after, Father Denarié arrives with Mr David's truck and a few students, to load our last luggage, some firewood and tapioca. Koi Nian is introduced to the officers as the one who will keep the water facility in good condition. A precautionary alert does not hinder the preparations of the Japanese. They bring equipment to build barracks. Five cars and two trucks create a clutter around the house. Soldiers repair the damaged power line in one place and install a cable. As we are leaving, a young officer approaches us, he speaks very good English and a little French. He starts with some courtesies, then continues with some Japanese propaganda and railing against the Anglo–Americans, mixing up the tittle-tattle with poor philosophy, identifying the emperor with Christ, God and Nature, the equivalence of all religions, saying that the Japanese could not prove all this but firmly believed it, and that, besides, we Christians could not prove our religion scientifically, for example, the birth of Christ from a Virgin. We talk a little, he says that he will come to the College to talk and we part good friends. We leave, and on the way we see teams of workers cutting our coconut trees from the *estate* to load them on trucks, by dozens.

Around noon everyone is reunited in the College, and Mariophile is for the third time under military occupation; the first two times in 1900 by the Italians and Russians successively, as they returned from the Chinese war against the Boxers.[22] The afternoon in the College is spent putting in order the material brought back from Mariophile. Towards evening, we start to know that on Monday morning, planes had done a lot of damage to the Sentul *workshops* in Kuala Lumpur. Father Aloysius learns by phone that an aunt and a cousin were killed.

February 21

Wednesday, at night, around midnight, raid alert; planes fly over, nothing more. In the morning, we start our new plantations between the kitchen and the Novitiate. There is enough land. We cut the old coconut trees, the very young ones not yet giving fruit, and keep only the trees in full yield. Our goats are in the garage, with the chickens. The cows are still at Mariophile. The students are working well despite their desire to leave, instead, to join their colleagues in Matang Tinggi where they

---

22 The Boxer Rebellion was an anti-imperialist, anti-foreign, and anti-Christian uprising that took place in China between 1899 and 1901. The Eight Nation Alliance, composed of American, Austro–Hungarian, British, French, German, Italian, Japanese, and Russian forces, defeated the Boxers and the Chinese army.

would be further away from the shelling. News from this Matang Tinggi group told us that as soon as they arrived, they had to leave their luggage behind and go to the Police Station of Bukit Mertajam by truck. The Authorities had not informed the local Police, the whole group was sent back to Matang Tinggi and confined in the house, without being able to circulate. The next day everything was fine.

The afternoon at the College is spent making arrangements and installations in the house. We work in the garden every morning, everyone without exception. In the evening, partly in the garden, partly in the shelters, partly put to various work. Working hours will be as during holidays, 8:30 to 11:00 (sunny time) and 15:30 to 17:20. The spiritual reading is at 15h00. That day, the government school, which occupies half of the College on the classroom side, was in session. There were not many students.

There were a thousand killed and wounded in K.L. where the *workshops* were razed to the ground.

February 22
Around midnight, precautionary alert, then raid alert. The planes fly over, very low. It seems they are laying mines in the North Channel.

Quiet day. In the morning, everyone cut down coconut trees and cleared the new garden. In the afternoon, we set up a library – a students' preparation room upstairs in the corridor – above the BMV statue (missing) in the middle of the central building. There is the fence made of screens that separates us from the Sisters' domain. Leaning against the partition of the Fathers' library, but on the outer side, benches and chairs are arranged to make an exercise room. The government school was running in the morning, with quite a few students.

February 23
Quiet day, after a night without warning. Work in the garden in the morning, in the evening, construction of a shelter for the Sisters in the drain that separates the houses of the Pulau Tikus church, from the path along the edge of the College property, behind the lavatory.

In Mariophile, the soldiers have not yet settled down, the work of installation continues. En Voon, our *kapala*, settled where the students used to guard the garden, gets Japanese permission to plant around his hut. Koi Nian is urged by them to become the guardian of the entire property, and to ensure that no one enters it. He must bring his rice card to the Japanese. He is told (as well as two other vegetable growers in the neighborhood of his house) not to plant for a few days; then he will be told whether he can plant or not. We continue to have En Voon to dig up the tapioca and bring it to the College.

The Sisters' cooking pleases everybody and we are very satisfied.

February 24
During the Community Mass, precautionary alert, then raid alert. After breakfast, *all clear*. Then alert again in the morning, very extended. The enemy planes fly a long

time over the town. Very little noticeable reaction. Some gunshots. Perhaps there was a bomb thrown into the distance. Works in the garden continue in the morning. In the afternoon, we carry on working on the Sisters' shelter (extreme necessity). Father Sélier of Balik Pulau being indisposed, Father Dérédec goes to keep him company.

February 25

Quiet night and day. However, an enemy plane was seen above us, but no alert. For the first time in more than three years, we sing the High Mass and Vespers in the College Chapel. Father Georgius Mg Kiat of Rangoon officiates. The Community of Sisters (about thirty people, including the girls) are positioned on benches, enlarging the choir. At Mariophile, we can still extract a little tapioca and daily we receive a quantity large enough for the 3 Communities. As the Japanese had put barbed wire to close off most of the land where we and our servants planted, we can no longer sell tapioca. We made some twenty thousand dollars selling this tapioca. Koi Nian, it seems, has permission to plant. The news arrives that yesterday's planes hit the harbour and the area surrounding Singapore, where there was a lot of damage. It is said that the battle for Malaya has begun. In Penang, the crossroads are guarded by military posts. Koi Nian and En Voon were able to get into the Mariophile kitchen to repair a pipe. The first dormitory is fully occupied, there are black mosquito nets on the beds. The battle is raging in Burma, where the Japanese counterattack strongly after having lost Mandalay. In Japan, Iwojima Island is occupied. Berlin is under a colossal raid. In the Philippines, the Bataan Peninsula has fallen completely.

February 26

Quiet night and day. Clearing in the morning and putting in order in the evening. Small theft in the kitchen at night, two Sisters' aprons pulled from the outside with a hook.

February 27

Quiet night and day. Works are actively continuing. We bring our four cows back from Mariophile and install them at the College, in the wooden shed between the kitchen and the Novitiate. At night, the Brothers apprehended a tapioca thief in their garden.

February 28

Precautionary alert at night. The planes pass, but no reaction. Shortly after the alert, the dogs bark at the kitchen. Nobody stirred, neither from the alert, nor the barking. Too bad, because the thieves were operating in the kitchen. They probably got in over the wall of the servants' bathroom which is enclosed in the kitchen. They snatched some provisions and some objects; little, but nowadays that amounts to several hundred dollars. They operated at leisure with the light of the moon. In the morning, new precautionary alert, we see a B-29 circling loftily, no reaction.

March 1

Beginning of the month of St Joseph, with the observations of the vow of 1943. St Joseph has so far answered us. Our night vigil around the kitchen waiting around for the thieves was not fruitful. We shall continue to watch, and someone will now sleep in the kitchen. Five students go to Mariophile with the cart, get permission to go to the house and bring back some bamboos and tapioca sticks.

March 2

Particularly hectic night. The watch of the kitchen surroundings by a Father and five pupils leads to the capture, a little after midnight, of the thief two days before, who happens to be an old acquaintance, Norbert Loh, called Anthony, the youngest son of our former cook, Ah Kong. After a blow from a stick well planted, he plays dead, but we tie him, interrogate him, and lock him up; we keep a close watch on him in a room near the kitchen. At daylight, he is identified by all the staff so that we can keep an eye on him in the future, and he is delivered to the Police Station, where he first receives a beating. Again, in the night, soon after the capture, a precautionary alert, and shortly after that, a raid alert. Enemy planes are flying very low and are sowing mines in the Channel. Two of these mines explode soon after, and their commotion strongly shakes the house, first felt from the ground and then from the air. Then, the *all clear* is sounded and next, a tuberculosis student from Swatow has a strong hemoptysis – we apply ice on his chest! Fortunately, the fridge that we brought back from Mariophile was overhauled the night before and gives us ice. In the morning, there is again a precautionary alert, then a raid alert, then *all clear*, then once more, a precautionary alert lasting several hours. In the afternoon, the Bunkyo Kacho, Hirano-san, comes to the College and gives a substantial supplementary compensation for the portion of Mariophile requisitioned by the Navy – in addition to what had been taken initially – comprising 6 acres of rambutans and 20 acres of coconut trees, that is $15.90 compensation for each tree. We wonder if they want to cut all these trees, or merely reserve the emplacement and the fruits. The Kacho informs us again that henceforth one cannot enter the part of the *estate* which is surrounded by barbed wire. He assures us that we can stay in the College and that the warning he gave at the time of the move, regarding the idea of another move, is no more applicable, and that we can plant without reservation. He promises to give us *changkols* and is very friendly, asking for explanations about the Stations of the Cross (Siew Tat, the Catholic inspector of schools, is with him as interpreter). We offer him refreshments which he takes with pleasure and with great simplicity, chatting very amiably for half an hour. He offers to help us if we have any difficulty, and recommends that we contact the Navy Staff who is billeted at Alan Loke's residence, next to the Novitiate.

March 3

Quiet night and day. Continuation of works.

March 4

Sunday. We begin a series of lectures, given in turn by the Fathers, on various religious and secular subjects, to replace the interrupted regular classes. Father Monjean starts with a talk on the prophets of the Old Testament, considered in relation to each other, and how they gradually brought about more amplitude and clarity.

Quiet night and day. It rains almost every day, which is very good for our garden. We buy 3 piculs of rice for more than 5 thousand dollars! It's obviously a *black market*! Mariophile's Japanese go to Koi Nian to ask for... the cows! He answers: '*Lain orang punya, sudah pergi lain tempat!* In fact, they graze luxuriantly in the College yard as they never enjoyed such beautiful grass. The Japanese from Mariophile summon, for tomorrow, the squatters who planted vegetables on our land in Mariophile. We have our new census lists established as a result of our move and the division of the Community into two. News of the two Fathers and nine students of Matang Tinggi is good but they have a shortage of water. Besides, the land is not very fertile there. We send to them, through the Sisters who go to Bukit Mertajam, various objects and cash.

March 5

Quiet night and day. The servants who had planted on our land receive two hundred dollars each as compensation. The *towkay* from Chulia Street, Tye Choon Yew, receives $300, which is the maximum received. The thirty or so other planters summoned get 100 or 200 dollars each. The Japanese fence up with barbed wire the space that they reserved for themselves in Mariophile, and the area along the main road – from the cement road until the European Swimming Club – including the hill slope, up to our boundary. Koi Nian and En Voon are among those who are allowed to remain in the compound and therefore do not receive compensation. The Japs dig a tunnel behind the Fathers' house, between the kitchen and the Chapel; they also dig elsewhere in the Hill. We receive 52 x $5 compensation for our cement poles, removed from our houses at Kelawei Road.

The start of fishing for the students. At Mariophile, we were not allowed to fish; here, by blending in with the Brothers who obtained a special authorization from the Navy to fish in front of our property, off limits to everyone else, we can fish, but the initial catch is quite poor.

March 6

Quiet night and day, except that at daybreak a thief comes to take the tapioca in the school garden in front of the portico and runs away when he hears a door opening. The school seems to work normally, the students are quite numerous. It is mainly the Brothers and Sisters who teach and take care of games and students' work. There are also some lay teachers. The *Headmaster*, a Chinese who was the *headmaster* of an English school before the war, is a brave man who does not create any difficulty and refers all business to his assistant, Catherine Loh, the sister of our former student Michael Loh, who died from a chest infection in Penang. The Deputy *Headmaster* is

Mr Gim Boon, a convert who lodges with his family in the *fabrica* of the students. A Swatow student, Jo Joannes, who had a hemoptysis attack just days ago, is admitted to the hospital. We try to get him admitted for free under a dispensation granted to the Brothers by the government, but without success. The Brothers submitted a list of people included in their Novitiate; the hospital refers to it and does not find the name of the student. So, we pay $2 a day, but we get a separate room for the student, which is satisfactory. As the food for the Brother who is in the hospital is already being sent daily from the College, under the Sister's care, we send the student's food in the same manner. Good fishing today for our students. The Brothers who have a boat and a large net do not catch so much.

March 7
Quiet night and day. Rain in the afternoon, which gives the students a well-earned rest. Our goats give us some milk.

March 8
Quiet night and day. The news comes that Vivian de Souza, seminarist from Malacca, sent back to his family by Bishop Devals, but who remained at the College pending the result of his application for admission to Rajaburi, has been accepted in this mission. It is a letter from Monseigneur Pasotti which announces the matter, transmitted by the Japanese Embassy in Bangkok and the Penang Police, brought to the Novitiate by Chong Ean himself. This letter announces that Father Jacques Cheng, pastor of Hua Phai, is appointed Apostolic Vicar of Chantaburi and was consecrated in Hua Phai on February 11th.

Our boy Lee Chong announces his determination to leave us, at least for a while, and to stay in the hospital neighbourhood to take care of his friend's house, who is moving to the other side of the Straits. In reality, he fears that if he remains with us, he will be subjected to the law which enrolls all domestic servants in Japanese organisations.

March 9
Quiet night and day. We build a henhouse under the verandah of the big study room to transfer the hens brought from Mariophile, hitherto put in the garage with the goats.

March 10
Quiet night and day from the point of view of the alerts, but productive in some unforeseen ways. Immediately after breakfast, the Assistant Director of the Novitiate, Brother John, comes with two Japanese, a Navy officer and a Naval M.P., to inspect the lodgings of the French residing at the College. First, they ask for the list of French Fathers living here and, while the Superior is typing the list, with age and occupation, the Japanese go to inspect the quarters of the Convent. The Superior joins them, gives them the list and is requested to remain there while they search

Mother Saint-Louis's place. Then the Japanese come back to the Superior and have his room shown, and those of Fathers Denarié and Monjean, in the Fathers' quarters, no search, but identification of the rooms only, with a harmless question here and there. The officer speaks very good English, has studied in America, and says that one of his brothers is Catholic. He also speaks a little French. He is very discreet and apologises for having to do what he does, and utters his thanks at every moment. He inquires about the Fathers' place of origin in France and speaks with emotion of the good bouillabaisse of Marseille. He leaves, but returns half an hour later to inquire about Fathers Pittaut and Paroissin. In the meantime, a Japanese man was prowling around. Around noon, another Japanese comes to the College to inquire about Father Meissonnier this time, and asks if he was with us when we left Tanjong Tokong to come here. We wonder what all that was about. Around 17:00, a Navy officer, Captain Hikada, C.I.C. of the Navy, who resides with many other officers at Alan Loke's house next to the Novitiate, arrives. He is accompanied by the same officer as the earlier one, who acts as interpreter (though the Captain obviously knows English). He makes himself at home in the parlour and summons the French residents of the College, that is, besides Mother Saint Louis, Fathers Rouhan, Denarié and Monjean. He introduces himself as Commander-in-Chief of the Navy in Penang, and says he comes to bring a message, as he considers us the representatives of the French in Penang. He regrets that certain events occurred in French Indochina the day before. Perhaps the Fathers know about them? On receiving our negative answer, he continues. For a while now, French cooperation was leaving much to be desired. This proceeded to such an extent that, yesterday, Japanese troops were forced to seize power in several towns in Indochina. The Navy knows that the French Missionaries in Penang do not get involved in politics and deal only with religious matters. So, it allows them to stay where they are, but they must commit themselves to doing nothing that may interfere with the Japanese strategy. We thank and commit ourselves to conduct ourselves accordingly. For our outings, no restriction, but we are asked to stay at home except for urgent business, otherwise we take the risk of provoking criticism against the treatment of the French by the Navy, and the latter might be obliged to change its attitude. The Captain kindly invites us to look for him if we have any difficulty. He shakes our hands as he leaves.

We think that as the Philippines had fallen to the Americans, the Japanese feared a landing in Indochina and took their precautions. Perhaps, they had also wished to make Indochina declare war on America, without success. The newspaper, in the evening, said that following difficulties in Indochina, Japan had to take certain measures in that country.

Kuala Lumpur is seriously bombarded by plane.

March 11
Sunday, quiet night and day. The other French Fathers (Fathers Balloche, Souhait, and Reboud) present in town did not hear anything from the Authorities or the Police. Around noon, a policeman from Pulau Tikus comes to inquire about the

names and ages of French nationals living in Pulau Tikus.

March 12

In the morning, a precautionary alert during Community Mass, nothing more. In the evening, Father Piffaut phones from Simpang Ampat Exchange to say that everything is fine. So, they have not been bothered [by the Japanese] there with Paroissin and the attitude towards us, which we were told to be purely local, also extends to them. Works continue. The garden is progressing; unfortunately, the rain, so favourable at the beginning of our stay here, stopped. We plant mainly sweet potatoes, *kangkong*, Dutch coriander, ladies fingers, amaranth, beans. We find more manure nearby than in Mariophile. The construction of individual shelters continues. Fishing in the evening. The shrimp nets yield nothing, or almost nothing, but the seine gives us ten *katis* of fish, crabs, and shrimps. The Brothers also have good fishing with their boat. The construction continues, of individual shelters, all kinds of shallow wells of a diameter just enough to be able to squeeze into, half covered with light materials and turf. There are about twenty of them, more or less completed.

March 13

Quiet night and day. A message comes from Bahau that the last bombings of Singapore have damaged the Convent, and that the Sisters – more than 20 of them – who were still there, were coming to Bahau. It seems that the surveillance around us is getting tighter. Since Saturday, the 10th, we do not go outside anymore; at least not those of us – the Frenchmen in the College – who do not have urgent reasons to go out.

March 14

Quiet night and day from the point of view of the alerts. But the situation darkens for the French. News from the newspaper suggests that the Japanese Authorities are taking action against the French in Indochina and elsewhere. It is said that the Siamese Authorities have been informed to take the same attitude towards the French as in Japan. It can be assumed that these daily notes might be interrupted at short notice...

March 15

Quiet night and day. The fatal predictions are not verified. The work continues. We finish the henhouse under the verandah of the study room, but that does nothing for the chickens rapidly dying of sleeping sickness.

March 16

Quiet night and day. Malaria rages in Tanjong Bungah and the families of our servants who stayed there are very hard hit. In town, many arrests (Chinese etc.). The situation becomes serious in Europe as well as in the Pacific. The Allies crossed the Rhine at Cologne and entered the Rhur. The Russians are in Danzig. The Americans occupy

Iwoshima. Terrifying raids are launched from there to devastate the cities of Japan.

March 17

We, Father Aloysius, Father Rouhan, Brothers James and Assistant Director John, repay the previous Saturday's visit by Captain Hidaka, Commander-in-Chief of the Navy in Penang, to the College. He receives us very kindly in his small living room at the Residence of Alan Loke by the seaside near the Novitiate. He has with him two of his collaborators, Ota-san, who seems to be his secretary, and an interpreter, the one who came with him to the College.

[Back to the notebook.]

Captain Hidaka offers us coffee (it is 9:00 local time). He speaks English, but slowly, and most of the time, he uses his interpreter. We thank him for the kindness he shows us. He encourages us to go through him for any requests we have to make to the Government. He has already arranged for us to have meat from the Navy supplier and at the same terms as the Navy, that is to say, beef at $10 a *kati* (instead of $35 in town and pork at $20 a *kati*, not found elsewhere) at the rate of thirty *katis* per week. He tells us he had an audience with Pius XI in Rome in 1935. He was in Kwong Tche Wan during this war and was in touch with a missionary from Japan who was mobilized there and served as interpreter, Father Bour, formerly at Hakodate. He tells us that he has in his possession films that Dr Brodie had taken at the Convent between 1928 and the war, and put them at the disposal of the Sisters, with his own projector, if they wished to see them. They will be able to keep the films. He told us that things are settled in Indochina and we can expect to remain in peace where we are until the end of the war. He goes down the flight of steps to accompany us. We promise him all our goodwill and he warmly shakes our hands.

March 18

Quiet night and day.

Alarming news arrives from Kuala Lumpur where alerts are heard almost daily, the raids are frequent and bombings are terrifying, around Sentul and the Chinese church. The city is deserted from 10:00 and the population only returns in the evening because there is no raid at night.

Schools are on vacation since yesterday and here we are with a fortnight of calm, which will take us to Easter Monday. It was a curious sight to see the College during the day when the Pulau Tikus Government Primary School, one of the four big schools of Penang, was filling up the College buildings: ground floor and first floor, from the portico almost to the end of the building, dormitories, and large study room, divided by partitions. There were about three hundred children, boys and girls up to eighteen years old, but mostly little ones. Taught by Brothers, Sisters, teachers, and lay mistresses. Many games in the courtyard, school gardens in front of the facade, teams of girls watering the vegetables under the direction of a mistress, and boys who manoeuvred like soldiers under the command of a Brother.

It seems, as Captain Hidaka said yesterday, that a sudden change has occurred in Indochina. The local newspaper published a statement of a former Japanese ambassador to the government of Indochina where he highly praised Admiral Decoux and his sincere cooperation. The paper also says that the shelling in Japan is appalling and that there are hundreds of thousands of victims. 'Neither we nor heaven can resist such assaults'. The new incendiary bombs used by the Americans exceed, says the newspaper, all that one can imagine.

March 19

Quiet night. Feast of Saint Joseph. Solemn Mass, with Adoration of the Blessed Sacrament, in observance of the wish made in 1943.

Father Chin Thomas, Vicar of Father Koh at the Chinese Church, sings Mass.

Good news from the Piffaut–Paroissin group in Matang Tinggi. But the prospects of establishing the entire Community there, if it comes to that, are not very encouraging. Especially because of the lack of water, or more exactly, the difficulty of getting it. Three cases of fever there. Here, students and Fathers feel more tired than at Mariophile. Change of diet, perhaps?

March 20

Quiet night and day.

Everything becomes more expensive. A *kati* of low-quality bananas is selling at wholesale price for two dollars and at a retail price for 4.50! As our supply of bananas brought back from Mariophile has just finished (after a long month), we have to buy some, at least from time to time. People run after everything. We must see when there has been a gust of wind, how the people of the neighbourhood come, really running, to pick up the branches of coconut trees as they fall. As for the cows coming to graze on the roadsides and on our land, it is a gang of kids who, armed with shovels and buckets, literally pick up the dung from the animals' backsides.

March 21

Quiet night and day, except that there was great agitation of planes in the morning. It was then known that an enemy squadron was over Aceh in Sumatra.

March 22

At night, precautionary alert around 00:30, airplanes continue flying very low for some time, to make a turn over the southern pass. Nothing else.

March 23

Quiet night and day.

March 24

Quiet night.

During the morning, three cars or *lorries* come to the Novitiate, seven first-generation Eurasians are interned, three Brothers, three *boarders*, and a servant. They are not allowed to take any books with them, but they are easygoing about their beddings, personal belongings, and money. Nothing for the French. For the past eight days, the newspaper has not given any news of Europe and almost nothing about the situation in the Pacific. We pick our first meal of the vegetables planted since our arrival: *kangkong* and Dutch coriander.

March 25

Quiet night and day. Some books are sent to the internees indirectly, but we have no means of communicating with them. Ninety-six Eurasian families are in prison. This one is full. Forty-five people are crowded in a corridor. Palm Sunday, we carry out the function according to the *Memoriale Rituum*, but without singing the Passion, so as not to tire those who would have had to do the singing. Many of our servants from Mariophile come over.

March 26

Quiet night and day. The American Brother (Michael), who is in hospital, is brought to the Novitiate by the M.P. to fetch his suitcase from there, and then sent back to hospital. It is said to him that when the internees leave Penang, he will have to join them. The M.P. also arrives at the Novitiate for the Brothers, the Sisters and us, with census sheets where all the inhabitants must be registered, with their country of origin, current nationality, names, age, sex, occupation, the nationality of their parents, and indicating the distribution according to rooms and numbered dormitories. Same measure with the Fathers of Pulau Tikus, with Father Koh, and at the Indian Church, for the orphans too. We have eight days to complete the lists. We also know that April 7 is the date for finalising the situation for several categories of people.

March 27

The internees leave for Singapore by special train. Quiet night and day. The garden works are actively continuing. Four kids have been born since the beginning of the year, all alive. Deliveries of beef and pork at very low prices by the Navy supplier are very satisfactory and we have a meat diet, almost back to normal; much less than before the war of course, but then, we were eating too much meat!

We are always on the alert, our suitcases ready, and we expect an arrest from one moment to the next. Attached, a specimen of a note that the Mother Superior sent to our Superior during Vespers, in the Chapel; it is fortunately not internment this time, but we never know.

March 28

Quiet night and day. We begin the services of the *triduum* of the Holy Week by the Tenebrae of Wednesday evening. The students, though few in number, are doing well by singing. The process of getting our eleven farmers of Matang Tinggi to obtain the special rice ration for the *settlers* is successful and we send them a document for this purpose, signed by the *Food Control Office*. The news from Matang Tinggi is good. Attached, a specimen of a note, brought by an Indian Sister, which maintains the connection between the Reverend Mother and the convent of Bukit Mertajam. Three cases of malaria, but not serious. The difficulty of water supply is the most serious.

March 30

Quiet night and day. According to some serious information, the number of internees these days barely exceed one hundred. The reason for this internment is that in the United States, the first-generation Japanese descendents were interned.

Our twelfth kid, since the beginning of the year, is born. All twelve are alive. The Holy Week services are running normally. The Altar of Repose is installed in one of the small chapels flanking the new sacristy. A veil separates this chapel when there is a function at the High Altar. The ration of rice for the next month is cut to 2 *katis*, namely, 1 *gantang* for each adult and 2 *katis* only for children (up to 12 years!). The oil is reduced to ¼ *kati*. Fishing brings little. Students go there only when the tide is the most favourable, and still only bring back a ½ bucket or, at most, 1 bucket of fish, crab, and shrimps. A large packet of letters from Ireland and England arrive for the Convent, the most recent are from April of the previous year. Letters of internees in Japan and India, too. The local newspaper finally broke the news, after almost fifteen days of silence, about the debacle of the Germans on the Western front. The Rhine is crossed everywhere, the American reach Darmstadt. And the Americans also land at Ryou Kyou.

Captain Hikada graciously lends us his splendid projector Paillard (Swiss brand) to view the films of Dr Brodie on the Convent etc. that came into his possession. According to the Reverend Mother, the projector would have also belonged to Dr Brodie. Negotiations for Seminarist de Souza, who is transferred to the Rajaburi Mission, to obtain a passport, continue slowly. The request made four months ago for two Annamite seminarists, for a return passport for Annam, has been unsuccessful.

March 31

Holy Saturday. Quiet night and day. Ceremonies as usual, but the Prophecies are not sung, the celebrant reads them. A letter arrived from Rangoon yesterday, sent by Father Mascarenhas through the Indian Independence League,[23] but censored by it, so that only the beginning and the end of the letter remain. It announced the death of Father Cathebras of Rangoon, R.I.P., but almost nothing else other than the repeated announcement of the death of some Fathers, Indigenous and European (Father Nicholas among others, so far not reported). We give the students some rest

---

23 The Indian Independence League, also known as IIL, was a political organisation operating from the 1920s to the 1940s to organise those living outside India to seek the removal of British colonial rule over India. During the Japanese Occupation in Malaya, the Japanese encouraged Indians in Malaya to join the Indian Independence League.

these days; they have not had one since the big fatigue due to the move, and because of the urgency of starting the garden.

April 1

Easter. Quiet night and day, but at night some enemy planes fly over and circle around persistently. It is said that a Japanese transport was sunk in the South Pass by a plane on Saturday morning. At the General Hospital, there might be three hundred wounded. Services were sung as usual on that day. We receive from Mariophile the ration of fish, delivered as if we were still there. In fact, at Pulau Tikus, we have not received anything yet in the way of fish distribution, although we moved here a month and a half ago. It's as though we have just received our *Fish Card*. When will there be a distribution? Sometimes, there is also fresh pork distribution. Almost nothing! Fortunately, the meats provided by the Navy store, at low prices, are quite abundant.

April 2

Easter Monday. Quiet night and day. In the morning, we hear noises like a cannonade in the distance. It's hard to guess what this might be. Day off for us. The Government school resumes after a fortnight's vacation. Half a day of classes, then there is a break and tomorrow, holiday again. An Italian Sister, exhausted, anemic to the last point, is sent to the hospital. Our student from Swatow, who is there, asks to come back, affected by the very frequent deaths that he sees there. We are requesting to be exempted from any coconut collection by the Government on our property in Pulau Tikus. Our servant, Ten Loi, leaves our service and goes to live in Tanjong Tokong. Father Selier of Balik Pulau is doing better, but Father Dérédec is still staying with him there. We are submitting a new census declaration (perhaps the twentieth since the arrival of the Japanese).

April 3

Quiet night and day. Resumption of work in the garden after the days of interruption coinciding with the Easter solemnities. The students are working very hard to bring back dung from the stables located in the Chinese cemetery, with our handcart *sacrificed* for this important work. It is with hundreds of dollars that we buy this manure, and transport it, from Tuesday up to Friday included, about eight carts a day. The students are very tired as a result of this.

April 4

Nothing special to note, except that the news brings us the announcement of the rapid progress of the Allied armies towards Cassel, Nuremberg, and Hamburg. We slaughter at the abattoir, and eat one of our heifers, a small one that was developing poorly. We only have three cows left.

April 5

It is decided to carry out a blood transfusion for an Italian nun who has become bloodless as a result of infection with *hookworms* and cannot recover her strength. Three of our students go to the hospital to examine their blood type and all three are found to be suitable donors. The most robust is chosen. In the afternoon, at Bukit Mertajam, precautionary alert.

April 6

At night, around 3:30 Tokyo Time (2h00 local), precautionary alert. The planes advance in two waves, nothing more. In the same night, we capture two *musangs* that make excellent curry for the evening. In the afternoon, Seminarist Henricus from Toungoo goes to the hospital to donate blood. The Chinese doctor, Miss Wang, is trying to find a vein and has difficulty. Two hours of work, six wounds to both arms, and a glass of blood as a result. The seminarist comes back without dressing, still bleeding and with fever. A real massacre. He has lost his appetite, and God knows he had a good one!

April 7

Quiet night and day. The seminarist who gave his blood is recovering quickly, despite a notable weakness. But the appetite is back! The Sister finds herself refreshed. The news given is that the Americans are arriving at Leipzig and the Russians at Vienna. The Japanese cabinet, Koiso, falls; an admiral apparently forms a new cabinet. The Russians reportedly denounced the non-aggression pact with Japan.

April 8

Sunday, quiet night and day. Good news about our tuberculous student at the hospital, and that of the Sister infested with hookworms as well. Many cases of tuberculosis around us. Among our former servants, Lee Chong, the boy, and Mah Hao, the former *lotor*. Soh Beng Keok, the manager of Kiki, died a few days ago.

The Sisters are bolder and move more freely around on the ground floor of our quarters than before, even after dinner in the evening, although they were asked to leave this area after the end of the students' prayer, immediately following supper. This is pretty much observed by the girls. Fortunately, the war is progressing fast and we can expect a close end to the abnormal situation we find ourselves in at the College. Without this perspective, it would be necessary to react against this promiscuity at dusk. Students are always instructed not to go into the courtyard at all, especially in the evening, and they observe it faithfully. They play *contra murum* in the part of the fronton which faces the cemetery, and with the rattan ball near the entrance of the cemetery. The evening recreation is spent either in the section of the verandas which is reserved for us, or between the kitchen and the Brothers' quarters. The rumour that Mariophile's chapel was full of rice is denied by En Voon, who saw it for himself, empty for the past few days. Soldiers no longer sleep at Mariophile but at the Sisters' bungalow by the sea.

April 9

Quiet night and day. It is announced that Rangoon is surrounded by the Allies. In Japan, Admiral Suzuki's cabinet was apparently formed with some difficulty.

We resume – *Deo Gratias* – classes after two months of interruption (since the 11th of February exactly). In the meantime, we have given only three lectures to students on various topics to hold their attention. The class is in the central part of the building, on the first floor, between the portico and the balcony on the courtyard, against the partition of the Fathers' library. There are only those who have not completed their studies (fifteen). The schedule is this one (Tokyo Time, 1:30 ahead of the local time):

07:40 (06:10 local time) getting up
08:00 (06:30) meditation
08:30 (07:00) mass
09:20 (07:50) lunch
10:00 (08:30) work in the garden
11:00 (09:30) end of work
11:30 (10:00) personal study
12:15 (10:45) class
13:15 (11:45) end of class
13:25 (11:55) personal examination
13:30 (12:00) dinner and then recreation

For students who have finished their lessons, work from 10 to 12:30 (8:30 to 11:00), and they then rest, and join the others for the personal examination. Afternoon:

14:45 (13:15) rest
15:45 (14:15) end of rest
16:30 (15:00) spiritual reading or prayer
17:00 (15:30) work in the garden
19:00 (17:30) end of work
19:30 (18:00) supper, then immediately, evening prayer
21:00 (19:30) Rosary, visit to the Blessed Sacrament
21:45 (20:15) chapel closes
22:30 (21:00) bedtime

We keep the prayer after dinner, abnormal time, to give the staff of the Convent time to put the refectory and kitchen in order before leaving this quarter for the night.

Sunday and some holidays, High Mass at 10:00, Vespers at 16:30, Spiritual Readings at 17:15.

For the moment, Theology only. We will try to add small classes soon. The group at Matang Tinggi does not seem to advance with the garden (there are too few of them, having four sick students out of nine) so they might not be able to start classes anytime soon. Father Monjean teaches Dogma, Father Rouhan Morals, and there is no Philosophy (the only two teachers are at Matang Tinggi). Father Denarié is in charge of the whole garden, without classes.

Certainly, no new student has come to us this year. Joseph Reutens, who was supposed to come from Bahau, could not obtain a passport.

April 10

Quiet night and day. A Eurasian from Syonan tells us that Father Michel would be at Bukit Timah. The internees arrested two weeks ago would have been taken there, too. The naval base of Seletar – formerly guarded so jealously – was smashed to pieces and would now be open to the general public. *Leaflets* were scattered, communicating three points (in Japanese and Malay):

1. stay clear of military installations targeted by the bombing
2. do not cooperate with Japs
3. Berlin is *habis*

A bottle of coconut oil in Penang costs $32. A picul of corn, with a special licence to purchase at controlled price, $1,080; without the license, $1,800. We planted a lot of sweet potatoes, but the result is problematic. The Brothers gave up totally because of the disappointing results.

April 11

Quiet night and day. We have not been out of the College since Captain Hidaka's visit. Neither has Father Baloche. Father Souhait sometimes comes to the Novitiate; once a week, he is at the College to confess the Sisters, and would also carry the Sacraments to the sick at Pulau Tikus. Father Riboud usually stays at home, he goes out once a week to do his business and comes to dine at the College. Here, it is Father Aloysius who does all the work outside. The girls at the Convent were instructed not to come into the kitchen area after the students' supper. For Easter, they were allowed to come and help the Sisters who are doing the clearing up after the end of our meal. So, they came over and continued to do so for several days until the Reverend Mother called them to order. The Sisters make good food that pleases everybody. The blood donor's arm is still bruised and painful, he does not pay attention to the infections. We wanted to call the doctor. The students have been productive and we already find something to eat in the garden. Good fishing by the students, around ten *katis* (fishes, crabs, shrimps). We buy sugar at $3,000 per picul. Teh's death in Tanjong Tokong village is announced. His son is faithful and brings us some fish. We still receive from there some ration of fish – up to twenty *katis* each time – whenever there is a distribution at Tanjong Tokong, which is very irregular. Sometimes, every two weeks. But here, in Pulau Tikus, our fish card has not yet earned us a single fish! The agriculture officer, who had helped us at Mariophile at the beginning of the war, also brought us some tapioca as a gift, and sweet potato leaves to plant. He is very helpful, this Tan Ah Kim.

Heard this double declaration at a Jikeidan conference from the Japanese presiding over it. First, General Yamashita, who led the command during the conquest of Malaya and then in the Philippines, has not disappeared, he is still leading his troops in the Philippines. Secondly, English submarines came near Penang, boarded fishing boats, and asked for all sorts of information. Those who are caught playing the enemy's game will be punished with death.

The Japanese collect all medicines, even from among *private practitioners*.

In the evening, we play Gregorian records with a phono that the Sisters still have here.

The tricycle always renders us the greatest service in bringing the provisions from town etc. We increase the production of the garden by bringing in manure. The Sisters, on their side, water their garden by recruiting the schoolchildren. The chickens we brought from Mariophile are almost all dead from sickness here.

Good understanding reigns between us and the Government school. The *Headmaster* is not a Catholic but seems a good man and gives a free hand to his Deputy *Headmaster*, who is a convert, and to his Deputy headmistress, who is the sister of one of our alumni. It is a spectacle to see, every morning, the school staff doing the *taiso* or educational gymnastics. The pupils – boys on the right and girls on the left – are in the courtyard facing the *lusorium*. Teachers, along with the exercise instructor, stand within the arches of the *ambularium* facing the pupils, along with the mistresses; the Sisters walk along the middle of the lines of girls, taking care to correct the movements of these young ladies. Except for the Sisters, everyone is doing the Swedish gymnastics movements to the sounds of a piano keeping rhythm with the movements. Our students who are, at this time, taking a break (between the end of lunch and the beginning of work in the garden), enjoy watching this from the verandah of the fourth dormitory.

April 12

Quiet night and day. A lot of sick people among the Brothers – Visitor Brother Paul and another Brother are feverish or dysenteric. Brother Superior James is very weak and has an upset stomach. The Brothers are cooking for themselves, and not very impressively. Also, the Sisters start to do for them what they do for us and prepare their meals, for all their Community. We learn about President Roosevelt's death from cerebral hemorrhage.

April 13

Quiet night and day, although it is claimed from various sides that B-29s came in the morning, that they were shot at, and that there was an explosion from a bomb. News from Matang Tinggi arrives. See leaflet attached [not attached]. It seems to be fine in the end. Our student in the hospital is rather better, he has put on weight. Sister Xaverine is getting better too.

The rain, which had been scant for more than a week, has returned for two days, and the appearance of the garden is much improved. Already, we harvest more vegetables than we did on average at Mariophile, especially *kangkong* and Dutch Coriander. We have planted a good cover of sweet potatoes but we are skeptical about the results, at least for the first harvest, which is always weak when we start to plant in any place. The ground then adapts little by little, if you put a lot of ash, and you always have to plant potatoes only at the same place. We buy as much provisions as we can, rather than keeping paper – even with prices between $1,000 and $2,000 for commodities like corn, *mee*, *ragi*. We bought 2 piculs of sugar at $3,000 per picul, brown sugar, but it keeps well and we shall sell it with great profit in a while.

April 14

Calm night and day. A Brother, who was expected to be interned because he belongs to the same category as those who were recently taken away, is summoned by the police. Anxiety, but he is rewarded with a *badge* like ours, and he returns to the Novitiate; he gets off with a scare.

April 15

Quiet night and day. News from Matang Tinggi by our ex-student Fair, who is coming from there. One student is a bit tired, the Fathers are doing well, Father Piffaut thinks of coming to Penang the following week. The garden starts to be productive (Dutch Coriander, especially). The land that they cultivate is just around the Fathers' house, where the Fathers stay on the first floor and the students on the ground floor. So, our breakdown so far is:

At the College in Pulau Tikus are three Fathers of the College (Rouhan, Denarié and Monjean), plus Father Aloysius seconded from the Mission to the College, and acting as a Procureur, and at the same time as assistant to the Superior. Also at the College is Father George Mg Kiaw, from the Rangoon Mission, working in the Malacca mission while waiting for his possible return to Rangoon; he is the vicar of Father Riboud of the Tamil Church, but is saying Mass, sleeping and taking his meals at the College (his continual presence at Penang Road is not required, and he is less exposed here than there, in case of bombing), twenty-nine students, with one permanently at the hospital (T.B.).

In Matang Tinggi, two Fathers (Piffaut and Paroissin) and nine students (all from Malacca).

In Singapore, interned (Changi? Bukit Timah?), the Procureur, Father Michel.

In Bahau, a Catholic Agricultural Colony, Father Messonier, head of agriculture at one of the *mukims*.

In Mariophile, nobody! In all, six Fathers and thirty-eight students.

April 16

Quiet night and day. For three days, we have received our rice from the Eurasian Store (*Kyoei Koshi*), but at Bagan Jermal, neither the Chinese *kedai* nor the Malay *kedai* received theirs. People suffer and eat what they can, some *sagu* (at $12 per *kati* today) or tapioca. It seems that instead of weighing the rice distributed to the dealers, the Government measures it to the *gantang*, and the *gantangs* are not filled when measuring. When the dealers come to distribute, they weigh (6 *katis* = 1 *gantang*) and do not get their full measure. Hence the difficulties. The factory that the Japs have set up in the Novitiate annex school is working night and day. Carpentry, it seems. Brother Paul, Director of the Novitiate, suffering from dysentery and incoercible vomiting, receives the Extreme Unction. We gather that the government does not come around anymore to pick the coconuts on our ground in Pulau Tikus. We will have all the harvest at our disposal, for food. Captain Hidaka had the Paillard cinematographic projector taken back from the Convent with 3 rolls of films, including 2 taken by Dr Brodie at the Convent.

April 17
Finally, the ration of rice for the month is distributed in Bagan Jermal, to the great relief of the population.

We buy, despite the astronomical prices, a lot of fish, corn, *ragi* and dried *mee* especially. Better to have food in the store than notes in the safe. We still buy some bottles of arrack as medicine in case of cholera. It does not appear that the cases reported in Kedah have compromised public health on this side. But there is an epidemic of intestinal flu, from which many people are dying. It seems that the illness of Brother Paul, who is better today, comes from that. Sister Xaverine at the hospital is not much better and the red blood cell content of her blood, improved after the blood transfusion, has dropped to the same level as before.

April 18
Quiet night and day. Departure of Vivian de Souza, who in November was sent back to his family by Bishop Devals, but whom we kept at the College until he was admitted to the Rajaburi Mission and was able to leave. From December, his pension will not be accounted for by the Mission of Malacca.

The Government School is working regularly. There are around five hundred pupils, mostly occupied with singing, physical exercise, and gardening. In the courtyard, many girls, who are already twenty years old, are doing choreographic exercises which may not be of very high quality but, however, do not leave our seminarists indifferent. During our midday meal, all the pupils disappear and there are only a few Masters or Mistresses who prolong their presence here for an hour or two. The commotion and cries of these schoolchildren while we conduct our classes are quite tiresome.

19 April
Quiet night and day. En Voon who comes from Mariophile tells us that there are no troops in the cantonment there, but only guards and workers who make partitions everywhere, arranging them here and there. He has with Koi Nian the guard of the *estate* occupied by the Japs. He has permission to cultivate. It seems that all the young trees around the house have been cut. It would mean the loss of all the young

durians that were so hard to plant. Thefts of wood are still committed despite the presence of the Japanese. There are Chinese who came to cut four or five *rubber* trees and take away the wood. The Malays do not dare anymore. We are getting fish rations at Tanjong Tokong and at Pulau Tikus, but it is not much, really. The students went fishing and got almost nothing. Brother Paul is better, but Brother Jacques is not well.

April 20
Quiet night and day. The newspaper says that Sabang, at the northern tip of Sumatra, was attacked by an enemy fleet, including a French Richelieu-class battleship.[24]

Today, no pupils at school, but a great meeting of *teachers* from all schools (including Malay) of Penang for physical exercises and lectures during the morning. These *teachers* are poorly paid, but they have advantages, such as two extra *gantangs* of rice, a free meal at noon that is brought from a central kitchen in Dato Kramat every day, etc. We buy rice at $160 per *gantang* – at the *black market*.

April 21
Quiet night and day. Three students are going to the bees on the Mariophile side, all day, and bring back a good quantity of honey. Brother Paul is doing better, but Brother Jacques remains severely indisposed, not feeding himself.

April 22
Quiet day. The students still find some honey in the attic of Mariophile. Rain is scarce. At Mariophile, the Japanese want to recall those who once planted on the land they occupied. They propose to go halves. The servants will agree to put in the work if they are allowed to plant what will mature in the long term, hoping that in the meantime...

April 23
Quiet night and day. It seems from the news that the end of hostilities in Germany should not be more than a week away. The rain has finally arrived in the night, and after a lull, most of the morning. The reaction of schoolboys and schoolgirls surprised by the rain near the College would have been worth capturing in a movie. Today, we start the secondary classes with this schedule: 10:00 – preparation, 10:30 – secondary class, 11:15 – recreation, 11:30 – preparation, 12:15 – Theology class, 13:15 – end of class. This week, only three days. From next week, these small classes (Liturgy, Canon Law, Pastoral, Sacred Scripture – three classes) will take up six days. During the class, the pupils of the school go up and down almost continually by the staircase of the *locutorium*, from which the location of our class is separated only by a series

---

24 The French battleship *Richelieu* was attached to the East Indies Fleet and participated in Operation Sunfish from 9 to 20 April 1945 on Sabang and Padang (North and West Sumatra), and in Operation Dracula (landing in Rangoon) on 3 May. She was in Singapore on 12 September 1945 to assist with the capitulation of Japan.

of screens. And the laughter, the calls of all these young girls, the sweet smells of schoolgirls, penetrate our atmosphere and constitute a very unusual atmosphere for our Theology lessons. Students still go to the bees on the Mariophile side and bring back an appreciable amount of honey and wax.

April 24

Quiet night and day. Distribution of sweet potatoes by the government, 1 *kati* per person, at $1.50 per *kati* only (instead of $5 or $6 on the *black market*), pretty good. The permit we were given to harvest coconuts within our entire property, between Burmah Road and the sea, is being used for the first time, and our Mariophile coconut cutter, Ah Pee, picks a hundred in the morning.

The newspaper announces that a junction of the Soviet armies could be done, on certain points that are indicated, with the Anglo–American armies. Which may well be a clue that it has already happened in reality.

April 25

Quiet night and day.

April 26

Quiet night and day. With the other neutrals, the French are summoned to the Keimubu *Special Branch* on April 27 at 10:30 (9:00 local time).

April 27

Quiet night and day. Early in the morning, we are told that it will not be necessary to go to the police. We are given sheets to fill for all those who are *Third Nationals* like us. It's the same information that has been provided ten times already. We fill up the sheets, nothing more. In the evening, the Annamites are summoned on Saturday at 15:00.

April 28

Still quiet. We learn that Pétain was released by the Germans, and that Goering has resigned.

April 29

Quiet. It has been a long time since any sign of approaching enemy aircraft is heard.

April 30

Quiet. We installed, for the school, a Japanese flag in the courtyard (in addition to the one in front of the portico outside). The shaft is attached to the guardrail of the verandah, at the top of the staircase of the clock, towards the study room. In the morning, at the beginning of the class, the flag is raised and the schoolchildren sing the hymn to the flag (instead of Kimigayo, which is sung only on grand occasions). When one of these functions is going on, it is pretty difficult to conduct our classes above the din. There are sports and games in the yard, some songs. It begins with an obeisance to the Imperial Palace [in Tokyo], which happens to be in the direction of the fourth dormitory, from where the students on the verandah get a full view of the proceedings.

May 1
Quiet. Letter from Matang Tinggi. They are going to start classes there too, but leaving out both Philosophies, and putting everyone in Fundamental Theology. A case of fever, but benign. The garden is productive.

May 2
Quiet. The news arrives that the passports of the two Annamites (Trinh of Bui-chu and Giam of Koutum) are finally ready, and they will be able to leave by train to Bangkok the following week.

May 3
Quiet. A hawker is instated in the passage between the *lusorium* and the cabinets, and sells delicacies like pieces of sugar cane, fried bananas, etc.

May 4
Quiet. Teacher's day. You have to watch their *Taiso* or educational gymnastics in the yard. Brothers and Sisters together, gesturing to the raucous command of a Jap.

May 5
Quiet. Students are reluctant to go fishing. We put the big net away. Trials with shrimp nets give nothing. We shall try the lines with multiple hooks.

May 6
Quiet. There was a Ceremony of Profession of Vows, Receiving the Habit, etc. in Balik Pulau for the Sisters. Mother Saint Louis went there for a few days on this occasion and she returned yesterday, on the 5th, with Father Dérédec, who had been there two months ago, to keep company with Father Selier, who was mentally fatigued. Father Dérédec resettled in the servants' room near the workshop.

May 7
Quiet. Benedictus, a seminarist from Malacca, arrives from Matang Tinggi to see his family in Penang and take some things for the students and the two Fathers. He gives some good news from there, a case of malaria, a light one (Jee). The others are fine. The garden is productive.

May 8
Quiet. Toward evening, the news comes to us that the Germans have surrendered unconditionally on the 7th at 2:40 in Reims.

May 9
Quiet. Benedictus leaves for Matang Tinggi.

May 10
Departure for Indochina of two seminarists, Trinh, deacon from Bui-chu, and Giam, acolyte from Kontum, who had completed their studies a year and a half ago and could not return home. They are passing through Siam and their journey is full of uncertainties, given the dilapidated state of the railroad which is constantly being bombarded. The news of the armistice in Europe is confirmed by the local newspaper.

May 11
Still quiet. Navy seaplanes aside, it is rare to see airplanes.

The workshop installed in the Novitiate annex school runs night and day and the noise never stops. There is a band of local children and young people who come every day to do gymnastics on our beach. There, too, towards the boundary with the Brothers' [Novitiate], the Japanese *motorboats* come to unload the equipment they need and they carry it to the school, crossing our land. But apart from them, and the Japs who lead them, we see very few Japanese soldiers on our land, by the seaside or at the College. Those who are quartered in the boys' and girls' school near the church are not showing up here and we only hear them singing. They do not bother the Fathers of Pulau Tikus (Father Baloche and Father Souhait) either. It is said that the battleship *Richelieu* is in these seas, that Rangoon has been recaptured. The price of the rice ration given by the government goes up from $0.10 to $1.80 and a part is delivered in *Nasi Krink*, which displeases the people a lot.

May 12
The Irish and Italian Sisters of Balik Pulau are summoned by the Penang police for the same formalities as us. We apply for them to do it in Balik Pulau instead. The situation is getting a little better at Poh Leung Kok for the orphan girls. The Sisters who are there have the opportunity to improve the lot of those children, who had been dying of hunger when they depended on the secular staff to secure their food. All the children are recovering, but many are in a desperate state.

May 13
The arrangement by which the Brothers of the Novitiate have their meals prepared in the College kitchen by the Sisters seems to work well.

May 14
Quiet. No news from our two seminarists who left for Indochina. As long as they do not come back, it's a good sign.

May 15
Still quiet. Our classes continue smoothly. Fishing by the Brothers, good catch of

crabs, but few fish, although they use their boat. They are more successful, even in catching fish, with the wide-mesh floating *crab net* than with the trawl net that they have almost abandoned. We try (given the obvious repugnance of our students for net fishing) the lines fixed at seabottom (*rawai*) but the result is not encouraging at first, even though the circumstances are favourable.

May 16
Quiet. The local newspaper contains nothing interesting anymore since it announced the capitulation of Germany, except for the intensive bombing of Japan (Nagoya) by hundreds of B-29s.

May 17
Quiet. Our former *dhoby*, Mah Hoa, dies of tuberculosis in a hut on the church grounds, in front of the bathroom of the College. He is baptized *in articulo mortis*.

May 18
Quiet. Received a letter from the Matang Tinggi group. All well, except for Jee who has malaria. The parish priest, Father Francis Lek, has it too. Father Piffaut takes his place for the parish work. They ask for funds but we scarcely have any, having put everything into provisions. Their Rhode Island Reds poultry is growing well. The Theology books sent to them by a Sister of the Bukit Mertajam Convent did not reach them. We are investigating. Here, a kid is born, the thirteenth one this year, but very weak. The milk which the goats provide us is reduced, it has gone down from a bottle of brandy to a glass only. At Mariophile, the Japs continue digging their tunnels behind the refectory, on the hill slope. They even work with explosives, it seems. Our servants recommence their agriculture in Mariophile. After chasing them away, the Japs called them back. Moreover, in service with us at the College, we only have Hin Min, the former rice cook, and Siong Tsann, the tailor; and in Mariophile, Koi Nian, employed by the Japanese, but always at our service. As for En Voon, although he has voluntarily ceased working for us five or six months ago, he comes regularly to see us and provides us all kind of services within his power. He has become very kind since he left us. Our garden is growing well, a lot of green vegetables. We have new spaces at the Brothers' [Novitiate], where there are many more open areas without coconut trees than here. The students are in good health and good spirits.

Indirect news from Father Meissonnier, still in Bahau, where he is ministering while cultivating at the same time. No news from Father Michel since the information given about him around Christmas. Nothing could be known about the Brothers who were interned two months ago, we do not know where they are. We continue to refrain from leaving the College. Father Aloysius runs the errands in town.

May 19
In a curious way, after repeated predictions the last two days that there was going to be a siren, the siren is heard in the morning, at 11:00, Tokyo Time, for the first time since April 6. Precautionary alert, nothing more. Planes pass.

The pupils of the school, at the first sound of the siren, fly like birds to their families, jubilant to see the classes finished before the hour. Io Ioannes, the student with tuberculosis at the hospital, is now well, and has the idea to stay there until the end of the war.

May 20
Quiet. The garden is productive. The amaranths (*bayam*) are splendid and in large quantities. A lot of *kangkong* and Dutch coriander too. The Jerusalem artichokes which had been planted by the Sisters before our arrival are also very good. But the long beans are damaged by many insects.

May 21
Quiet. Fishing is often good. We start with the seabottom lines (*rawai*) with many hooks. We take in *Sembilangs* and *Duris*.

May 22
Quiet. In cooperation with the Brothers who catch a lot of fish with their *crabs' nets* but cannot cope with the mending, we start giving them some help for that. They brought some nets here, and three or four students are working to repair them.

May 23
Quiet. Good understanding with the Government school always. We help each other, they put their coolies at our disposal, we give them some firewood, coconuts, etc. We cut branches of *sennas* to obtain firewood.

May 24
Quiet. A postcard arrives from Indochina; the first time this happens, by mail. It is for Father Piffaut, sent by one of his cousins, an officer in the Legion. It was posted early January of this year, in response to the card that the Father had sent him more than six months ago. Nothing interesting in this card, written (as is required) in Nippon-go. We have stopped the study of Nippon-go since we came back to the College.

May 25
Quiet. We begin to use the permit to pick all the coconuts on our College plantation. But it is difficult to find pickers and they ask for very high rates.

May 26
Quiet. The rain which had been too rare these days comes back quite frequently.

May 27
Quiet. We harvest the first sweet potatoes we planted when we arrived from Mariophile. Very encouraging, beautiful and healthy, very good, considerable quantity.

May 28
Quiet. Father Piffaut arrives unexpectedly, summoned together with Father Paroissin by the Penang Police to provide information on facts already repeatedly stated. He came alone thinking he could arrange matters for both. He arrives after the evening prayer, having left Matang Tinggi at the beginning of the afternoon. He says that the situation of the small community is satisfactory. Classes have started again but Philosophy is taught together with Theology. Spirits are high. Only one has fever right now; the others are in good health. The garden is progressing quite well.

May 29
The Holy Oils which came from Bangkok to Singapore – thanks to the goodness of Shinozaki-san who brought it himself, and then had it sent from Singapore via Monseigneur Olçomendy, through a son of Teh Kee, who carried it past all the checkpoints – finally reached us, but in infinitesimal quantity. Father Piffaut easily settles his affairs with the police, and prepares a few things that he will take with him to Matang Tinggi.

May 30
Father Piffaut leaves for Matang Tinggi.

May 31
Still quiet. *Corpus Christi*. Procession as usual. Few outsiders, the priest having recommended his flocks not to come for fear of arousing the suspicions of the Police. Very nice weather, the ceremony is successful. It is Father Chin Thomas who carries the Blessed Sacrament.

June 1
Quiet. The salt and sugar rations are further reduced this month: 3 *tahils* of sugar and 2 of salt per person.

June 2
Quiet. Students go fishing for small shrimps (*udang halus*) and bring back about ten *katis*.

June 3
Quiet. But in the evening loud clamour, songs, cheers among Japanese soldiers stationed all around. Unknown cause.

June 4
The trees of the property begin to bear fruits (rambutan and especially mangosteen). The students guard and pick them, and the Sisters distribute these among the three Communities.

June 5
Very good shrimp fishing by the students, twenty *katis*.

June 6
Still quiet.

June 7
Quiet. The Superior is summoned to Mariophile by the commander of the Marines to settle a case of tenants of a house belonging to us. Everything is going well. The Superior takes the opportunity to lightly examine the state of the property (he has not been there since the taking over of the Indochina government by the Japanese some two months ago). An *attap* hut has been erected on the edge of the main road by the sea, near bungalow no. 514. These people will have to be expelled at the end of hostilities (the brother of Chinese Swimming Club barkeeper Ah Sin). Near Koi Nian, the Japanese set up pig sties and raise ducks on a large scale.

June 8
Quiet. Feast of the Sacred Heart. Solemn Mass and (at the request of the Sisters), Adoration, another High Mass and Vespers. Up to thirty orphan girls of Poh Leung Kok came to spend the day here and take part in the Adoration. Great joy for these poor children. We feast them with mangosteens. They have become skeletal over many months, the Sisters of Poh Leung Kok being powerless to stop the pinching of the [missing word].

The *black market* is now spreading to the phone exchange. If we do not grease the palms of the phone operators when we ask for a connection, we always receive the same answer – *engaged* – and it is impossible to get anything else. Mr Sandanans, the manager of the Indian Agricultural Settlement of Batu Kawan, comes to see us and tells us of the great misery of these *settlers* who left Penang, attracted by beautiful promises. But the ration of rice is a month late there and people are dying of hunger. By contrast, the Chinese Settlement of Alma Estate is doing very well.

June 9
Quiet. Our sweet potatoes are very productive, and we replant them as we lift them.

June 10
Quiet. One of our goats is suddenly convulsed and we sacrifice her for fear of seeing her die. We attribute this to what she might have eaten, mangosteen husks. These fruits are abundant this year, and as we keep all the plantation yield for ourselves, looked after and plucked by the students themselves, they have plenty for their table.

There is enough to give some to the Brothers and to the Sisters. Father Aloysius takes an eight-day leave and goes to Bukit Mertajam and Taiping.

June 11
Quiet. We eat the goat killed yesterday; she makes for a delicious curry.

June 12
Quiet. We put a few students for the coconut harvest; two of them are climbers and pluck 3 trees in the morning and 2 in the evening so as not to tire themselves. 15 *katis* of small shrimp are caught by the students.

June 13
Quiet. Good news from Matang Tinggi, but one case of fever there. They ask for money to buy provisions; everything is expensive. A new bicycle costs $7,000. A pair of new leather shoes, $300. Still good shrimp fishing (20 *katis*).

June 14
A fire lights the sky above the town at the beginning of the night.

Always good relations with the school. We share with them the joyful abundance of our mangosteens. There are four hundred and fifty students. Among the teachers, there are eleven Brothers of the Novitiate (two other Brothers teach at the Malay School at Kelawei, with students almost exclusively Malay). There are seven Sisters on the school staff, but two of them teach at the Poh Leung Kok. The Sisters also have one teacher at Balik Pulau and three at Bukit Mertajam.

June 15
Quiet. Rumour has it that the English entered Siam in five places.

As we have a lot of coconuts, we sell them at the *black market*, at $5 each and above. As the price of the rice ration has become so high, the poor people withdraw ½ ration, sell it to the *black market*, and then buy the other half.

There were gleams of fire over the town the night before; it is said that a junk full of oil barrels has burned.

Our mangosteens are producing at the maximum. We have plenty for the Brothers, the Sisters and ourselves. We send over many times to the Poh Leung Kok where there are more than one hundred orphans. Father Dérédec, our distinguished guest, is indisposed, mild bronchitis, upset intestines, toothaches.

News from Bahau via a card from Seminarist Joe Reutens to his father. A new installation was completed for the Minor Seminary there. They have a small chapel and keep the Blessed Sacrament. Malaria is calming down a bit but almost everyone has had the scourge.

From time to time we receive some fruits (especially rambutans) from Mariophile by En Voon who works there with the Japanese. We organise a distribution of mangosteens (1,200) to the school students. That's $600.

June 16

Quiet. A team of students has been busy for fifteen days repairing the Brothers' nets (crab nets). It's a big job. We call the orphans of Poh Leung Kok for help. Two come in the afternoon to take a lesson and the students teach them how to do it. Thus, one can see seminarists and orphans mending a net together in the verandah in front of the refectory.

Nearly all the Japanese in the area belonging to the Navy are well disciplined and discreet. At the beginning of their stay, they were going to the surrounding houses but now they do not go outside – people do not like it, even though the Japanese did nothing reprehensible; and the chiefs ordered their subordinates to stay in their corner, that is, at the school of the Sisters and Brothers, near the Fathers' house. These Navy people are well disciplined and very decent. On the other hand, soldiers are like soldiers everywhere; these last few days they were looting rambutans from a nearby *kampong*. None of this happens here, fortunately; there are only the *flying foxes* (very numerous), squirrels and *musangs* to plunder our fruits.

June 17

Quiet. The picking of mangosteens continues, very abundant, thousands and thousands. We receive a large basket of rambutans from Mariophile. Miraculous fishing by the Brothers, on this Sunday, even as we read the Gospel of the *Duc in altum* and the two boats full of fishes...

June 18

Quiet. Very little news of the world, by any channel whatsoever. We only know that the battle is raging on in Okinawa, and that the bombings of Japan are frequent; in Europe, quiet, the four sectors of Germany are peacefully occupied by the *big four*.[25]

Two Japanese soldiers, apparently coming from the *workshop* set up in the Novitiate annex school, help us to pick the mangosteens. Nothing exaggerated. The problem of repairing the Brothers' nets has, it seems, been solved through the cooperation of eight girls from Poh Leung Kok; they are taught the art of netting and the nets to be repaired are brought to their home. Meanwhile, the Brothers are doing good fishing; 21 *katis* today is very precious, because, at under $60 per *kati*, we can only find rotten fish to buy.

June 19

Quiet. The rain we were waiting for so impatiently, for the last few days, arrives abundantly during the night and the day. Also, instead of working in the garden, a conference for everyone. As the fruits fall more when it rains, the area underneath our trees is invaded by bands of children and hungry people waiting for a *windfall*.

If the students did not take turns to keep watch, there would be a lot of depradations.

---

25   The 'Big Four' were France, Soviet Union, the United Kingdom and the United States.

Big accident: four nets which the Brothers had put out at sea disappeared during the night. Searches were made in vain. Probable theft.

June 20
Quiet. Rain. Conference for everyone. Afternoon a phone call for the Superior (it is convenient to have the telephone at the College!) It is the *shunin* of Bunkyoka, Chin-san (Mr Tan, former inspector of Chinese schools during the British period) who asks if we can organise at the College, for Saturday, June 23, a meeting of Christian Clergymen, followed by a refreshment service (coffee, fruit). The Bunkyoka will send 1 *kati* of sugar and 1 *kati* of coffee powder, and will give compensation for the fruits provided by the College. It is approved. Father Aloysius returns from his leave, bringing back good news from Taiping, Bukit Mertajam, and Matang Tinggi. Passports are completely put on hold in Malaya.

June 21
Calm. The rain continues regularly every night.

Feast of Father Aloysius. There was a nice concert last night by the students in his honour. Father Aloysius tells us about the exploits of communists in the interior, especially between Ipoh and K.L. They are well supplied by parachute drops and organise very bold raids. Everywhere, it is a mess, especially on the railway, by which we travel very often without a ticket, with the complicity of the local staff. In most areas, the law is held in contempt. We receive the notice for the Saturday meeting.

June 22
Quiet. The mangosteen harvest continues, still abundant, although it has decreased appreciably. We also harvest rambutans.

June 23
Quiet. At 15:00, meeting in the exercise room, which is now one of the classes of the government school. Gocho Chong had the classes finish earlier and arranged the tables back to the back, so that in the big space near the pulpit, we have 3 horseshoe tables after dinner, and the Sisters arrange 25 covers, laid out with fruits, coffee, and cakes of their confection. At the right time we take our places along the aisles: Catholics on one side (Brother Jacques, Father Rouhan, Father Souhait, Father Baloche, Father Riboud, Father Koh, Reverend Mother Saint-Louis and Reverend Mother Saint-Paula (Balik Pulau); Protestants on the other side (eleven); and, as they are more numerous, two of them sit on the Catholic side. Officials arrive, first, Bunkyoka Shunin Chin-san who is Methodist but very friendly, and Siew Tat, another Chinese from Bunkyoka, he is a very good Catholic, and then the Japanese, Bunkyo Kacho Hirano-san, with the director of the Religious Department of the Gunsei Kanbu in Taiping (where the civilian and military headquarters are located) – it is on the occasion of this person's visit that the meeting takes place – and two other officers of Bunkyoka: Miura-san, the director of the Penang Teachers'

College, and Matsuta-san, both old acquaintances who intervened actively during the removal operation, from Mariophile. These gentlemen introduce themselves, after sitting down, giving their names and ranks. Hirano-san explains that the visit of [no name]-san is motivated by the general tour of religious institutions that he is undertaking in Malaya to understand the mentality and views of various beliefs.

Hirano-san declares that he wants to go *worship* at the chapel, adding that next time he will go to a Protestant church. The officials come with us to the chapel where they bow and collect themselves for a moment. Then back to the portico, cordial greetings, invitation to come back, and the cars start. We cordially shake hands with about half of the Protestant ministers, the others having left during the visit to the chapel. Thus ends this memorable meeting; the two Chinese officials from the Bunkyoka thank us profusely upon departure, and give us $75 as compensation for expenses.

En Voon comes from Mariophile, bringing some Census lists because we are supposed to appear there again, with the mention that we left! He says that the steps from the altar in the chapel have been removed; that the refectory is divided into what seems to be bathrooms, because water pipes enter the refectory through the small round hole in the wall facing the hill; a pipe is also going up to Father Meissonnier's room. Some of the big pipes coming from the electric pump have been removed. A network of barbed wire, with cement poles, is laid from Koi Nian's place to the big durian tree in the valley. The pigs have not yet arrived but work on their enclosures is being done. Many rubber trees have been cut.

Father Dérédec is a little better.

June 24

Quiet day. Our students go fishing with the Brothers of the Novitiate, with their boat, and they bring back a good amount of fish.

June 25

Quiet. The *shop* of the Sisters – installed for over a year and a half in the room next to the Superior's office (now the office of the Gaucho or *Headmaster* while the Superior's office is installed in the student library, the books [from the latter] having been moved partly to the Fathers' library, and partly to the section of the verandah in the center of the main building which serves as classrooms, study rooms and exercise room) – is flourishing and little boy's pants are being sold at prices around $400.

In the afternoon, a Japanese motorcyclist from the Marines, stationed at Mariophile, comes to the College, asks for the Superior and, in good English, explains that for the water supply in Mariophile, changes are necessary and asks permission to connect Mariophile and the two bungalows by the seaside to the main pipe of the town, also to restore the pump, for which the electric motor had been brought here. All permissions given, he goes back immediately to fix everything accordingly. Very polite and reasonable this engineer of the Marines – a petty officer, it seems.

June 26

Quiet. The Japs living around us do not have bugles, but they shout in a voice resembling a bugle call to give orders. In some places, mariners have megaphones.

June 27

Quiet. In the morning, the Superior is called by phone to Keimubu; immediately when he reports, the policeman asks:

> *Where are Fathers Piffaut and Paroissin?*
> – In Matang Tinggi.
> *Who gave them the authorisation?*
> – It was by order of Bunkyoka that they went there.
> *You should have made a report.*
> – It was done, here is the copy.
> *But then we must have the original in our papers.*
> – Without a doubt.
> Let's go see.
> After a moment the policeman comes back:
> *It's in order. You can go.*

June 28

Quiet. Still no news of our students who left the previous months: de Souza for Siam, Trinh and Giam for Indochina.

June 29

The Community is treated with durians from Balik Pulau, thanks to the care and generosity of the Reverend Mother Saint-Louis.

June 30

10:00 local time, precautionary alert, airplanes on Sungei Petani.

A Japanese from Mariophile approaches very politely to talk about the water supply up there and takes delivery of the pump motor he wants to install.

July 1

Some foreign planes pass during the night. People expect something to happen.

July 3

Another addition to the College fauna; a piglet is brought by Mysi (Ah Moh) and given to the Sisters with the already existing one; they are stabled between the henhouse and the servants' rooms. The mangosteen season ends – what quantity! And quality! It has been a blessing for all these last weeks. We passed a basket to each of our three Japanese friends and benefactors.

The news comes to us that Singapore must be evacuated, and the civilians set out on various points of the Peninsula, as far as Ipoh.

July 4
We learn that Mac-Arthur is already settled in Balik Papan, with American troops in Banjarmasin too. The advance towards Malaya is accelerating.

Prices are still rising. A yard of black taffe $740, Father Koh's bicycle $18,000.

Monseigneur Olçomendy proposes to send money to Matang Tinggi's group ($5,000). We accept.

July 5
Ration of rice for the month, 3 *katis* for the men, 2 *katis* for the women. The newspaper admits the loss of Miri. Moreover, we know that Pontianak has also been lost for the Japanese. Large pieces of artillery were placed behind the Western Road cemetery and are being fired today.

July 6
The *kumiais* or monopolies for purchasing and selling materials and essential commodities have been dissolved and the trade becomes free again. In fact, the *kumiais* were boycotted and everything was going to the *black market* without the Japs being able to prevent it.

July 8
The shop of the Sisters, installed in the liturgy room, does splendid business; clothes, especially, are sold at incredible prices. Sometimes, there is more than a thousand dollars of turnover in the day.

July 9
The control on coconuts is lifted. As in the past, we continue to pluck them with a student climber.

July 13
B-29s fly over Penang. We are offered 4,500 dollars for our He-goat and 2,700 for three kids. We refuse to sell.

July 15
News arrives about the death of Father Bertie Ashness in Singapore.

July 17
Rumours about the bombing of Singapore after the February raids are refuted.

July 18
End of term at the Japanese School in the College. Family farewell, no Japanese, it

is Siew Tat who represents the higher authorities; already, it is said there will be no reopening after the holidays.

July 19
Greater activity of Japanese aviation.

July 20
We have a new-born calf. This gives us a herd of four cows and thirty-three goats.

July 21
The Brothers continue to enjoy good fishing. Today, they brought back 71 pounds of fish. On their side, our students bring back 10 *katis* of shrimps. There is plenty for the three Communities. The news from Matang Tinggi is not very good, five students have malaria.

July 23
Inoculation against cholera. There is no more oil ration.

July 25
At 1:00, we heard the siren, but nothing followed.

July 26
We meet starving people who do not refrain from proclaiming loudly: *Semua orang lapar*.

The Japanese bring down the large metal trolley-bus posts between Pulau Tikus and Gottlieb Road. In Burma Road, they are laid, part on the shoulder, part on the road; it's a real danger to the traffic. We can get quinine tablets *gratis* through Dr Don who, during these last months, has been our doctor. The health of Father Dérédec, who stays in the room adjoining the garage, remains poor. He does not get up very much. By night, we make some epic hunts to drive away a horse that the Japanese have allowed to wander everywhere and devastate the garden. They have the good sense to keep him locked up now. At 10:00 am, alert; nothing afterwards.

Our *buah kliang* of Mariophile, which had never been rented out, finds an amateur reaper for $450. The cow which recently calved starts giving us milk.

The Japanese have collected all radio devices. Allies have come so close lately that even longwave devices will soon be able to receive their broadcasts, hence, the measure that is being applied these days. An orphan of the Sisters in Poh Leung Kok, admitted to the hospital, responds to the doctor who asked her about her illness: '*I am hungry*'. In fact, the local people whom the Japanese put in charge of Poh Leung Kok cleaned out most of the rations, already so lacking, and the orphans would die of starvation if the Sisters do not bring them supplementary rations from outside.

July 27
The Japanese placed partitions in the Mariophile refectory, and they organised

bathrooms in there. They also made a gravel road from the house to the reservoir road through the rubber plantation.

July 28
The news informally circulates that the Allies have launched an operation in Phuket on the coast of Siam.

July 30
Bombing of Sungei Petani. The news [unreadable] Phuket is confirmed. Two expeditions of students to Balik Pulau to fetch *bakau* bark. They stay there for two days and bring back a good quantity.

The priest of the Chinese church and his vicar (who have just left the College) speak only in French between themselves, for fear of being spied upon.

The Japanese who occupy the schools of Pulau Tikus are proper and even kind to the neighbours. They invite the priest to come to pick up the coconuts in their *kampong*. For lack of bugle calls, everything goes very well *by screaming*. They are well disciplined, except on certain days when on the occasion of festivals or [unreadable], they drink, sing, and fight with great clamour, loitering outside with electric lamps – when there is no sustained blackout; they fall seated on the ground, it ends with a shower of blows from their chiefs to send them to sleep. But on ordinary days, they observe a great silence like a religious community.

The trolley bus continues to operate, just about every half hour. Apart from Koi Nian at Mariophile and En Voon at the College, we only have two servants left: the rice cook, Hon Min, and the tailor, Chong Tsam, who [unreadable] in the kitchen with the Sisters. Our boy Hong is in hospital with tuberculosis.

The fervour of the Christians diminished after the [unreadable] caused by the bombardments at the beginning of the year. Many young men are enlisted by the Japanese and cannot fulfill their religious duties.

August 2
At the end of the Mass, precautionary alert.

August 6
Occupation of the Bukit Mertajam convent by the Japanese.

August 7
The Japanese summon Reverend Mother Saint-Louis to Bukit Mertajam to arrange the evacuation of the Convent with the Church of St Anne.

There is talk of an ultimatum of the Powers [unreadable] expiring on [unreadable]. Favourable conditions are promised if Japan obeys and ceases hostilities.

Arrival to the Matang Tiggi Community of a new student, Joe Reutens from Malacca.

August 10

[unreadable]... to say ... shall be free on August 15th

Brothers fishing, 90 pounds of fish

Departure of Reverend Mother Saint-Louis for Bukit Mertajam

... [Ch]rysostome on the declaration of war of the Soviets against Japan.

Since [unreadable] days the factory installed by the Japanese in the Brothers' school on the edge of [unreadable] Road has stopped working by night ... The newspaper announces the invasion of Manchukuo [Manchuria] by the Soviets and by [unreadable] terrible bombs of a new kind, on Japan ... the evening, Chrysostome ... the prediction made ... new ... coming from Tokyo ... accordingly, of ... Japanese money ... a student of ... on a bicycle to ... warn the Fathers ...

[15 August, Japan surrenders. 3 September, British troops land in Penang. 12 September, start of the British Military Administration.]

[Pages from 11 August to 20 September of the notebook are missing,
The Diary is continued on loose sheets.]

September 21

Friday, heavy rain. The garden yields a lot of vegetables. Both the Brothers and we have stopped going fishing as the authorities give us *gratis* every day 14 pounds of meat and 14 pounds of fish, which are divided between the 3 Communities.

September 22

Saturday, we unearth the formic acid jars buried at the beginning of the Japanese occupation.[26] They are in perfect condition. The spot is behind the apse of the chapel at Mariophile. Little by little, the team there is putting the house back in order; whenever the students who are at the College go to Mariophile on Wednesdays, or those at Mariophile go back on Sunday night after having passed Sunday here, they carry materials with the handcart. It's a continuation of our countless handcart trips during the wartime. One of the three entrances of the underground [tunnel] dug by the Japanese behind Mariophile bungalow is crumbling and remains blocked.

In order to allow a class of Dogma to take place on Sunday morning, to replace that of Wednesday (prevented since the re-establishment of the walks), the Confessions are done on Saturday morning from 11h15 to 11h45. Then, singing class.

September 23

Sunday, Dogma class, preceded by a preparation (10h00–10h45), then class (10h45–11h45).

---

26 Formic acid is one of the acids (the other one is acetic) used for coagulating latex. One reason for the decline in rubber production during the war was the scarcity of acid and its prohibitive price.

The cutting of the branches of nine *angsana* trees, from the College courtyard towards the sea, is completed. The largest tree is left intact. Despite the rain, Father Paroissin and the ten students of Mariophile come over here for the day.

The Brothers pass a rumour that we will move to Mariophile and leave the College premises available to their school. On our part, we urge them to request the authorities to clear out the two Brothers' schools of Pulau Tikus, which contain equipment and provisions, declared *Enemy property*.

September 24

Implementation of a new schedule for the Community. Now, work in the morning for all, afternoon studies for all. The spiritual reading is put back into the last quarter of an hour before dinner.

During evening prayer, the College bells are tolling, afterwards, we hear the engine of a *car* and a hooting horn. It is Father Michel who returns; he left Singapore Saturday morning, by *car* all the way, and has travelled from K.L. in the same car with the Reverend Mother Saint Tarcisius. Twenty months of captivity! The hardest were the first six days in Penang Prison. Three days without food, lying on the cement, being treated like common-law prisoners. Then, very hard three-days' trip. As a result, the beginnings in Changi Prison seemed rather mild in contrast. We talk until almost midnight, so many things to tell each other! But it was necessary to let the traveler rest after three tiring days of travelling by *car*. The English troops occupy Ipoh.

September 25

Day of joy. Fathers and students from Mariophile come to participate in the College. Also present is the English army chaplain who is in charge of troops from K.L. to the Siam border. He takes care of sending our letters. His name is Father Schembley, an Englishman born in Bangalore and educated at St Sulpice.

Postal services resume, both in Malaya and overseas, without stamps, the weight limit is one ounce. Partial resumption of railway services as well.

We spend the day at Mariophile.

September 26

We continue to enjoy a free supply of meat and fish. The meat is refrigerated but not bad at all. Other internees arrive, those travelling by plane. The speeches of the Allied statesmen make us believe in the likelihood of a war against Russia. A letter from the Capitular Vicar, Monseigneur Olçomendy, orders the Collection for peace instead of the Tempore Belli Collection. The Mass rate is restored as before the war; it had been raised to $10 in Japanese currency, which was worth nothing at the end. Currently, we find the rate of exchange to be $1 British for $1,000 Jap notes.

September 27

With the letter from Monseigneur Olçomendy was a note of Father Michel; the first time we see his writing since his internment. Left Singapore on September 5th; this note reaches us on the 27th.

September 28
Classroom work continues more normally now that we are having class in the afternoon.

September 29
Father Michel is visibly recovering, eating and resting well.

September 30
Prices remain high; some go up. We live on our provisions obtained at the time of the Japs, and on the meat and fish provided *gratis* by the army, and so we do not spend a penny.

October 1
The season is very wet, which allows us to harvest abundantly in the garden.

October 2
College Day. The Malayans come from Mariophile to spend the day. The soldiers come to remove the two cars left by the Japs in Mariophile. We only have petrol from the big tank near...

[Two pages are missing from 2 to 8 October]

...Singapore. On the East coast, piracy is at its maximum. It is announced that Malaya will now be one, without the triple designation of the past, *Straits Settlements*, *Federated Malay States*, and *Unfederated Malay States*.

October 9
Free rice distribution to the entire population. We receive 4½ *katis* per person, equivalent to half the ration for the current month. The College telephone which had been cut by the telephonic central two weeks ago is restored, with no. 8 instead of 546.

October 10
Double Tenth,[27] rather calm. We decorated moderately. People do not have money, not even the English officers. The phone is connected to Mariophile, but it does not work yet. A *lorry* of R.A.F. is lent to us to bring some of our materials back to Mariophile.

A telegram from Singapore tells us that Father Celestinus (from Rangoon), on loan to Malacca after his Ordination in 1943, is on his way back here.

---

27 Double Tenth is the National Day of the Republic of China. It commemorates the Wuchang Uprising on 10 October 1911 (10–10 or double ten), which led to the end of the Qing dynasty in China and the establishment of the Chinese Republic on 1 January 1912.

October 11

Annual comedy for the Superior's feast. This is taking place in the verandah upstairs, which is abreast with the portico. The life of the Matang Tinggi group is enacted, the way it was there. An Annamite dressed in Jap costume appears on the scene, looking like a real Jap.

October 12

In the morning, Solemn Mass of Thanksgiving in honour of Saint Joseph, for our reunion after the separations of these last few years. In the afternoon, a traditional lottery. The biggest prize is for the Reverend Mother, and a student, escorted by Father George, brings her on the famous tricycle. Then, the two go to the wharf, looking for Father Celestinus from Rangoon who had been posted to Singapore since his Ordination. Before supper, Solemn Benediction with *Te Deum*. After supper, a movie, which the Sisters and their girls, who are working in the kitchen, are watching from the other side of the screen.

October 16

The town is still guarded by the military, there are sentries at crossroads and patrols by car. Communists put up posters everywhere in all languages, 'To relieve the poor, and to stabilize the livelihood of the civilians', the Malayan Communist Party. The letters do not arrive from Europe – neither from India, nor from Burma or Siam. However, Father Michel received a letter from a co-internee posted in Suez. Telegrams arrive well; the Reverend Mother received one from Paris. Cable and Wireless[28] resumes business and accepts telegrams. No telegram service to Japan, Siam, Indochina, and the Netherlands East Indies. Inside Malaya, it works as well as letters (pretty good).

The Sisters who are living in the College are leaving one by one, returning to the Convent. The Postal Savings Banks[29] have reopened from October 15th. The Electricity Supply Department puts right our electrical installations at the College and at Mariophile, *gratis*, thanks to the kindness of the chief, Major D.

October 17

Still no letters. Prices are very high and rising somewhat. A portion of *curry food* in an *Indian Mahommedan shop* costs $0.50.

---

28 Cable and Wireless traces its history to a number of British telegraph companies founded in the 1860s. With increasing competition from companies using radio communications, it was decided in 1928 to merge the communications methods of the British Empire into one operating company, initially known as the Imperial and International Communications Ltd, and from 1934, as Cable and Wireless Limited.

29 The British Post Office Savings Bank was created in 1861. Besides managing savings account, it also started to offer stocks and bonds in 1880.

October 18

A visit from Father Aloysius, who arrived late the night before, and stayed at the presbytery of Pulau Tikus with Father Edmund who accompanied him. He is well and says that the Japanese staff largely remained in Taiping until the 16th. He is going back to Taiping on the 19th. He also says that ten thousand Indian workers who were brought to Siam by the Japs, and who had no more patience to wait until they were repatriated to Malaya, had started to walk and the head of the column had reached Sungei Petani. They leave a long trail of corpses on the road, and most of those who arrived at Sungei Petani died of exhaustion soon after. Father Vendergon, who had gone down to Malacca to take some rest, was forced by the Military Authority to turn back, to go take care of this human tide surging down along North Kedah.

A student at Mariophile has malaria, extremely severe.

A letter from India arrives, via Japanese Red Cross, Tokyo. And that's all.

October 19

Prices go up, continue to rise ...

No pork to buy, the pork sellers refuse to open shop for four days because some of them were arrested for selling above the controlled price.

The first letters arrive from overseas by post; they are letters from India. The postal franchise ceases from this day and new stamps are put into service with surcharge B.M.A. MALAYA. A letter from Father Ouillon brings us the first news of Hong Kong.

October 20

The first letter of Europe finally arrives! It is for Father Michel, coming from his family in Belgium. His eighty-four-year-old mother is still alive.

The cost of living is always rising. The rice is $6 the *gantang*. Bold thefts multiply. The situation is more difficult than during the time of the Japanese because money is scarcer. In addition, malaria is in recrudescence and quinine is rare.

October 27

It was only yesterday that the Allies landed in Medan.

Great troubles in Taiping these days. The crowd refuses to obey the reading of the Riot Act and the troops must fire; there are dead and wounded. The rice for the month of October is given free by the government but the ration remains very insufficient, 9 *katis* for men, 6 *katis* for women and 3 *katis* for children, same as during the Japs' occupation. People are disappointed. Many daring robberies by an armed gang of thieves.

October 29

No beef. We take the risk (because the pork is too expensive) and, without permission, we kill one of our four cows (three years old). The Brothers and the Convent have a share in the treat. Today is the last day of the service for the Sisters in the College kitchen and refectory. Tomorrow, they will pack their things, and the day after tomorrow they will leave.

October 30
The kitchen is taken back by the staff of the College, the *kapala*, En Voon (who cooks for the Fathers at the same time), two servants, the rice cook, Hin Min, and the tailor, Siong Tsann, who cooperate in the kitchen with four Supersénateurs, volunteer students. They cook, clean vegetables and fish, etc. from 9:30 onwards. Usually, in the afternoon, they have practically nothing to do in the kitchen. Nice start under the amused eye – and with the always-ready assistance – of the Sisters, who are still here today. Abundant beef, vegetables. The curry comes from a shop…

[Two pages are missing from 30 October to 1 November]

… Novitiate and the Convent; we do not keep it for ourselves, having a lot of meat to eat. The first letter from Burma arrives by post today at the Brothers', coming from the Director of Mandalay. The cathedral and the Brothers' school are ruined, the Clergy House has resisted, the Brothers teach in a nearby house and also in Maymio.

November 2
Half a dozen letters arrive from Burma, sent by Bishops and Fathers. Tungoo's Mission was ruined, and Mandalay's as well, partly. But few casualties. These are our first letters from Burma to arrive by the normal way.

The robberies by armed gangs around the College are on the increase; they happen almost every night. We organise ourselves for the defence and we get ready to alert the police by phone.

Some distributors of the rations have yet to receive rice for the second half of October.

November 3
It is decided, in agreement with the Convent, that the Sister who was so far *Kapala Masak* at the College will come back every day, between 8:00 and 15:00, except on Sundays, and she will take over the direction of the kitchen. In addition, 5 Sisters who are teaching at Pulau Tikus will have a pied-à-terre in the old laundry room and will take their noon meals there. Ray's deliveries are quite regular, between 20 and 60 *katis* per day. The rice ration has been increased since 1 November. That's about 2 *gantangs* a month for an adult male, still insufficient! A dozen cases of cholera in Sungei Bakap.

November 5
First letter from France, it is from rue du Bac and contains two circulars dated August 15, 1945.

November 6
A coconut is $0.25 in town; this is reminiscent of the Japanese era.

Murders and *robberies* are increasing in a worrying way.

The *TongKoh Prumpuan* that stands in the kitchen seems very comfortable in the midst of her team of domestic seminarists.

We have fresh fish in abundance by buying it directly from Tanjong Tokong fishermen at $0.40 per *kati*.

November 8
The Brothers move their classes from the College to their Kelawei Road school. Soon, the College will be entirely cleared.

The street lighting resumes. The service had hardly been restored when the bulbs were stolen during the night. The series of murders in daylight and *gang robberies* prompted the authorities to proceed with a number of arrests.

November 12
The spate of armed robberies continues despite the violent reaction of the civil and military police. A letter from Bishop Provost informs us that the communications with Toungoo and Mandalay are still impossible from Rangoon, and that the students must remain in Penang until further notice, except for the two priests, Fathers Celestinus and Georgius. The Brothers lend us a Westinghouse fridge in good condition.

November 16
First letter from a Father's family in France. But it was posted in England and took about ten days to arrive. A letter from Bangkok, too.

Armed robberies continue.

The prices of commodities that have risen so far may perhaps go down, with *black market* rice at $180 a *gantang* instead of $5. We get our ration for the month, two *gantangs* per person, that is very little! The petrol left behind by the Japanese is being eyed by some Health department employees who want to use it against malaria, they say. But we clandestinely remove 200 gallons.

The horse that had fallen into our hands ('Joker', belonging to Lieutenant-Colonel de Buriatte) is taken back by the people of this gentleman.

November 17
Signing of the contract with Moses Chua Ah Moh for rearing pigs etc. in Mariophile.

November 19
In the night, thieves came to siphon off about 80 gallons of petrol and decamped.

November 20
We mount guards at the tank. Some men have made two attempts to steal petrol. The students sent them running. Dutch women in uniform can be seen in town. Dutch soldiers have landed in Prai and there are some administrative elements

in Penang. The Military Government's instructions are that everyone stays in his place, no movement. It takes five days to go to Singapore, and it is difficult to get a passport. The communists unscrew the bolts of the railway and, sometimes, it is necessary to walk about twenty miles on foot. Severe restrictions on the use of radio. But news from Rangoon and Hong Kong shows that it's worse elsewhere than here.

November 21
Letter from France, by ordinary mail, this one posted in France.

We draw another 50 gallons of petrol and the tank is empty.

November 25:
Thefts of planks in Mariophile. We get some Catholic Chinese (Moses and [unreadable]), to take over the pigsty left by the Japs near the end of the football field. Two Dutch nurses, helmeted and equipped, come to the High Mass and receive Holy Communion.

News from H.K. via Father Chorin (Bangkok) who describes what ruins the Japs have left there. It's a lot worse than in Penang.

November 26
News of Captain Hidaka by Father Vong. He was in Kulim, well treated by the English, having his own *car*. He sent Brother James his grateful recollections and his thanks for speaking on his behalf. He was soon to go to Batu Pahat, a prison camp.

A Chinese man returning from Medan says that the Japs patrol the town, well-armed, together with the British, to maintain order. The Japanese currency is still used over there at the rate of $1 British currency = $20 Japs. The Dutch currency is boycotted.

Finally, some news arrives from the Salesians[30] of Bangkok. It appears that de Souza, who left on April 18 from here, finally joined them.

November 29
The widespread shortage of rice in the world is officially announced. We anticipate a reduction of the ration, and the campaign for the production of foodstuffs, tapioca in particular, is revived. Prices go up.

November 30
It is decided that Fathers George Maung Kiaw and Celestin Hton Kin would go to Rangoon by air. They are the first to be sent this way, just as they were the first to be ordained priests here. Two servants, who had been faithful and helpful throughout the war, Hin Ming and Siong Tsann, leave us to open a tailor shop in town.

---

30 The Salesians of Don Bosco (SDB), also known as the Salesian Society, officially named the Society of St Francis de Sales, is a Roman Catholic religious institute founded in the late nineteenth century by Italian priest Saint John Bosco to help poor children during the Industrial Revolution.

December 1
Oral exams, both in Mariophile and at the College, the holidays will begin after the retreat that takes place from the 4th to the 7th.

December 2
The two Fathers from Rangoon, Father George and Father Celestin, leave by plane for their mission at 11:00, from Butterworth (Mata Kuching Airfield, in military terms, no. 60 Staging Post). They are expected to reach their destination in about six hours. Arrangements for the departure of two students (one from Rangoon and one from Mandalay) by junk to Moulmein continue, the permits to leave Malaya are granted by the Military Authority; but the captain of the junk is asking for a big amount of money for the food during the journey which is supposed to last forty-five days – nothing less than $125 per person. It is true that food is very expensive. We also arrange for the holiday of the seminarists from Malacca. There is only a limited number of rail passes: fifteen a day; also, the complacency of the railway staff is required to allow them to travel together.

December 4
Departure of two seminarists, Mg Htun Lin from Mandalay, and Jerome from Rangoon, by junk, scheduled trip from Penang to Moulmein forty-five days, for $125 per person.

December 5
Beginning of the Community Retreat.

December 8
Beginning of holidays. Malayan students are going on vacation. For a few days, the English people's supplier provided the Brothers with bread, meat, and preserves. Then a counter-order arrived and it was stopped.

Only six students remain at Mariophile; the others prefer to stay in the College.

December 9
Departure of Benedictus Michael, Reader from Malacca, his classes completed.

December 12
Departure of 3 students from Bangkok, their studies completed (Lao, Saul, Vinh). They leave by bus; the railway does not work yet for Siam. From Penang to Alor Setar, first section, $6 per person.

We have the temporary authorisation to travel around freely by trolley bus.

December 13
The phone is installed in Mariophile and, at night, this ease of communication is very helpful.

The news comes to us regarding the appointment of Monseigneur Lemaire as Superior General of the Foreign Missions.

December 14

Crimes and robberies are multiplying. A victim, among others, is Father Baloche at Pulau Tikus; thieves entered his house at night, by forcing a window bar, and took some small things. From this day (officially), classes end for the Brothers' school, which is still operating in the College, taking over the primary school of the Japanese government since September 1945. The primary school itself had continued the classes opened here by the Sisters following their set up in the College. The last day of class would have been, in fact, on the 13th; and on the 14th, the whole school goes to a movie show in town.

The British military settles in the New Spring Tide, which has been requisitioned for the use of convalescents en route for repatriation, or for those needing meals. It is named: St Andrews on the Sea, Holiday home (Church of Scotland Huts). It was the organisation that came to the College two months ago looking for space.

December 17

Hope to ship the rest of our Supersénateurs to Burma soon. A 200-tonne boat is prepared by the B.M.A. (British Military Administration) to fetch provisions and will take a few passengers. But the thing is still uncertain. There are now 3 Dutch chaplains in the region for the troops stationed in Penang and in Sungei Petani: Father Looters S.K.D., Father Loof (Secular), and Father Vrom Jesuit. They will have a Solemn Mass for Christmas and one of our seminarists will be Sub-deacon.

The fish is again very expensive, ray at $0.40 and above, after a few days at $0.30. And yet it is *ayer jalan*. Fortunately, there is the *Bunga Ayer* at $0.25 a *kati*, excellent.

We sell few piculs of loose sheets of the old *Histoire de l'Eglise* by Father Walloys, as paper wrappers, at a price of $50 a picul. More news arrives from France. Father Denarié remains the only one to have received nothing from his family so far. All the students of Malacca *ad unum* have gone to their families. Fathers Piffaut and Meissonnier also left for the Cameron Highlands. A pass is necessary to travel on the railway, it serves as a substitute for the ticket, $4 up to Singapore, $2 to KL.

December 25

Splendid Christmas, celebrated in a big way, everywhere, with beautiful weather. The celebration at the Assumption Church, with many soldiers, was particularly successful. At the College, we had a pre-war programme for the eve and the night, but because of the very small number of students, and their state of fatigue, no mass was sung during the day.

December 26

The news that the seas are infested with pirates north of Pulau Langkawi stirred in us some fears about our companions traveling by junk.

The festivities are saddened by the news that rice [rations] will be cut off entirely in rural areas, including Tanjong Tokong. People say that the English should at least give as much as the Japanese. We receive news of the arrival of the three Siamese seminarians who left on the 12th and arrived in Bangkok on the 18th. Long journey, tiring and expensive. Siam is totally cut off from Burma and Indochina.

December 31

The year ends with a big disappointment about the rice. The rural districts (Balik Pulau, Province Wellesley, Tanjong Tokong, etc.) are without the ration for the second half of December, and face the prospect of no longer receiving the Government's rice ration until further notice.

Pirates infest the north of Langkawi and the junks do not dare to go looking for supplies.

The Dutch overrun Penang more and more, many Dutch Fathers, one Secular, five Jesuits, fifteen from various orders (Capuchins,[31] Picpus[32]...)

1946

January 1

The usual session of greetings took place last night, with a reduced strength, two Fathers and fifteen students in all, in the *lusorium* (first time since 1940). Also, the ceremony was reduced to its simplest expression: a song, the wishes of the students, the riposte, a second song; and it was done. But the songs were very well executed (remarkable, because for several months, the students were singing poorly in the chapel); but there was a promise of a picnic in Balik Pulau shortly.

January 4

Picnic in Balik Pulau. Big success. Trolley to Ayer Hitam and then through the pass on foot. Back in the opposite direction. Students left at 6:15, returned at 18:30. Extremely happy.

January 6

Two military chaplains come into retreat at the College. A Jesuit Father, Vroom, and a Secular Father, Luf. Both very nice.

---

31 The Order of Friars Minor Capuchin (abbr. OFM Cap.) is an order of friars within the Catholic Church, an offshoot of the Franciscans. The Order arose in 1525.

32 The Congregation of the Sacred Hearts of Jesus and Mary is a Roman Catholic religious institute of brothers, priests, and nuns, which emerged amid the religious upheaval caused by the French Revolution. The priests are also known as the Picpus Fathers, because their first house was on Picpus Street in Paris.

January 9
Last vacation day. All the Malayans, who had gone off in full force for their *Christmas Holidays*, come back sick, except one.

January 10
A day that marks an epoch. Resumption of the normal regime, after four years full of adventures, uncertainties, almost daily changes in the agenda. We return to the old hours of rising and bedtime, and the complete programme. But from 17:30 to 18.30, there is compulsory manual work instead of free time. As compensation, free recreation after meals is maintained as it used to be during the war, until further notice.

The Supersénateurs, fifteen in number, have a special *ordo diurnus*, some are still cooking under the expert guidance of Sister Johanna.

N.B: seven Directors at the resumption: Father Rouhan, Father Michel, Father Denarié, Father Monjean, Father Piffaut, Father Meissonnier, Father Paroissin, the same as in 1941. Everyone has stood firm. *Deo Gratias.*

There are fourteen students to continue the courses, eleven in Theology (all in Special because all did the Basic last year) and three in Philosophy, all from Malacca.

In addition to that, there is a Supersénateur at the hospital, TB case, there for more than six months already. So, counting everybody, thirty students.

The prospects of the Supersénateurs' return remain vague. Junks to Burma are on strike, and there are pirates in Langkawi. No communication by boat with Indochina. For Hong Kong, there is a boat that asks $250 per person. People on their way to Rangoon had to turn back, unable to disembark for lack of proper papers; and the Penang Authorities do not know what these papers are about. We have to wait. No new students in view.

The government has reversed its decision to give a rice ration only to urban areas with more than 5,000 inhabitants. As a consequence of the allocation of equal rations for the entire country, our ration falls from 2 *gantangs* to 10 *katis* (instead of twelve) per month. It's pathetic!

January 15
A student from Malacca, Gregory Jee, who had gone on vacation, writes that he has decided not to continue. His departure is set for December 8.

January 16
First walk since the resumption. It is not yet back to *normal* because, temporarily, one modifies the traditional schedule for Wednesdays. After Mass, *privatim* meditation, then at 6:15, breakfast. Free time until 11:30, dinner.

Armed robbery in College Square at 16:00, in a house. Things are going too far.

January 20
Rations are distributed very irregularly. January's salt has not arrived yet, neither has December's. We have 11 *katis* of rice for the men this month. The rice in the *black*

market is worth 3 dollars the *gantang*. We were promised distributions of *corned beef* but nothing came.

January 22
Robbery by a gang, just opposite the main Police Station on Penang Road. There is no limit to insolence!

January 23
The first printed magazines from Europe arrive, an October issue of *Missions Catholiques* and one of *Union Missionnaire du Clergé*.

January 25
First letter from the Seminary of Paris (there had been only one circular so far) written by Fathers Lobes and Belleville.

January 29
It is said that the English soldiers rent out their revolver at night to whoever wants it.

January 30
General strike in Malaya, following the arrest of a communist leader.

The trolley buses try to run but are stopped by the strikers. Malcolm MacDonald, son of Ramsay MacDonald, is appointed Governor of Malaya.

Since the resumption of classes on the 10th, the system of two teams of Supersénateurs, five per team, alternating a week at the College, a week in Mariophile, works satisfactorily and ensures the security of Mariophile with Father Paroissin permanently up there.

This does not prevent criminals from entering bungalow no. 514 and pulling away some of the electrical installations.

February 1
The system for the security of Mariophile, organised since the resumption, is working and there are no thefts up there. Father Paroissin teaches students up there, in addition to the classes he conducts here at the College.

February 2
Candlemas[33] with candles and procession. It is a pleasure to see the ceremony again, omitted in recent years. The news comes of the happy landing on January 16th, of the two students who left in a junk on December 4th.

February 10
Priestly Ordination of Vinh and Saul, formerly from Bangkok, now at Chanthabury.

---

33   Candlemas (or Candlemass) is a Christian Holy Day commemorating the Presentation of Jesus at the Temple, based upon the account in Luke 2:22–40.

February 11
Anniversary of the announcement of our expulsion from Mariophile last year. The matter has turned out really well. But what a memory!

February 15
Anniversary of the fall of Singapore. Communist elements are trying to celebrate this event in Singapore and Penang. There are fights and fatal casualties.

February 16
Tremendous explosions. A Japanese depot exploded near Butterworth. The thefts and murders continue in a worrying way. Despite the death penalty against those who possess weapons.

February 18
We solemnly celebrate the BB Martyrs of this day, for the first time in years. The postal workers' strike, which lasted eight days, ends.

February 19
The student who is in the hospital has a hemorrhage.

February 20
Day marked by a sad event; the student who used the electric iron to prepare the hosts forgot to cut off the power when he finished. The iron is no longer usable. It will not be easy to repair it. Will it be necessary to revert to the old iron which was used at Mariophile during the war years? The preparation will be very slow and tedious!

February 21
The student at the hospital has a fresh hemorrhage. He is demoralised.

Our iron for the hosts, which was *grilled* (the student who used it having forgotten to turn off the power at the end of the session), will not be easy to repair here.

February 22
The authorities inform us that because of the serious difficulties that exist in Burma, no passport will be issued for this country. So, we are looking for a ship on which the students could embark as sailors, with a landing in Rangoon. For that we have to find a compliant captain.

February 23
Important arrival of wheat flour. Prices fall immediately. There is also a lot of *pulut* available. Serious disorders in India. A wind of independence is sweeping through the empire.

February 25
Rumors of war with Russia. The crime wave that had grown so alarming in Penang

seems to be diminishing. Letters from France take two and a half months to arrive by surface mail and many seem to be lost. A package sent by plane on February 9 arrives.

February 28
The canned meat falls to $0.40 a pound.

March 1
Finally, bungalow no. 514 by the seaside in Mariophile is rented out. Since October 1944, we have had no income from it and the looters had damaged it quite a bit. We begin the fulfillment of the vow to Saint Joseph, it is the first of the five years during which he binds us.

March 2
We still cannot find a ship for our Supersénateurs. There are boats for Burma with available space, but you cannot get a passport.

March 5
Finally, a letter from Indochina arrives. It is Bishop Cassaigne of Saigon who writes. His Vicariate was very much affected, six priests massacred, twenty on the run or held as hostages by the rebels, Major Seminary scattered, incalculable material ruin.

March 6
The community is vaccinated against smallpox.

March 7
We celebrate Saint Thomas with sung services for the first time since 1941. In the evening, cinema. Letters from France, including one for Father Piffaut, from his mother, dated October 10, 1945.

March 10
We have abundant distribution of Australian sausages, rather good quality, at low prices. Finally, we receive the flour so long promised. But it seems that it is adulterated and we dare not use it to make the hosts.

March 13
A letter arrives from Monseigneur Robert, still signing as Superior General, dated January 29, announcing the recall of at least thirteen missionaries to Paris in the near future, and requesting information on the personnel by way of preparation.
Visit of Father François, coming from Ipoh.

March 14
The Capitular Vicar, Monseigneur Olçomendy, had announced his arrival from Singapore by plane this morning. He did not arrive and nothing was received to explain this absence.

March 15

Still no news of the Capitular Vicar.

The bakers are again selling wheat bread at twenty cents a pound of bread.

March 16

The Capitular Vicar telegraphed, 'trip by plane canceled, shall be coming next week.'

The heat remains oppressive despite recent showers.

March 17

Father Riboud's Jubilee at the Indian church. It's very simple, but very nice. Atmosphere very pleasant in this parish, coming together, all spontaneous, almost without preparations.

March 18

Preparatory fasting to the Feast of St Joseph according to the wishes of the Community.

Monseigneur Olçomendy arrives by train. He seems to be fine.

March 19

St Joseph's Feast. Solemn Mass, exposition of the Blessed Sacrament until the Solemn Salvation. Monseigneur Olçomendy is with us for this first Thanksgiving to Saint Joseph since the liberation, in observation of the vow that will bind us again for four years.

Priestly Ordination of Lao and Souza in Bangkok.

March 20

Monseigneur Olçomendy, after spending twenty-four hours at the College, leaves us for the town.

March 25

Priestly Ordination of Goh (Malacca) in Bangkok.

March 28

Visit of Father Dalson, English military chaplain, in residence in Taiping.

April 1

The B.M.A. gives way to the Civil Administration. Everyone wanted that. As far as we are concerned, we have more than one reason to be indebted to the British Military Administration.

The sultans are protesting against their position in the new Malayan Union – they are reduced to the role of *advisers*. They do not consent; they abstain from going to the installation of the civil government, and all Malays must wear a white band around their *songkok* for eight days as a sign of protest.

April 13

We finish the classes today; the written exams took place at the beginning of the week, and the oral exam will be on the 15th; there are only ten theologians and three philosophers.

We are still struggling to repatriate our students. A letter was sent by the College to the Bishop of Rangoon, asking him to obtain permission for our Burmese students to return home.

April 21

Easter. Solemn Mass. The students are numerous enough (twenty-eight) to be able to sing well despite the many ministers of ceremony. Tomorrow, seventeen students will leave for Mariophile and eleven will stay here. During holidays, some will transfer from the College to Mariophile and vice versa. We must keep both places occupied because thefts are still frequent. It is in the harbour that looting is the most prevalent. It is said that half of the goods are stolen. Also, importers have given up ordering goods and the lack of basic necessities continues. It is said that it will be better when the Harbour Board starts to work again. Now it is still under Military Control.

23 April

There are no more Dutch people in town. All their troops are gone. The installation went well yesterday at Mariophile, but at night there an incident that could have ended with the destruction of the first dormitory; the fire started in a bed (as a result of burning tobacco falling from a pipe) while the students were at the evening prayer. Fortunately, there was a student on duty; he extinguished the fire at the start without difficulty.

May 3

Arrival of a letter from the Superior General recalling Father Meissonnier to Paris.

May 5

Departure of three Annamites students, Nam from Saigon, Reader; Thien and Ngia, Secular, their studies completed; waiting for five months for an opportunity to leave. They take away their books.

May 8

Departure of Father Philippe Meissonnier, recalled as professor in Paris. There are six Fathers remaining. All present. The three Annamites embarked yesterday on a tanker belonging to the navy of the government, for their passage (free) (without passport) from Singapore to Saigon.

May 9

Community picnic in St Jean for the first time after a 4-year hiatus. 13 participants altogether.

May 10
Father Paroissin, who went to Singapore, returns. He was able to get a new motorcycle there.

May 12
Sunday. For the last time, the students of the College go up to Mariophile to sing the Sunday services. At the end of the week everyone will come down and, for the first time since the end of August 1945, Mariophile will remain under the care of a servant. We farm out the fruits of the plantation for $450.

May 13
Father Meissonnier was able to get a free passage from Singapore to Amsterdam aboard a Dutch boat where he will serve as chaplain.

May 18
For the first time since the return of the English in September 1945, Mariophile remains without Fathers or students; a guard is put there just like before the war, and with the holidays ending today, everyone goes down to the College.

May 20
The long-awaited permission finally arrives; the government of Burma no longer objects to the departure of our Burmese students. Immediately, we make the requests to establish the return permits and vaccinate the students as the regulations require. We do the same for the three students of Swatow. The phone is removed from Mariophile.

June 16
The departure of the Swatow students seems close at hand, but no news regarding the departure of the Burmese students; no boats, the biggest ones avoiding Rangoon because of the bad condition of the port, and the small ones abstaining for fear of bad weather accompanying the monsoon.

J. Reutens, sick (fever and rheumatic pains), goes home to seek treatment.

June 17
The wave of theft and crime rises again. In broad daylight, at noon in MacAlister Road, passersby are accosted and relieved of all their precious things, including their bicycles. In remote corners, Batu Itam for example, it is the same; people armed with revolvers are looting isolated houses. And when the honest people ask for hunting guns to defend themselves, they are refused.

June 20
Corpus Christi. Procession, temporary altar in the *lusorium*, itinerary through the verandas, Brothers and Sisters are participating.

June 22
Delay in the departure of the three students of Swatow who were supposed to embark tomorrow. Their boat is damaged and has to first proceed to Singapore for repairs. Received a letter from Father Meissonnier writing from Suez on June 5 and expecting to arrive in Amsterdam on June 20.

June 23
The *Sunday Gazette*[34] has an article on the [unreadable] Fathers.

[It is clipped in the Diary, in English]

MORALS AND MORALE: This column was talking last Sunday with a reliable informant who disclosed that in the confusing days following the fall of Penang, a group of British soldiers who had lost their way on the mainland, were led to safety by a quiet, modest Chinese catholic priest who at the risk of his own life and with the Japs fast catching up only a few miles away, had driven for hours showing the troops the way to escape. [Added by hand, Father Teng]

This is one of many war-time good deeds done quietly and without much ado by the Christian Fathers here who, like the Christian Brothers to whom the column paid tribute the other week, had stayed on throughout the occupation, contributing, as always, to the maintenance of Penang's morals and morale.

Their work has, perhaps not been as generally acknowledged as it should be, but this is because they neither sought nor desired publicity. Theirs was the unrecorded story of the war – a story of self-sacrifice and devotion to duty which had made possible the continuation of the Christian way of life in the darkest period of Malaya's history.

The three Annamites who left on May 5 write that they arrived safely in Saigon, but the two of Thanh Hoa cannot, for a while, think of going to Tonkin.

June 26
Still difficult to arrange the return of our Burmese students. We begin to prepare an itinerary for them from Penang to Rangoon via Calcutta.

July 12
Still no progress for the departure of the students. Arrival of Monseigneur Olçomendy, who came to visit Penang.

July 13
Arrival of Ah Kwang, the Hylam, with his leg amputated; he was discharged from the hospital, where he lost a leg and gained the baptism. He will stay in the small room

---

34   The *Sunday Gazette* was the Sunday edition of the *Pinang Gazette*, started in 1932 but interrupted during the war; it returned in 1945.

near the students' toilets, arranged for our former boy Lee Chong who is leaving to return to China. Like him, he [Ah Kwang] will watch this corner during the absence of the students who are busy elsewhere. The bishop of Toungoo writes, requesting for five students to be sent by plane (four from Toungoo, one from Kengtoung). We immediately begin to take the steps towards this departure; we will send three first, then two, in order to avoid a total disaster in case of the loss of a plane (a plane going to Burma has totally disappeared, days ago).

July 15
A student, Basil Pinto, fell from a rambutan tree while picking fruit, and was transported to the hospital. A fracture of the spine, it is feared.

July 16
Departure of three students from Toungoo by plane: Sebastianus, Aloysius, and Ernest, their studies completed a long time ago, all three Minored, taking their books with them.

July 17
Pinto has a slight fracture of the spine.

July 18
The Community is vaccinated against typhoid, first injection.

July 19
Departure of a student from Toungoo: Marinus, Minored, his study finished, and Khee Chong from Kengtoung, Secular, his study finished, take their books with them, both by plane to Rangoon.

As the wind was very strong, the plane carrying them had to turn back and in the evening, after supper, much to our surprise, Khee Chong called us on the phone from the Staging Post of Mata Kuching in Butterworth from where the students had flown in the morning.

Pinto has fever, following the insertion of catheters for urination. So, we have three students out of twenty-one permanently living outside, two are sick in the hospital and one is with his family, having rheumatism for over a month.

July 21
The rice ration given by the government in recent weeks is pathetic, 1 *kati* per person per week. On the other hand, the rice *black market* at 4 dollars per *gantang* is flourishing. We can have as much as we want, and this rice arrives by the ferry at Michell Pier, brought by Chinese ladies, old or young, by children even, with bags or baskets containing less than 20 *katis*, to escape the regulations on the transport of rice, as everyone knows. The rice comes from Kedah and Siam.

July 25
The Community is vaccinated against typhoid, second injection.

July 27
For the first time in many years, an official invitation arrives at the College for a Garden Party at the Residency. It is sent by the Governor General who is in Penang these days; the function is in honour of the Malay delegation which comes to deal with affairs related to the constitution of the Malayan Union, so unpopular with the Malays.

Our Supersénateurs, numbering six, go to Bukit Mertajam for Saint Anne's [Feast]; they will be in charge of singing at tomorrow's Sunday ceremonies.

July 28
In the absence of Supersénateurs; given the very small number of students (eleven) who are present, we inaugurate a reduced system of services at the altar.

July 29
Departure of Michael Then from Sarawak, going on holiday, and we do not want to take him back following the decision of the Council of December 1945, for lack of a vocation. Secular, 2nd year of Theology, he carries his books with him.

August 1
Pinto is operated at the hospital; there is a double fracture of the neck and his case is very serious; few survive, says the surgeon. In addition, the bladder is paralysed and the catheters placed there cause severe haemorrhage; also, operation is done at the same time on the neck and at the bladder.

August 2
Finally, we manage to take tickets for the four Burmese who are waiting to be sent home, but to Mergui only. From there, they will have to manage by themselves. They are supposed to leave on the 7th. The boat of Father Michel, who is going on leave, is also announced as departing on the 7th. As for our three Chinese from Swatow, the boat they should take is still out of order, we do not know where it is.

August 7
Departure, to Mergui and later to their respective missions by the Straits Steamship *Tung Song*, of four students (three from Mandalay: Jackson, Chit Maung (Acolytes) and Henricus (Secular)), their studies completed.

At Mariophile, we are repairing the water piping system badly damaged in some parts by the Japs who, on a more positive side, had water conveyed [by pipe] from the town to the students' bathroom. We fit up (discreetly) a *stopcock* between the water inlet pipe of the town and the lower pipes of our system (the water from town does not have sufficient pressure to reach the kitchen). The piping between the student bathroom and the *Rubber Plant* is restored, but with old ¾ inch pipes which will not last long.

August 8
Last day of (excellent) services of Sister Johanna at the College. This time, the Sisters have completely left the College.

August 9
Oral exams and holidays. Malayan students are going home. We remain with only seven students, so we shall not go to Mariophile, where kitchen facilities are not restored yet; it will probably be the same in December. We are so few that, until the end of the holidays, we will have neither High Mass nor Vespers but only Salutation.

August 11
Beginning of the rainy season.

August 12
Departure on leave of Father Michel.

August 13
End of the free service of bread and biscuits by the army for the benefit of the Brothers and us, too. This has served us well all these past months; this lasted for almost a year. That same day, the Town Council decreed that the free water granted to the College, for a period of ten years in 1934, has ended and would not be renewed.

August 14
The pupils who left on the 7th of August arrived safely at Mergui, as announced by a telegram. For the first time since our forced exodus from Mariophile in February 1945, we cook our food at Mariophile for lunch, and then up there on Wednesday. Up till now, the food was still being brought cooked from the College by tricycle.

August 21
For the first time since before the war, some Mass wine reaches us. This is Australian wine, made under the guidance of the Jesuits, very good and sweet, having only one disadvantage, that is, the cost of $3.15 a bottle (including $2 of duty!)

August 24
Departure of three students from Swatow, their studies finished, Io and Tang, Acolytes, Kwang Seng, Exorcist. It is (after a year of English reoccupation, or almost so) the end of the repatriation operations of our Supersénateurs; two still remain in the Province but of their own free will, having left the seminary, and one in the hospital, with a fractured neck, in treatment.

August 26
The five remaining students go for a picnic in Taiping and come back only on the 28th.

September 7
Last day of vacation. Picnic in Telok Bahang with the *lorry* of Mariophile. A splendid day for the students. We propose to do it again sometime on Wednesdays or during free days.

September 8
The students come back, twelve at the College and one at the hospital. The latter is much better, walking, eating alone, but must remain in the cast.

September 9
Beginning of classes. The annual retreat is postponed until the end of the year. We start again at Mariophile to tap *rubber* (interruption since December 8, 1941). The sale is $50 a picul, we give $0.20 to the tappers by *kati*.

Appendices

Timeline

PENANG FORTRESS

1936	Penang is officially termed a Fortress after the construction of Batu Maung Fort
7 Jul 1937	Marco Polo Bridge Incident. Japan invades China
3 Sept 1939	Phoney War. France and the United Kingdom declare war on Germany.
Jan 1940	Conscription of able-bodied British males aged 18–55.
25 Jun 1940	Armistice is signed between France and Germany. Germany occupies the northern part of France, while an Axis-friendly government based in Vichy and headed by Philippe Pétain controls the southern part.

1941

Jan	Passive Defence Services organise air raid exercises on Penang Island.
Feb	Situation deteriorates, Medical Auxiliary Services and Local Defence Forces are put in place on Penang Island.
21, 29 Jul	France authorises Japan to use airport and port facilities in Indochina.
Aug	Two U.S. Navy cruisers pay a friendly visit to Penang.
Sep	Report states that Penang sends 63 per cent of its export to the U.S. and only 2 per cent to Japan.
Oct	Census enumerates 59 Japanese men and 18 Japanese women living in Penang.

ATTACK ON PENANG

8 Dec	Japanese troops land on the beaches of Kota Bharu (Kelantan).
	Japanese air raid on Butterworth and Bayan Lepas airfields. The firing of Anti-Aircraft (AA) batteries can be heard, but there was no blackout that night in Penang.
9 Dec	All British bombers except one are wiped out by a Japanese air raid on Butterworth. From then on, blackout every night until the departure of the British soldiers.

10 Dec	*Prince of Wales* and *Repulse* are sunk in the South China Sea.
11 Dec	'Black Thursday', air bombing of George Town, machine-gunning of the streets. The people flee the city. Looting starts.
12 Dec	Second day of air bombing. A decision is made to evacuate European civilians.
13 Dec	Third day of air bombing. In the evening 650 European women and children are evacuated.
14 Dec	Evacuation continues. Public services are collapsing.
15 Dec	The battle front moves to Kedah, north of Penang.
16 Dec	Destruction of facilities by the British and final evacuation from Penang.
17 Dec	Bombing and looting continue. Creation of Penang Service Committee (PSC) headed by the *Straits Echo* editor, Manicasothy Saravanamuttu, who replaced the British flag in Fort Cornwallis with a white flag.
18 Dec	At 9 am, the PSC broadcasted, 'Penang is an Open Town. The British have evacuated. Please stop the bombing…'. The Japanese planes drop leaflets asking for order to be maintained.

JAPANESE OCCUPATION

19 Dec	Japanese Occupation of Penang begins.
23 Dec	PSC becomes the Peace Preservation Committee (PPC) for several months. Its first act was to collect all weapons.
24 Dec	Compulsory registration of Eurasians.
25 Dec	Event organised by the Indian Independence League, attended by 10,000 people.
	Fall of Hong Kong.

1942

2 Jan	Asdang House Conference where the Japanese set the tone of their governance.
15 Feb	Fall of Singapore, no more free Englishmen, except in hiding.
18 Feb–4 Mar	Sook Ching (purge through cleansing) massacres in Singapore.
March	Tokyo time is imposed (1h30 ahead of Singapore).
5, 6 & 7 Apr	Extension of Sook Ching in Penang by the Kempeitai.
20 Apr	Deadline for the 'donation' of 50 million Japanese dollars from the Chinese community of Malaya and Singapore, including 5 million from Penang. The deadline was met only on 25 June after borrowing 22 million from a Japanese bank.

Apr	Schools reopen, teaching is conducted in Japanese, Malay and Tamil languages. English is banned as medium of instruction.
	The Kempeitai starts to use the Penang Prison as interrogation and execution centre.
Aug 1942 –Feb 1943	Two battles marking the turning point of WWII – Japan lost the battle of Guadalcanal and Germany lost the battle of Stalingrad.
Oct	Second round-up of the Penang population by the Kempeitai. Chinese schools reopen, Mandarin is not allowed as a medium of instruction, but Chinese dialects are.
10 Nov	Germany invades Vichy's France.

1943

Feb	Another round-up of the Penang population by the Kempeitai.
Mar	New Kempeitai chief, Captain Terata, replaces Major Higashigawa.
15 Jul	Arrival in Penang of the first German U-boat.
25 Jul	Prime Minister of Italy Benito Mussolini is arrested and replaced by General Pietro Badoglio.
8 Sep	The surrender of Italy to the Allies, signed on 3 September, is made public.
20 Dec	Formation of the Labour Service Corps in all states of Malaya.

1944

11 Jan	German U-boat 178 and Japanese cruiser *Kuma* are sunk off Penang port by the British submarine *Tally Ho*.
Feb	Marimuthu, the chief warden of Penang Prison, is assassinated.
6 Jun	The Allies land in Normandy, France.
25 Aug	Paris is liberated from German occupation. Charles de Gaulle becomes the head of the Provisional Government of the French Republic. Philippe Pétain is taken to Germany. In Indochina, Jean Decoux assumes full powers.
20 Oct	The American landing on the island of Leyte marks the beginning of the Philippines battle.
Nov	Allied bombing of Penang and Singapore, testing the new long-range B29 bombers.
16 Dec	U.S. troops defeated the Japanese troops on Mindoro island in the Philippines.
16 Dec 1944 –25 Jan 1945	The Battle of the Bulge, the last German offensive in WWII.

1945

11 Jan   Major air bombing over Penang, government buildings and the Post Office are destroyed.

24 Jan   Bombing continues.

1 Feb   Bombing (Penang Library lost over half of its collection of rare books).

3 Feb–3 Mar Battle for Manila.

19 Feb–26 Mar U.S. troops capture the island of Iwo Jima.

21 Feb   U.S. troops capture the Peninsula of Bataan in the Philippines.

9 Mar   Fearing the landing of U.S. troops, the Japanese take over French Indochina and create the Empire of Vietnam, the Kingdom of Kampuchea, and the Kingdom of Luang Phrabang, under their control. Most of the French are arrested, put under house arrest, or killed.

9–10 Mar   U.S. planes bomb Tokyo.

7 Apr   Admiral Kantaro Suzuki becomes Japan Prime Minister.

2 May   British forces reoccupy Rangoon.

7 May   Germany surrenders to the Allies. The war ends in Europe.

1–21 Jul   U.S. troops land and take Balikpapan.

26 Jul   Potsdam Declaration (U.S. ultimatum to Japan to surrender).

6 Aug   U.S. drops the atom bomb on Hiroshima.

9 Aug   U.S. drops the atom bomb on Nagasaki. The Soviet army enters Manchuria (Manchukuo).

15 Aug   Emperor Hirohito surrenders.

20 Aug   The capitulation is reported in the Japanese newspapers.

21 Aug   The Japanese surrender is published in *Penang Shimbun.*

OPERATION JURIST

24 Aug   The Royal Navy fleet (Task Force 11) leaves Ceylon for Penang with 43,000 troops.

25 Aug   Emperor Hirohito orders the Imperial Army to cease operations.

28 Aug   HMS *Nelson* reaches Penang.

1 Sep   The British fleet anchors in Penang.

2 Sep   Signature of the Surrender aboard USS *Missouri* in Tokyo, marking the end of WWII, and the surrender of Rear Admiral Jisaku Uozomi aboard HMS *Nelson* in Penang.

3 Sept — 600 Royal Marines land at Weld Quay in Penang at 8h00.

4 Sept — Japanese soldiers are concentrated in Gelugor before being evacuated to the mainland. All political prisoners are released from Penang Prison.

6 Sept — Official ceremony on Swettenham Pier. The Japanese army officially surrenders in Penang.

7 Sept — Official visit of Lord Louis Mountbatten, Supreme Allied Commander, Southeast Asia Command.

8 Sept — Victory March in Penang.

BRITISH MILITARY ADMINISTRATION

12 Sept 1945 — British Military Administration is established. The Japanese Dollar is immediately replaced by the Straits Dollars, except in Penang, at least for few weeks.

16 Sept — Five banks open.

Sept — Estimated total number of deaths of Penang people during the war: 6,000 (2,000 by Kempeitai, 1,500 during air raids and 2,500 building the Burma–Thailand railway line).

10 Oct — The creation of the Malayan Union is announced in British Parliament.

21 Oct — Beginning of the week-long Perak Disturbance, four deaths in Taiping on 22 October.

1946

29 Jan — General strike.

15 Feb — Second general strike (anniversary of the fall of Singapore). In Penang, a fire hose is used to disperse the crowd.

MALAYAN UNION

1 Apr 1946 — The Federated Malay States, the Unfederated Malay States and the Straits Settlements (minus Singapore) form the Malayan Union. Penang conserves its free port status.

28 Sept — In Penang, the War Crimes Trial of 32 Japanese and three Taiwanese ends with the sentencing of 14 accused to prison sentences of five to seven years and 21 to death (eventually, only 20 were executed).

Currency and Units of Measure

Currency

1 dollar = two shillings four pence sterling (60 dollars = 7 pounds)
In 1939, the Straits Dollar was officially replaced by the Malayan Dollar,
(but the introduction of the Straits Dollar was postponed till after the war)
In 1942, the Malayan Dollar was replaced by the Japanese Dollar
In 1945, the Japanese Dollar was replaced by the Malayan Dollar

Malaysia adopted the Metric System in 1972.

Length

1 mile = 1.609 metres
1 furlong = 201 metres
1 chain = 20 metres
1 yard = 0.91 metres
1 foot = 30.48 centimetres
1 inch = 2.54 centimetres

Surface

1 acre = 4,047 square metres = 0.40 hectare
1 rood = 1,012 square metres = 0.10 hectare
1 pole = 25.29 square metres

Volume

1 gallon (Malay, *gantang*) = 4.55 litres
1 quart (Malay, *cupak*) = 1.14 litre

Weight

1 picul (Malay, *pikul*) = 100 catties = 60.48 kilograms
1 catty (Malay, *kati*) = 0.60 kilograms = 604.80 grams
1 tael (Malay, *tahil*) = 1/16 catty = 37.80 grams
1 pound = 0.45 kilograms = 450 grams
1 ounce = 0.02 kilograms = 28.35 grams

List of Catholic Missions
mentioned in the Diary

BURMA (MYANMAR)

Kengtung (Kengtung) Apostolic Prefecture of East Burma, under the Pontifical Institute for Foreign Missions (Italian missionaries).

Mandalay (Mandalay) Apostolic Vicariate of North Burma, under the MEP.

Rangoon (Yangon) Apostolic Vicariate of South Burma, under the MEP.

Toungoo (Taungoo) Apostolic Vicariate of East Burma, under the Pontifical Institute for Foreign Missions (Italian missionaries).

CHINA

Chaotung (Zhaotong) Apostolic Prefecture and town of Yunnan, under the MEP.

Lanlung (Anlong) Apostolic Vicariate and county of Guizhou, under the MEP.

Manchuria (North East China) Apostolic Vicariates of Kirin (Jilin) and Moukden (Shenyang), under the MEP.

Nanning (Nanning) Apostolic Vicariate and capital of Guangxi, under the MEP.

Pakhoi (Beihai) Apostolic Vicariate and port of Guangxi, under the MEP.

Swatow (Shantou) Apostolic Vicariate and port of Guangdong, under the MEP.

Tatsienlu (Kangding) Apostolic Vicariate and town of Sichuan, under the MEP.

Yunnan Fu (Kunming) Apostolic Vicariate and capital of Yunnan, under the MEP.

INDOCHINA (VIETNAM, CAMBODIA AND LAOS)

Bui Chu (Bui Chu) Apostolic Vicariate in Central Tonkin, under the MEP.

Kontoum (Kon Tum) Apostolic Vicariate in North Cochin, under the MEP.

Laos (Laos) Apostolic Prefectures of Luang Prabang and Vientiane, under the MEP.

Quinhon (Qui Nhon) Apostolic Vicariate in East Cochin, under the M.E.P.

Saigon (Ho Chi Minh City) Apostolic Vicariate in South Cochin, under the M.E.P.

Thanh Hoa (Tanh Hoa) Apostolic Vicariate in Central Tonkin, under the M.E.P.

KOREA

Seoul (Seoul) and **Taiku** (Daegu) Apostolic Vicariates, under the M.E.P.

MALAYSIA

Malacca (West Malaysia and Singapore) Apostolic Vicariate, under the M.E.P.

Sarawak (Sarawak) Apostolic Prefecture, under the St Joseph's Missionary Society of Mill Hill (English missionaries).

SIAM (THAILAND)

Bangkok (Bangkok) Apostolic Vicariate, under the M.E.P.

Chanthaburi (Chantaburi) Apostolic Vicariate, under Thai bishop.

Rajaburi (Ratchaburi) Apostolic Vicariate, under the Salesians of Don Bosco (Italian missionaries).

The Seven Orders

Upon completing each stage of study, the students of the CG received their sacraments and were thus inducted into the clergy and ordained to Minor or Major Orders. Only Minor Orders were ordained at the CG, sometimes the Sub-diaconate and Diaconate. Ordination to Priesthood was performed only by the Apostolic Vicar (Bishop) of the Mission.

Layman (non-ordained member of the community)

Tonsured (prerequisite to receive Minor and Major Orders to become a cleric) in December, first year of Theology

Minor Orders

1. Porter (door-keeper, symbolic office) in September, second year of Theology
2. Lector or Reader (read the Sacred Scriptures, except the Gospel) in September, second year of Theology
3. Exorcist (the office became purely ceremonial) in September, third year of Theology
4. Acolyte (assistant of the Priest or of a Deacon) in September, third or fourth year of Theology

Major Orders

5. Subdeacon (Subdiaconate) in September, fourth year of Theology
6. Deacon (Diaconate) in September or December, fourth year of Theology
7. Priest (Priesthood) in December, fourth year of Theology

In 1972, the Minor Order of Tonsure was discontinued. The Minor Orders were renamed Ministries, and only the Ministries of Lector and Acolyte were retained. The Major Order of Sub diaconate was discontinued and the Subdeacon's functions were taken over by the Acolyte. Since 1983, the Major Orders have been replaced by the Sacred Orders or Holy Orders:

> Diaconate (Deacon)
>
> Presbyterate (Priest)
>
> Episcopate (Bishop)

List of People mentioned in the Diary

I. THE CLERICS

1. MEP priests based at the CG
2. MEP priests based in Penang
3. MEP priests in the Diocese of Malacca (Peninsular Malaya and Singapore)
4. MEP priests based in Asia
5. MEP priests based in France
6. Malayan parish priests in the Diocese of Malacca
7. Other Catholics Priests
8. Brothers of the Christian Schools or Lasallian Brothers
9. Dames of Saint Maur or the Infant Jesus Sisters
10. Protestant Christians

II. THE LAYMEN

1. The British, the Americans and the Australians
2. The French
3. The German, the Italians and the Japanese
4. The Malayans

I. THE CLERICS

1. MEP priests based at the CG

Belleville, Georges, was born in 1914. Assigned to Penang's CG, he was expected to embark at Marseille on 15 September 1939, but as the war had started, he was mobilised. He only arrived at the CG in October 1946 to replace René Paroissin as director and taught Philosophy. He was posted to Taiping in 1952, Butterworth in 1957 and Tapah in 1977, and finally St Francis Xavier's Church in Penang in 1984. After retirement, he was the chaplain of the Catholic hospital of Ipoh from 1990 to 1995. He returned to France and passed away in 2000.

Denarié, Georges, was born in 1889 and trained at the Pontifical Gregorian University of Roma. He was a director at the CG from 1917 to 1958. He retired in France and died in 1960.

Deyrat, Joseph, was born in 1906. He was a director of the CG from 1931 to 1935 and taught Philosophy. He was sent to Japan in 1935 and stayed until 1977. He retired in France, where he passed away in 1980.

Lobez, Pierre, was born in 1909. He was a director of the CG from 1934 to 1939. He returned to France, where he was mobilised and imprisoned in 1940. After teaching at the Paris seminary, he came back to the CG in 1954 and taught till 1967. The following year, he was Procureur in Singapore. He retired in 1972 and stayed at the Home of the Little Sisters of the Poor in Penang, where he passed away in 1982. He is buried in the Kelawai Road Catholic Cemetery.

Meissonnier, Philippe, was born in 1909. He was a director of the CG from 1935 to 1946. Trapped in Kuala Lumpur in 1944, he was called by Adrien Devals to assist him in *mukim* VI of the Bahau Catholic Settlement. After the war, he returned to Paris to teach at the Seminary. He came back to Singapore in 1949, where he passed away in 1986.

Michel, Henri, was born in 1889. A Belgian, he was a director at the CG from 1915 to 1922. He taught at Bièvres' seminary near Paris from 1923. He came back to the CG in 1927 and stayed until 1946. As Belgium was an enemy of the Axis powers, Father Michel was first placed under house arrest, and then was incarcerated in Singapore. After the war, he served as the Procureur in Singapore. He retired in Belgium, where he passed away in 1988.

Monjean, Hubert, was born in 1896. He was trained at the Pontifical Gregorian University of Roma. He was director at the CG from 1923 to 1949, where he taught

Philosophy. After the war, he was a Visitor to people affected by leprosy on Jerejak Island, off Penang Island. In 1949, he returned to France, and became the archivist of the MEP in Paris until his death in 1957.

Pagès, Justin, was born in 1865. He reached Penang in 1890 and was made the Superior of the CG. Then he became the Superior of the Minor seminary in Singapore until 1944. He retired at the Procure of Singapore. He died in the Singapore Hospital in 1944.

Paroissin, René, was born in 1912. He was a director of the CG from 1937 to 1947, where he taught Moral Theology and then the Holy Scriptures. He returned to Paris in 1947, where he taught at Bièvres' seminary. In 1961, he was supposed to come back to Penang, but was finally posted to Moulins-sur-Allier as chaplain. He retired in 1991 and passed away in 1998.

Piffaut, Pierre, was born in 1899. He was a director of the CG from 1925 to 1965, where he taught Sciences and Moral Theology. He retired in France and died in 1975.

Rouhan, Marcel, the purported author of the Diary, was born in 1896. He was trained at the Pontifical Gregorian University of Roma. He was a director of the CG from 1925. He replaced Justin Pagès as Superior in 1930. Rouhan returned to France on 19 November 1946. He came back to Penang in 1951, but returned permanently to France in 1953, where he died in 1980.

2. MEP priests based in Penang

Baloche, Jean, was born in 1887. He was first posted to Kuala Lumpur in 1911, then to Penang in 1932. He was parish priest at the Church of the Immaculate Conception in Pulau Tikus from 1936 to 1950. He died in Penang in 1953.

Dérédec, Noël, was born in 1885. He arrived in Penang in 1911. He was assistant priest at the Assumption Church, George Town. During the war, he took up residence at St Francis Xavier's Church with Louis Riboud. He retired in France, where he died in 1947.

Riboud des Avinières, Louis, was born in 1888. He reached Penang in 1921. He became the parish priest of St Francis Xavier's Church in George Town in 1936, where he stayed as priest in residence until he passed away in 1960.

Souhait, Jean-Baptiste, was born in 1885. He arrived in Penang in 1907. From 1933 until 1947, he was the parish priest of the Assumption Church. As the church was practically closed during the war, J.B. Souhait took up residence at the Immaculate Conception Church in Pulau Tikus with Jean Baloche from 1942 to 1943. He passed away in 1950 in Penang and is buried in the Kelawai Road Catholic Cemetery.

Selier, Marcel, was born in 1911. He was sent to Ipoh in 1936. He was the parish priest of The Holy Name of Jesus Church in Balik Pulau from 1939 to 1947. He took up residence in the New Village of Machang Bubuk (a few kilometers from Matang Tinggi) in 1948, when he was building a new church in Kulim, which opened in 1957 to replace the Church of Pagar Teras. He passed away in 1973 and is buried near the ruins of the former Church of Pagar Teras, located on the Penang–Kedah border.

3. MEP priests in the Diocese of Malacca (Peninsular Malaya and Singapore)

Bécheras, Edouard, was born in 1879. He arrived in Singapore in 1905, and was posted to Malacca and Bukit Mertajam. He was back in Singapore after the First World War. In 1935, he established the Sino–English Catholic School (now the Catholic High School) in Singapore. At the end of 1943, he was in Bahau, in charge of the Chinese area, *mukim* V. He returned to France for holidays and passed away aboard a ship, en route to Singapore, in 1957.

Berthold, Hippolyte, was born in 1911. He arrived in Singapore in 1938 and taught Latin in the Minor Seminary. He followed the Minor Seminary to the Bahau Agricultural Settlement at the end of 1943. After the war, while resting in Cameron Highlands, he was attacked by communist insurgents. He returned to serve in Singapore. He became blind in 1983 and passed away in 1995.

Devals, Adrien, was born in 1882. He was first posted to Penang and then took up different posts around the Peninsula. In 1934, he replaced Bishop Barillon as the Apostolic Vicar of Malacca. He was placed in charge of the Agricultural Settlement of Bahau in 1944. His right foot was wounded – either by a hoe, or a spider bite. It turned gangrenous and had to be amputated. He passed away in the Seremban hospital on 17 January 1945.

François, Jules, was born in 1884. He arrived in Penang in 1907. He was in charge of the Chinese community in Malacca in 1910. After the First World War, he was back in Malacca, where he will be remembered as one of the prime movers behind the establishment of the Portuguese Settlement. He was also a member of the Malacca Historical Society. He was posted to Ipoh in 1938, where he passed away in 1955.

Olçomendy, Michel, was born in 1901. He was first posted to Kuala Lumpur, then Taiping, and finally Singapore. He was made Capitular Vicar in 1945 and Bishop in 1947. In 1953, he was elected Archbishop. He retired one year before passing away in 1977.

Ouillon, Jean, was born in 1879. He reached Hong Kong in 1902. In 1922, he was sent to take care of the Procure in Singapore, where he died in 1947.

4. The MEP priests based in Asia

Cassaigne, Jean, was born in 1895. He reached Saigon in 1926. He was first sent to the Moi tribes. In 1941, he became Bishop of Saigon. He resigned in 1955 because he contracted leprosy and died in 1973.

Cathebras, Pierre, was born in 1876. He was posted to the South Burma Mission and passed away in Rangoon (Yangon) on 1 May 1944.

Chorin, Louis, was born in 1888. He arrived in Bangkok in 1913. After learning Chinese, he was put in charge of the printing press. In 1925, he became the Procureur. In 1947, he was nominated to the position of Bishop in Bangkok. He died in Bangkok in 1965.

Ferlay, Joseph, was born in 1874. He was sent to Siam in 1897. For most of the time, he was placed in charge of education in the Mission of Bangkok (Siam). He passed away at the Procure of Bangkok in 1948.

Gérard, Léon, was born in 1874. He was sent to the Mission of Northern Manchuria in China. He died in 1951.

Perros, René, was born in 1870. He was sent to Siam in 1894. Most of the time, he was in charge of the Seminary. In 1910, he became Apostolic Vicar, retiring in 1947. He died in 1952.

Provost, Frédéric, was born in 1877. He was sent to the South Burma Mission in 1900. He served as Apostolic Vicar in Rangoon from 1929 until his death in 1952.

Sion, Jean, was born in 1890. He was sent to Cochinchina in 1920. In 1941, he was nominated Apostolic Vicar of Kontum. He passed away during a trip to France in 1951.

5. MEP priests based in France

Boulanger, Louis, was born in 1871. He was sent to India, from where he returned to France in 1900 and taught at the Seminary. He was a stretcher-bearer during the First World War. In 1921, he became the assistant of Monseigneur Budes de Guébriant, the General Superior of the MEP. He retired due to poor health and passed away in 1942.

Lemaire, Charles, was born in 1900. He was sent to Manchuria in 1930. He was elected the Bishop of Kirin (Jilin, Manchuria) in 1939. He was appointed General Superior of the MEP on 16 November 1945, but reached Paris only on 23 July 1946. When he was not reelected to the post of General Superior in 1960, he was sent to Hong Kong, where he retired and passed away in 1995.

Robert, Léon, was born in 1866. He left for the Far East (China / Japan) in 1888. In 1921, he was the assistant of the General Superior. He replaced Monseigneur Budes de Guébriant as General Superior of the MEP, when the latter passed away in 1935. As his service was prolonged due to the Second World War, he resigned only at the age of 80, on 13 November 1945.

6. Malayan parish priests in the Diocese of Malacca

Aloysius, Ignatius John, of Indian descent, was trained in the CG. He was the parish priest of the Saint Louis church in Taiping from 1936 to 1944. Following the invasion of France by the Allied Forces on 6 June 1944, the French priests feared losing their Neutral status and consequently getting arrested. They requested Bishop Devals, Apostolic Vicar of Malacca, for a local priest to take over the direction of the CG, if necessary. IJ Aloysius was chosen and arrived on 4 August 1944. He later became General Vicar to the first Bishop of Penang in 1955.

Ashness, Bertin Justinian, of Eurasian descent, was born in Penang in 1897. He studied at the SFI in Malacca before entering the CG in Penang. Joining the Maryknoll Society (Catholic American Foreign Mission), he was ordained as a priest in New York in 1924. He proceeded to Kongmoon (Jiangmen) in China but left because of unrest in 1925. After a stay in a Carthusian monastery in England, he came back to Malaya. He was assistant priest at St Michael Church in Ipoh in 1936. In Singapore, he became the priest of the Sacred Heart church in 1937, and then of the Holy Family church in 1944. He passed away in Singapore on 12 July 1945.

Chin, Thomas, of Chinese descent, was assistant parish priest at Our Lady of Seven Sorrows Church in Penang from 1944 to 1948.

Edmund, John, of Indian descent, was parish priest at St Anthony's Church in Telok Intan and Saint Mary's Church in Tapah from 1936 to 1947.

Koh, Moses, was the first Chinese priest of Our Lady of Seven Sorrows Church from 1938 to 1948.

Lek, Francis, of Chinese descent, was parish priest at the church of Our Lady of the Sacred Heart in Taiping in 1944. He became parish priest at the church of the Holy Name of Mary in Matang Tinggi in 1945 and at Saint Anne's Church in Bukit Mertajam from 1945 to 1948.

Teng, Joachim, of Chinese descent, was born in Singapore and educated at the CG. He was serving in St Francis Xavier's Church in Malacca in 1937. He was the parish priest at Saint Anne's Church in Bukit Mertajam from 1938 to 1945, and at the church of the Holy Name of Mary in Matang Tinggi from 1940 to 1945. He was arrested and detained by the Japanese for one week in 1944.

Vendargon, Dominic, of Indian descent, was educated at the SFI Melaka and at the CG in Penang. He was parish priest at the church of Christ the King in Sungei Petani from 1941 to 1948. He was visiting priest of Saint Michael's Church in Alor Setar in 1943 and 1944; part of this time, Kedah was under Siamese administration (18 October 1943–2 September 1945). He became the first Bishop of Kuala Lumpur in 1955, and the first Archbishop of West Malaysia in 1972.

Vong, Paul, of Chinese descent, was parish priest at the church of the Holy Name of Jesus in Balik Pulau from 1937 to 1939. He was the last priest to serve in the Sacred Heart church in Pagar from 1940 to 1948.

7. Other Catholics Priests

Borromeo, Charles, was the Roman Catholic Archbishop of Milan from 1564 to 1584 and a Cardinal. He was a leading figure of the Counter-Reformation movement against the Protestant Reformation. In that role, he was responsible for significant reforms in the Catholic Church, including founding seminaries for the education of priests. He is honoured as a Saint by the Roman Catholic Church, with a feast day on 4 November.

Cheng, James Louis (Giacomo Luigi), was the first Thai Bishop of Chanthaburi from 1944 to 1952 where he passed away.

McCarthy, Edward J., joined the Maynooth Mission to China, founded in Ireland in 1916, later known as Missionary Society of St Columban. In 1935, he moved to the Philippines. In January 1941, he visited Penang on his way to Bhamo in the Kachin state of Burma, where he was arrested by the Japanese and interned until 1945.

Pasotti, Gaétan, an Italian, was a Salesian of Saint Jean Bosco. He was Bishop of Rajaburi (Siam) from 1941 to 1950, and he passed away in Thailand.

Schembley, Father, was an Englishman born in Bangalore and educated in a Saint Sulpice seminary. He became a Catholic army chaplain.

8. Brothers of the Christian Schools or Lasallian Brothers

Blais, Michael Paulin, a French Canadian, was a teacher, a disciplinarian, and a musician. He was known by the nickname Lau Hor (or 'Tiger' in Hokkien). He walked around with a cane under his arm. He founded the SXI orchestra and, later on, the SFI orchestra. He was the musical director of the Saint Francis Xavier Pageant in Malacca in 1952. During the Japanese occupation, he was under house arrest at the General Hospital. On 27 March 1945, he was sent to the Sime Road Camp in Singapore. He died in Canada in 1983.

Byrne, James, (Jacques, in French), an Irishman, was trained in Paris. He arrived in Penang in 1887 at the age of 18. He assisted the director of SXI in 1901, and then replaced him. He became the Visitor (or Provincial, head of a Lasallian Brothers District) from 1912 till 1925, and again from 1929 to 1946. He promoted the formation of lay teachers. He was known as 'Cardinal Jacques'. He received the OBE and passed away in 1947. A street is named after him in Pulau Tikus.

Coates, John Edward, was originally from Hong Kong. He was the assistant director of the Novitiate and was later posted to SFI in Malacca.

Gallagher, Paul, was Visitor from 1925 to 1929. He was Director of SXI for twenty years. During the war, he was the Director of the Novitiate. He opened schools in Kedah and Perlis. From 1950, he took over the schools of the Mill Hill Fathers in Sarawak.

9. Dames of Saint Maur, or the Infant Jesus Sisters

Saint-Charles was born Marie Delebarre in France in 1903. When Mother St Tarcisius left for Singapore in 1942, she took over as Head of the Convent in Penang and, the same year, went to head the Convent in Singapore. In 1944, she was one of the settlers in the Bahau Agricultural Settlement. She succeeded Mother

St Tarcisius as Superior of the Convent in Penang in 1946. She was the Provincial (head of the Infant Jesus Sisters provincialiate) of Malaya from 1954 to 1964, and from 1965 to 1971, of Singapore only (after the separation of Singapore and the Federation of Malaysia).

Saint-Louis was born Philotea Cardon in France in 1887. She arrived in Penang in 1919. She replaced Mother St-Charles as Head of the Community in Penang in 1942. After heading the Convents in Taiping and in Cameron Highlands, she retired in Cheras Convent in 1964, where she passed away in 1986.

Sainte-Paula, an Italian Sister, was the Superior of the Balik Pulau Convent during the Japanese occupation.

Sainte-Johanna, of Chinese descent, was born Maria Kang in Malaya in 1904.

Sainte-Rose, of Chinese descent, was born Dorothy Chan. She was one of the three pioneer teachers of the Sacred Heart school in Balik Pulau in 1930, and later became its third headmistress. She served as the headmistress of St Joseph School in Pulau Tikus during the war.

Saint-Tarcisius was born Françoise Salles in France in 1875. Sister Salles Saint Tarcisius sailed to Malaya in 1904. In 1924, she was promoted Superior of the Penang Convent and head of the Infant Jesus Sisters Provincialate of Malaya. Over the next 30 years, she established more than 30 convent schools in Malaya. In Penang, she founded Butterworth Convent in 1930, Sacred Heart Convent (Balik Pulau), and St Marguerite Convent (Bukit Mertajam) in 1934, and Datuk Keramat Convent (George Town) in 1935. She was awarded the OBE in 1936. In September 1942, she left Penang for Singapore. She was back in Penang in September 1945. In 1946, Mother St Charles replaced her as Superior of the Convent in Penang, but she officially only retired at the age of 80, in 1954. She spent her last 10 years at the Convent Light Street and the Cheras Convent, where she passed away in 1964.

10. Protestant Christians

Harvey, Frederick W., was a Major of the Salvation Army. Together with his wife, he started the Penang branch in 1938, providing free education for 150 children in the vacated YMCA building at Logan Road. When war broke out, his wife was safely evacuated to Australia with their son, but he refused to leave Penang, although ordered to do so. Harvey continued working with Eric Scott in temporary hutments outside the town, to provide relief to those who had fled the bombing. He was incarcerated in the Penang jail and sent to Changi. The family was reunited in Penang after the war.

Scott, Eric Hammond, was the Anglican Vicar of St Mark's Church in Butterworth since 1939. When war broke out, Scott was allowed free movement in town for a short period, but was later placed under house arrest at St Nicholas' Home for Blind Children (under the care of the Anglican Church). He was not allowed any contact with the children in the home, but was permitted to hold public services in the chapel. In the latter part of 1942, he was transferred to the civilian internment camp in Changi. Soon after the Japanese surrender, Scott flew back to Penang, before taking up a post in Sarawak.

II. THE LAYMEN

1. The British, the Americans, and the Australians

Brodie, (Dr) William Hugh, became Penang Municipal Health Officer in 1934. He left for England on leave before the war and came back after. A Freemason, he was a member of the Scotia Lodge (services held at the Art Deco masonic temple at Western Road/Jalan Utama since 1933) and elected Grandmaster in 1947. He retired in 1948 and joined *the P&O* as ship's surgeon. He passed away in New Zealand in 1954.

Conaghan, George H., was an Irish Catholic lawyer. His father was T.E. Conaghan. Like his father, he joined the firm Wreford and Thornton, 29–31 Beach Street. He later became the principal of Conaghan, Wreford & Thornton. He was appointed in 1945 to head a Special Court to investigate the cases of collaborationism during the occupation.

de Buriatte, Ernest Arthur, was born in London in 1887. He was a partner in the Penang legal firm Presgrave and Matthews, made judge of the Federated Malay States Supreme Court in 1937, and nominated a member of the Straits Settlement Legislative Council in 1941. During the war, he was Commanding Officer (Lieutenant-Colonel) of the 3rd Battalion of the Straits Settlements Volunteers Force (Penang and Province Wellesley Volunteer Corps). First imprisoned in Changi, he spent most of the war in various camps in Thailand. After the war, he returned to his practice in Penang. He finally retired in England where he died in 1953.

Evans, (Dr) Leonard Wynne, was born in 1891, son of a doctor. He started as Medical Officer in Kelantan in 1921 and was subsequently posted to Singapore. When the Japanese attacked, he was working as the Chief Medical Officer at the Penang General Hospital (since September that year). Refusing to evacuate with the other British nationals, he stayed behind to take care of the wounded. The Japanese allowed him to continue to administer the hospital for a while, but when he refused to cooperate, they interned him a year later in Changi. He was awarded the CBE in 1946, when he was deputy director of medical services of the Malayan Union. He passed away in 1979 after an accident.

MacArthur, Douglas, In March 1942, he moved to Australia where he became the supreme commander of the Allied forces in the southwest Pacific. After more than two years of fighting in the Pacific, he fulfilled his promise to return to the Philippines. He formally accepted the Japanese surrender on 2 September 1945.

MacDonald, Malcolm John, was a former Labour Member of Parliament (MP), who was appointed Governor-General of British territories in Southeast Asia (1946–1948), and then Commissioner-General for Southeast Asia covering regional affairs, during the period of the Malayan Emergency. He was the son of **James Ramsay MacDonald**, first Labour Party politician to become Prime Minister of the United Kingdom in 1924, serving again in 1929–1931, and in the Coalition Government, 1931–1935.

McKern, (Dr) Albert Stanley, was born in Sydney in 1885. He settled down in Penang in the early 1920s and ran a successful medical practice. He built an architecturally acclaimed family home, Elysian, in Tanjung Bungah (later used by the RAF). He invested in several seaside properties, one at Batu Ferringhi which became the Lone Pine Hotel in 1948, and a piece of land in Tanjung Bungah which was leased to the Société Financière des Caoutchoucs (Socfin) in 1952, to build a managers' holiday bungalow, Villa Aremi, later the Tanjong Country Club and today replaced by a condominium. McKern died in a prisoner's camp in Sumatra two months before the end of the war. He bequeathed a trust which yielded USD4 million, ten years after the death of the last trustee in 1997, to finance medical research related to pregnancy, labour and the puerperium at his alma maters: Yale, University of Sydney, and University of Edinburgh.

Regester, Paul John Dinsmore, was an advocate and solicitor in Penang with the law firm Hogan, Adams & Allan, which represented the CG's interests. The legal office was located above the Barkath Store in Union Street.

Roosevelt, Franklin Delano, 32nd President of the United States from 1933 until his death on 12 April 1945.

2. The French

Decoux, Jean, Governor-General of French Indochina from July 1940 to 9 March 1945, representing the Vichy French government.

de Gaulle, (General) Charles Chairman of the Provisional Government of the French Republic, 3 June 1944 to 20 January 1946.

Pétain, Philippe, Chief of the French state, 11 July 1940 to 20 August 1944.

3. The Germans, the Italians, and the Japanese

Political Leaders of Germany:
Hitler, Adolph, Chancellor (30 January 1933 to 30 April 1945)
Göring (Goering), Hermann, President of the Reichstag (30 August 1932 to 23 April 1945)

Prime Ministers of Italy:
Mussolini, Benito (31 October 1922 to 25 July 1943)
Badoglio, Pietro (25 July 1943 to 8 June 1944)

Prime Ministers of Japan:
Koiso Kuniaki (22 July 1944 to 7 April 1945)
Suzuki Kantaro (7 April to 17 August 1945)

Japanese Governors of Penang:
Lieutenant General Shotaro Katayama (1942–1943)
Major General Masakichi Itami (1943–1944)
Lieutenant General Shinohara Seiichiro (1944–1945)

Hidaka, Captain Shinsaku, was Chief of Staff of the Rear Admiral Commanding the Penang Naval Headquarters. He was also referred to as the Commander-in-Chief of the Penang Navy. During the Japanese occupation, he lived at Allen Loke's villa, next door to the Novitiate, and had cordial relations with the Fathers. Captain Hidaka complained to Lieutenant-General Ishiguro about the brutal actions of Higashikawa, head of the Penang Branch of the Kempeitai, causing the latter to be transferred and replaced by Captain Terata. Captain S. Hidaka was on board the HMS *Nelson* in 1945 when the Japanese surrendered.

Manaki, Takanobu, was a Major-General attached to the Military Service Bureau (Ministry of War). In November 1941, he was made Deputy Chief of Staff of the

25th Army in Malaya. He convened a meeting at Asdang House on 2 January 1942, before the army advanced southward to Singapore.

Mori, Hirano, was the Bunkyo-Kacho, chief of the Bunkyo-ka (Department of Education and Religious Affairs) in Penang. He was a Buddhist monk in Japan before the outbreak of the Pacific War.

Shinozaki, Manura, was a Japanese journalist before the war, based in Singapore where he was arrested for intelligence-gathering activities. After the Japanese victory, he first worked for the Kempeitei, then he oversaw the Overseas Chinese Association and the Eurasian Welfare Association. He was in charge of the Catholic Settlement of Bahau in December 1943 (explaining his connection with the bishopric of Singapore) and of the Chinese Settlement of Endau. After the war, he was a prosecution witness in the War Criminal Court and expelled from Singapore in 1948. He published his autobiography *Syonan, My Story: The Japanese Occupation of Singapore* in 1975.

Yamashita, Tomoyuki, was a Japanese general. After his victory over the British, he was nicknamed 'The Tiger of Malaya'. In 1945, he assumed the defence of the Philippines during the American reconquest.

4. The Malayans

Aparajoo, (Dr) Ratnam, became a surgeon at the Penang General Hospital during the war. He was awarded the OBE in 1946.

Baboo, or **(Dr) (Haji) Shaik Mohamad Baboo bin Ahmad Albakish,** was Acting Chief Medical Officer at Penang General Hospital in 1941. He studied medicine in Singapore and entered Penang General Hospital in 1917. He retired in 1949 and opened Baboo Dispensary at Dato' Kramat Road.

Ivan, Allan, was a Catholic Eurasian who rented a bungalow from the CG in Tanjung Bungah in September 1942. An apprentice jockey, he worked for horse trainer George McGill. On 18 December 1941, he journeyed by boat, then bicycle, to Sungei Petani to inform the Japanese army that the British had left Penang. He was accompanied by Izumi, a Japanese barber at Argyll Road, and another Japanese civilian; they were arrested but freed shortly afterward.

Loke Wan Wye or **Alan Loke** was a son of Loke Yew, a leading Chinese tycoon in Malaya. He commissioned Scottish architect David McLeod Craik to design the Loke Mansion or Loke Villa in the Art & Crafts Style. The sea-facing Loke Villa was built in 1924 next to the Novitiate. He died in 1941.

D'Oliverio, (Miss) L.M., was the elder sister of **Mrs A.D. de Mello**. Miss D'Oliverio served as matron of the Poh Leung Kok Home from 1930 until the start of the Japanese occupation. After the war, Miss D'Oliverio resumed her position until she resigned in 1965.

de Mello, **Mrs A.D.** (died 1930), was the first matron of the Poh Leung Kok Home.

de Mello, (Mrs), also known as **Mrs Mary Capel,** was the daughter of **Mrs A.D. de Mello**. The Japanese appointed Mrs Mary Capel to take over as matron of the Home from her aunt, Miss L.M. D'Oliverio, until the end of the war. Mrs Mary Capel was the last matron of the Home, serving from 1965 to 1977.

Saravanamuttu, Manicasothy, was born in Ceylon. He studied at the University of Oxford in England and became a newspaper journalist in Ceylon. In 1930, he arrived in Penang to work as sub-editor for the *Straits Echo* and was promoted to editor the following year. At the outbreak of war, the last British nationals were evacuated from Penang in 16 December 1941. The following day, Saravanamuttu took it upon himself to haul down the British flag from the flagstaff at Fort Cornwallis. He chaired the Penang Service Committee and organised a Volunteer Police Force to keep public order, remove corpses from the street and prevent looting. Upon the arrival of the Japanese, he was arrested and jailed for nine months. During the occupation, he became an arrack producer. With the return of the British, he resumed the publication of the *Straits Echo*. After the independence of Ceylon, he embraced a diplomatic career. He represented Ceylon in Malaya and Singapore, then Indonesia and, finally, Thailand. He passed away in 1970.

List of Places mentioned in the Diary

Asdang House: or Asadong House, on Northam Road, was the former Nova Scotia, built at the end of the nineteenth century by the Khaw family. Asdang House was occupied by the Japanese during the war and was finally destroyed in 1993 (a mock building has been rebuilt since).

Assumption Church: The first Catholic parish in Penang consisted mainly of the Eurasians who accompanied Captain Francis Light to settle in Penang. They arrived on 15 August 1786, and celebrated the Feast of The Assumption. The church of the Assumption was initially built at Church Street, and the presbytery, at Bishop Street. The present church was built on Farquhar Street in 1860. The Assumption Church was upgraded to a cathedral serving the new diocese of Penang in 1955. However, it lost its status as a cathedral when the seat of the bishop was moved to The Cathedral of the Holy Spirit in 2003. The church was successfully restored in 2017 and started a Roman Catholic Diocese Museum on its grounds.

Bagan Jermal: Situated between Pulau Tikus and Tanjung Tokong, it used to be the limit of George Town in the mid-twentieth century.

Bahau: A place in Negeri Sembilan where the Japanese administration founded a Catholic Agricultural Settlement for the Eurasian and Chinese Catholics of Singapore. The prime movers were Bishop Adrien Devals, the Apostolic Vicar of Malacca, and Mamoru Shinozaki, who was overseeing the Overseas Chinese Association and the Eurasian Welfare Association. The first batch of settlers arrived in December 1943. Each settler was supposed to receive 3 to 4 acres of land, materials and food until he could support himself. A church, a dispensary, a school, and other facilities were built. By 1945, the population was estimated to be more than 5,000. Although it was named Fuji-Go (literally, 'The Beautiful Village'), the Bahau settlers suffered from harsh living conditions, malnutrition, disease, lack of medical facilities and years of hardship. The settlement was abandoned after the war.

Bahau was one of more than thirty agricultural settlements established by the Japanese to address the food shortage. Among the other known settlements were a Malay settlement and an Indian settlement on Bintan Island, as well as a Chinese settlement called 'New Syonan' in Endau (Johor). A number of agricultural settlements were established in Province Wellesley, a Malay settlement in Bertam estate, an Indian settlement in Batu Kawan, and Chinese settlements in Bertam Estate, Alma Estate, and in Malakoff Estate. The last was founded by the Penang Overseas Chinese Association on 20 November 1944 with 100 families (though planned for 3,300). The Penang Shimbun wrote 'the people are happy, the food plenty'. The College General Agricultural Settlement at Matang Tinggi received the special ration of rice accorded to the agricultural settlers.

Balik Pulau: Literally, 'the other side of the island'. A market town surrounded by fruit orchards in the southwest of Penang Island. The French mission founded its third parish here in 1848. The Infant Jesus Sisters opened their first school in 1930, followed by the Brothers in 1937.

Batu Kawan: An island within a large estuary in Province Wellesley (Seberang Perai). St John the Baptist, a small wooden chapel, was built on Bukit Tambun across the river in 1830. The parishioners were Chinese agricultural settlers, as well as French sugarcane planters from Mauritius who established Jawi, Val d'or and Malakoff plantations. This French Catholic parish closed down in 1890.

Bel Retiro: Literally, the 'Beautiful Retreat', in Spanish. The rest house was built on top of Penang Hill in the late eighteenth century as a retreat for the superintendent, later Lieutenant-Governor or Governor, of the Penang settlement.

Bukit Mertajam: Mertajam Hill is the site of the Cherok Tokun stone, an ancient Buddhist relic. The first wooden chapel on Bukit Mertajam was built in 1846 by Fr Adolphe Couellan, a French priest who studied at Sainte-Anne-d'Auray in Brittany; he thus dedicated the church to St Anne. The early parishioners were the Chinese farmers who had relocated from Batu Kawan. St Anne's church was erected in 1888 and became an important pilgrimage site during St Anne's Feast. The IJS opened their Convent School in 1934. Joachim Teng was the parish priest from 1938 to 1945, followed by Francis Lek Chee Kok from 1945 to 1948.

Cameron Highlands: A Mandailing adventurer, Kulop Riow, introduced this tableland on the border between Perak and Pahang to British colonial surveyor William G. Cameron. It was developed as an agricultural settlement and a health resort. The MEP built their retreat house and the IJS opened a Convent School at Tanah Rata, the administrative town, in 1935. The Convent School was used as a hospital by the Japanese during the war.

Chinese Swimming Club: Located in Tanjung Bungah, the club was established in 1928 by Chinese swimming enthusiasts in reaction to the 'Whites-only' policy of the Penang Swimming Club.

Convent Light Street or The Convent: The oldest girls' school in the country. Seeing the progress of English Protestant Missionaries in school recruitment, the MEP requested the help of the Holy Infant Jesus Sisters (also called Dames de Saint-Maur), to introduce girls' education in Penang. The IJS reached Penang in 1852. They first established a school near the Assumption Church in Church Street, and then moved to a large coastal site in Light Street in 1859. During the war, the Convent was occupied by the Japanese Navy, causing the IJS to move to the CG in Pulau Tikus.

Convent Pulau Tikus: The Holy Infant Jesus Sisters took over the St Joseph parish girls' school located behind the Immaculate Conception Church and opened Pulau Tikus Convent School in 1922. During the early 1950s, the IJS built Pulau Tikus Convent Secondary School across the street from the church.

Elysee Hotel: German soldiers where billeted at this hotel on Farquhar Street from 1943. It was demolished after the war and replaced in the 1970s by the Merlin Hotel, one of the first high-rise buildings in Penang, today the Bayview Hotel.

European Swimming Club: The Penang Swimming Club was founded in 1903 in Tanjung Bungah. It was an exclusive 'Whites-only' club until the 1960s. The German submarine crew frequented this club to use the swimming pool in 1943 and 1944.

Holy Name of Jesus Church, Balik Pulau: A chapel was built in 1855 to serve the parishioners of Balik Pulau, mostly Hakka farmers. The Holy Name of Jesus Church was rebuilt in 1894.

Hutchings School: A primary school next to St George's Church on Farquhar Street, named in honour of the late Rt Rev Robert Hutchings, Anglican Chaplain in Penang, who helped establish the Penang Free School in 1816. Hutchings School started in the former premises of the Penang Free School, after the latter moved to Green Lane in 1928. The school building was occupied by German soldiers in 1943.

Immaculate Conception Church: Driven out by Burmese attacks on Siam, a small community of Eurasians, mostly Catholic, fled to Penang and settled in Pulau Tikus. They founded the parish of the Immaculate Conception and built a small wooden church in 1810. The church was rebuilt in brick in 1900. The community established a primary school in a large wooden building called 'Noah's Ark'. The Lasallian Brothers took over the school in 1906. The school building and the Eurasian village next to it, called Kampung Serani, were demolished in 1994.

Malacca: The port of Melaka was established in the late fourteenth century and became known as the seat of a renowned Malay Sultanate, until it was captured by the Portuguese in 1511. The Roman Catholic Vicariate of 'Malacca', covering Malaya and Singapore, was created in 1888, superseding the Vicariate of Western Siam. Even though the Vicariate reestablished the old Portuguese See of Malacca, the residence of the new bishop was located in Singapore.

Machang Buboh: Also Machang Bubok, Machang Bubuh, Machang Bubuk. A town mostly populated by Chinese farmers of Hakka origin relocated from Batu Kawan. Fr Cardon (MEP), who served as parish priest between 1905 and 1914, was a curator, ethnologist, historian, journalist, and naturalist. During the Malayan Emergency, the Chapel of St Anthony was built in Machang Bubuk New Village.

Mariophile: Literally, 'for the love of Mary, the mother of Jesus'. The CG's retreat was built on land given by Captain Francis Light to the MEP. It is located in Tanjung Bungah on the lower slope of Pearl Hill, which the local Malays call Bukit Paderi, meaning 'Fathers' Hill'. A canon dated 1785 is found in the compound. St Joseph's Chapel was added in 1884. In 1984, the College General Seminary relocated from Pulau Tikus to Mariophile, where a new seminary was built and inaugurated in 1995.

Matang Tinggi: Also Permatang Tinggi. A town with Chinese Catholic farmers relocated from Batu Kawan. Claude Tisserand, College General Superior from 1834 to 1849, built a spacious house for a Minor Seminary named 'St Mary College' which he ran from 1850 to 1860. The parish received its first resident priest in 1893. A church and a presbytery were erected in 1906 and rebuilt in 1927. A primary school was added, which had to close down during the Japanese occupation. Joachim Teng was the parish priest from 1940 to 1945, and Francis Lek from 1945 to 1948.

Maymio (Pyin Oo Lwin): a hill town in the region of Mandalay.

New Springtide Hotel: Also Springtide Hotel. A popular seaside resort located in Tanjung Bungah. Its swimming pool was used by the German submarine crew in

1943 and 1944. At the end of 1945, it was turned into a convalescent home, named 'St Andrews on the sea, Holiday Home. (Church of Scotland Huts)'.

Nilgiris: The Nilgiri Hills, located in western Tamil Nadu (India), was the summer capital of the British. The MEP ran St Theodore's Sanatorium, Nilgiris, from 1900.

North Beach Road: The coastal road in Pulau Tikus ran along the College General seafront. It was later extended and renamed Gurney Drive.

Our Lady of Seven Sorrows Church: The church of Our Lady of Seven Sorrows was established in 1888 by Father Emile Barillon for Chinese parishioners in George Town. It was enlarged a few times and finally rebuilt in 1958.

Poh Leung Kok: Also Po Leung Kuk. The Society for the Protection of the Innocents or Welfare Organisation for the Protection of Women and Girls, the Poh Leung Kuk Home was located in Babington Avenue since 1926.

Province Wellesley (PW) or The Province: Better known as Seberang Perai. A strip of land in southern Kedah was annexed to Penang in 1800, and the province named after Richard Wellesley, who served as the Governor of Madras and Governor-General of Bengal between 1797 and 1805.

Pulau Tikus: Literally, 'Rat Island'. A small rocky island off the northern coast of Penang Island. The western part of George Town along the north beach is also named 'Pulau Tikus' after the nearby island. The Catholics, especially the French and Eurasians, had a significant presence in Pulau Tikus. The Fathers of the CG moved in as early as 1809.

Sacred Heart Convent: The school of the Sacred Heart, also known as the Balik Pulau Convent, opened in 1930. It was started by three Sisters of the Holy Infant Jesus, Sr Saint Rose, Sr Saint François, and Sr Saint Geneviève. The medium of education was Chinese. After the school closed down on 21 October 1990, the premises were converted into a home for the elderly and retired Sisters of the Infant Jesus.

St Francis Xavier's Church: The parish was founded by François Hab (MEP) for the Tamil-speaking community in 1857. The present church was built on Penang Road in 1902 and damaged during the war. Father Louis Riboud rebuilt the church in 1953.

Saint Jean: A holiday bungalow owned by the CG, located above the Teluk Bahang fishing village, on the northwestern slope of Penang Hill.

St Joseph's Novitiate: The Lasallian Brothers acquired land next to the CG in 1915 to build a training college and quarters for novices. The first building opened in 1918, and by 1925, the St Joseph's Novitiate was completed, adjacent to the College General. The land was sold in 2008, but the building was retained and incorporated into a shopping complex.

St Joseph's Orphanage: Father François Hab (MEP), who founded St Francis Xavier's Church, also started an orphanage in the church compound in 1865. The orphanage was renamed St Joseph's Home and continues to cater for underprivileged boys and girls.

St Nicholas' Home: A charitable institution for blind and visually impaired children was founded by the Medical Mission of the Anglican Church in Malacca in 1926. The Home moved to Penang in 1931, and to its present location on Bagan Jermal Road in 1938. A kindergarten was added in 1941.

St Xavier's Institution: The first Catholic Free School was founded by Fr Garnault in 1787 and the first wooden school was rebuilt in brick by Fr Boucho in 1825. Three Brothers of the Christian Schools, known as Lasallian Brothers (one American and two French), arrived in Penang in 1852. They took over the Catholic Free School and named it after St Xavier, the Great Apostle of the Indies. In 1858, the school moved to the present location and was christened St Xavier's Institution. A three-storey school building was erected in 1895. The school was occupied by the Japanese Navy during the war and destroyed by Allied bombing in 1945. A new school complex was rebuilt on the same site and reopened in 1954.

Sungei Pinang: The Pinang River on the eastern side of Penang Island was the location of an early indigenous settlement on the island, before the arrival of Captain Francis Light.

SXI Branch Schools: In 1906, the Lasallians took over the community school in 'Noah's Ark', Pulau Tikus. A new secondary school building was added next to St Joseph's Novitiate in 1930. The primary and secondary schools became known as St Xavier's Institution branch schools (SXI Branch or SXB). During the war, when the St Xavier's Institution premises on Farquhar Street were occupied by the Japanese Navy, the Lasalle Brothers moved the school to several locations in Pulau Tikus: the CG, the Novitiate, the new SXI secondary school building facing Kelawai

Road, and the branch school in 'Noah's Ark'. Towards the end of the war, the SXI secondary school building in Pulau Tikus was used as a factory by the Japanese. A private mansion at 457, Burmah Road, was acquired for the St Xavier's Institution branch school after the war, and a new primary school building was erected behind it in 1962.

Tanjung Bungah: Literally, 'Flower Cape'. Mariophile, the CG's country retreat, is located at the eastern end of Tanjung Bungah. The Penang Swimming Club and the Chinese Swimming Club are located in the vicinity.

Tanjong Tokong (now, Tanjung Tokong): Literally, 'Temple Cape'. This is said to be the first Chinese settlement on Penang Island, established in the late eighteenth century by a Hakka Chinese pioneer named Zhang Li. Deified as a local pioneer deity, 'Tua Pek Kong' (literally 'grand uncle') is venerated as the 'God of Prosperity' in a temple next to his grave in Tanjung Tokong.

Glossary

CHINESE TERMS

bee foon	also *bee hoon*, rice vermicelli.
Chingay	a procession held in celebration of the birthdays of Chinese deities; includes street performances where performers balance giant flags 7 to 10 metres in height and about 30 kg in weight
kongsi	company, business partnership; amongst overseas Chinese, the word *kongsi* was also applied to clan organisations, whose members shared a common descent, and to other social organisations
look teou	also *ludou*, mung bean (*Vigna radata*)
mee	fresh noodles dried under the sun
Poh Leung Kok	also Po Leung Kuk; Society for the Protection of the Innocents, or Welfare Organisation for Protection of Women and Girls, founded in Penang in 1888
Sook Ching	meaning 'purge through cleansing'; Japanese military operation which often resulted in the systematic killing of perceived hostile elements among the Chinese population
towkay	business owner, boss

FRENCH TERMS

Boche	derogatory name for a German person
Chant du depart	the *Song of the Departure*, written by Claude Dallet in 1852, with music by Charles Gounod, sung at the end of the farewell ceremony in the MEP chapel in Paris, the day before the departure of the new missionaries for their Mission; not to be confused with the French revolutionary song of the same name, written in 1794 by E.N. Méhul (music) et M.J. Chénier (lyrics)

matefain	also *matefan*, a thick crepe made with potatoes
Missions Catholiques	*Catholic Missions,* a weekly published from 1868 to 1964. It was run by the Society for the Propagation of the Faith, founded in 1822
néo-myste	newly-ordained priest
Procure	also Procure house, the place where the Procureur lives
Procureur	the cleric in charge of the domestic, financial, material, and temporal needs of the Community. At the beginning of the war, the Procureur of the College General was Fr Michel, while Fr Ouillon was the Procureur of the Mission of Malacca, based in Singapore
Rue du Bac	literally, 'Ferry Street'; the address of the MEP headquarters in Paris since 1663
Sénateur	student of the College General yet to complete his studies, usually Minored or Sub-Deacon
Supersénateur	student in the College General who has majored and is already a Deacon
Union Missionnaire du Clergé	*Missionary Union of the Clergy,* published from 1925 to 1956 by the Missionary Union of the Clergy, founded in Italy in 1916 by Paolo Manna (former missionary in Burma and Superior of the Pontifical Institute for Foreign Missions)

INDIAN TERMS

cangee	also *congee,* a kind of rice porridge
dhoby	laundryman
ragi	finger millet (*Eleusine coracana*)

JAPANESE TERMS

Bunkyo	also Bunkyo-ka; Education Affairs Department
dai jin	also *daijin*; important person
Dai Toa Senso	Greater East Asia War
Gaucho	also Gocho or Kocho, *see* Kacho
Gunsei Kanbu	also Kambu; Military Administrative Office
hancho	also *honcho*; team leader
Jikeidan	Self Defense Corps, Vigilante Corps

Kacho	also Kocho, Kucho; Head of Department
Kumicho	chief, senior leader
Kanname-sai	also Kannamesai; imperial festival for the year's new rice harvest, celebrated on October 17, when the first harvest of crops for the season is offered to Amaterasu Omikami, the Sun Goddess
Katakana	a component of Japanese writing system, used specially for transcription of foreign language words into Japanese based on phonetics
Keimubu	Civil Police Department
Kempeitai	also Kenpeitai; Military Police, both conventional and secret police
Kimigayo	usually translated as 'His Imperial Majesty's Reign,' the national anthem of Japan
kumiai	also *kumi, komiai*; association, committee
Kyoei Koshi	trading company
Naiseika	Internal Affairs Department of the Japanese Navy
Nippon-go	also Nihon-go; the language spoken by the Japanese
Nissan Jidosha	Nissan Motors; originally Jidosha Seizo, the company changed its name to Nissan Jidosha in 1934 when it moved into mass production of small car, and then upgraded to the production of trucks and military vehicles during the war
O Hayo	also *ohayo*; the informal and short form of *ohayo gazaimasu*, meaning 'good morning'
rimpo	also *rimpo hancho*; small group leader, neighbourhood watch team leader
seicho	government office
shinbun	newspaper; the *Penang Shinbun* was an English daily first published on 8 December 1942 (replacing the *Penang Daily News*, published between 10 March and 7 December 1942) under editor Eric Porter Balhetchet (who became the President of the Penang Eurasian Welfare Association on 16 December 1942, editor of *The Straits Echo* after the war, and was appointed Justice of the Peace in 1953)
shunin	person in charge, senior staff
Syonan	also Syonan-to or Shōnan-tō, literally 'Light of the South Island'; name given to Singapore by the Japanese during the occupation

taiso	also *rajio taiso*, radio exercises, warm-up calisthenics, performed to music and guidance from radio broadcasts

LATIN TERMS

Achatina	a genus of medium to very large sized tropical land snails, terrestrial pulmonated gastropod mollusks of the *Achatinidae* family
ad libitum	at leisure
ad orientem	towards the East (with one's back to the people), instead of *versus populum*, facing the people
ad tempus	temporally
ad unum	to one
ambularium	ambulatory
BMV	*Beata Maria Vergine*, Blessed Virgin Mary
capsarium	a dressing room
contra incendium	against the fire
contra murum	against the wall
Corpus Christi	body of Christ; the feast of Corpus Christi is a Christian liturgical solemnity celebrating the Real Presence of the Body and Blood, Soul and Divinity of Jesus Christ in the Eucharist
Deo gratias	thanks be to God, and *Sancto Josepho:* Saint Joseph
De Spiritu Sancto	of the Holy Spirit
dimissionales	or *litterae dimissionales*; letters of discharge given by a bishop to allow his subject to be ordained by another bishop outside his jurisdiction
Duc In Altum	to draw in deep water; referring to the instruction by Jesus to Simon (Peter) to cast his net into deep water (Luke 5:4–6), resulting in a 'miraculous catch of fish'
fabrica	workshop where things are made or repaired
in articulo mortis	at the point of death
in plano	flat, plane
lapsus calami	slip of the pen
lavarium	bathroom
locutorium	parlour, room for conversation

lotor	laundryman
lusorium	recreation room
Memoriale Rituum	'Reminder of the Rites', first published by order of Pope Benedict XIII in 1725, as a 'reminder of the rites for carrying out in small parochial churches some of the principal functions of the year'
modus vivendi	literally, 'mode of living'; agreement of mutual accommodation
NB	stands for *Nota Bene*, meaning 'note well'
ordo	*ordo diurnus*, agenda or daily schedule
O res mirabilis	'O what an astonishing thing'; from *Panis angelicus* (Latin for 'Angelic Bread'), the penultimate strophe of the hymn *Sacris solemniis* written by Saint Thomas Aquinas for the feast of Corpus Christi
prandium	breakfast
privatim	privately
Propaganda	*Propaganda Fide* or *Sacra Congregatio de Propaganda Fide*, the Sacred Congregation for the Propagation of the Faith founded in 1622 to spread Catholicism in non-Catholic countries
RIP	*Requiescat In Pace*, Rest In Peace
Tempore Belli	in times of war
Tenebrae	darkness; it is a religious service of the Christians held during the three days preceding Easter, and characterised by the gradual extinguishing of candles
Te Deum	Latin Christian hymn composed in the fourth century; from its incipit, *Te deum laudamus*, 'Thee, O God, We Praise'
Triduum	three days; it is a period of three days of prayer usually preceding a Roman Catholic feast

MALAY TERMS

angsana	also *senna* or *sena*, Pokok Angsana (*Pterocarpus indicus*)
attap	also *atap*; roofing, thatch of palm leaf, especially nipa palm (*Nypa fruticans*)
ayer jalan	literally 'water from the street (drain)', of poor quality
bakau	a generic name for mangrove; red mangrove (*Rhizophora mucronata*)

barang	things in general, luggage, one's belongings
bayam	amaranth, spinach (*Amaranthus*)
bunga ayer	also *ikan bunga air*; fish belonging to the sprat family (four species in the genus *Clupeichthys*)
buah kliang	black plum; *pokok jambu keling*, tree (*Syzygium cumini*) producing black plums, also called *pokok jambu keling*
changkol	also *changkul*; large hoe for digging
chupok	also *cupak*; a quart (1.14 litre)
duri	also *ikan duri*; Sagor catfish (*Hexanematichthys sagor*)
habis	finish
jaga	watchman
janggus	cashew; *pokok janggus*, cashew tree (*Anacardium occidentale*)
kachang hijau	also *kacang hijau*; green gram, mung bean (*Vigna radata*)
kampung	village; in English, kampong is translated as 'compound': enclosure
kangkong	also *kangkung*; water convolvulus (*Ipomoea aquatica*)
kapala	also *kepala*; head, chief person; *kepala masak*, chief cook
kedai	shop; *kedai kopi,* coffee shop
Kling	an Indian person, specifically a Tamil from the Coromandel coast of Southeast India (though now considered derogatory, the term is etymologically related to the kingdom of Kalinga)
kueh bakul	literally, 'basket cake'; a Chinese New Year cake made with glutinous rice, often eaten with taro or sweet potato
Lain orang punya, sudah pergi lain tempat	meaning, 'these belong to someone else, they have already gone somewhere else'
makan besar	big meal, feast, banquet
Mata Kuching	longan (*Dimocarpus longan*); name of the Royal Air Force airfield which opened in Butterworth in October 1941 (Mata Kuching Airfield, in military terms, is no. 60 Staging Post)
matamata	also *mata-mata*; policeman
mukim	parish or precinct, an administrative division between the *daerah* (district) and the *kampung* (village)
musang	Asian palm civet (*Paradoxurus hermaphroditus*)

nasi krinh	also *nasi kering*; rice dried after being cooked
padang	field, open ground, sports ground, esplanade
padi	rice (*Oryza sativa*)
Pendirian Timor Asia Raya	literally, The Stand for Greater East Asia, Japanese military policy
pulau	island
pulut	glutinous rice (*Oryza sativa* var. *glutinosa*)
rawai	a fishing method using a line of unbaited hooks
sagu	sago (*Metroxilon sagu*)
sembilang	also *ikan sembilang*, eeltail catfish, whose tail is elongated in an eel-like fashion, from the *Plotosidae* family, catfish
Semua orang lapar	meaning 'everyone is hungry'
sengkuang	jicama, yam bean (*Pachyrhizus erosus*)
sepak takraw	Southeast Asian footvolley, played with a small rattan ball
songkok	traditional Malay headgear usually made of black or embroidered felt, cotton or velvet, commonly worn by Muslim males
TongKoh Prumpuan	also *tokoh perempuan*; eminent woman
tokong	the place of worship (temple) and the divinity
tujuh ekor	literally, 'seven tails'; seven of a type of animal, tail being the numerical coefficient for an animal.
udang halus	also *geragau*, small shrimp that resemble krill (*Acetes indicus*)

Sources & Bibliography

PRIMARY SOURCES

Located in the archives of the Seminary in Penang

– CG 007: College General presentation to the Japanese Authorities on 16 May 1943

– CG 054 to 056: Minutes of Council of the College General, 4 volumes, from 1847 to 1968

– CG 066: 1931–1946 Diary of the College General

– CG 068: Journal I Diary 1944 (10/01/44 to 16/01/45)

– CG 069: Journal II Diary 1945 (17/01/45 to 17/03/45)

– CG 070: Journal III et IV Diary 1946 (21/09/45 to 09/09/46)

UNPUBLISHED SOURCES

Memoir of (Brother) Michael Blais FSC, JSM, 'Malaya. War Time (Penang, Singapore, Calcutta, New York, Montreal, Quebec) and Malaysia (1946–1980)', typewritten text, undated.

Patary, Bernard, 'Homo Apostolicus. La formation du clergé indigène au Collège général des Missions Etrangères de Paris, à Penang (Malaisie), 1808–1968: institution et représentations'. PhD Thesis, History, Université Lumière Lyon 2, 2009.

BOOKS

Abu Talib Ahmad, *The Malay Muslims, Islam and the Rising Sun: 1941–45*, Kuala Lumpur: MBRAS, 2003.

Barber, Andrew, *Penang at War: A History of Penang during and between the First and Second World Wars 1914–1945*, Kuala Lumpur: AB&B, 2010.

Barber, Noel, *Sinister Twilight: The Fall of Singapore*, Glasgow: William Collins Sons & Co, (1968) 1985.

Batumalai, Sadayandy, *A Bicentenary History of the Anglican Church of the Diocese of West Malaysia (1805–2005)*, Melaka: Christ Church, 2007.

Cheah Boon Kheng, *Red Star over Malaya: Resistance and Social Conflict during and after the Japanese Occupation of Malaya, 1941–46*, Singapore: NUS Press, (1983) 2012.

Chen Yen Ling, *Lessons from my School: The Journey of the French Nuns and their Convent School*, Kulim: IJ Enterprises Sdn Bhd, 2019.

Chew, Maureen K.C., *History of the Catholic Church in the Diocese of Penang*, Penang: The Titular Roman Catholic Bishop, 2016.

Chew, Maureen K.C., *The Journey of the Catholic Church in Malaysia 1511–1996*, Kuala Lumpur: Catholic Research Centre, 2000.

Chin, C.C. and Karl Hack (editors), *Dialogues with Chin Peng: New Light on the Malayan Communist Party*, Singapore: NUS Publishing, 2004.

Chin Peng, *My Side of History*, Singapore: Media Masters, 2003.

Corfield, Justin and Robin, *The Fall of Singapore – 90 Days: November 1941–February 1942*, Singapore: Talisman Publishing, 2012.

Decroix, Paul, *History of the Church and Churches in Malaysia and Singapore (1511–2000)*, Penang: P. Decroix, 2005.

Destombes, Paul, *Le Collège général de la Société des Missions Etrangères de Paris 1665–1932*, Hong Kong: Imprimerie de la Société des MEP, 1934.

Hodgkins, Fiona, *From Syonan to Fuji-Go: The Story of the Catholic Settlement of Bahau in WWII Malaya*, Singapore: Select Books, 2014.

Jacques, Michael, *The Man from Borneo: An Autobiography*, Petaling Jaya: SIRD, 2010.

Jacques, Michael & Alias, *A Sign of Faith: La Salle Brothers' 300 years, 1680–1980*, n.p, n.d.

Khoo Keat Siew and Neil Khor Jin Keong, *The Penang Po Leung Kuk: Chinese Women, Prostitution and a Welfare Organisation*, Kuala Lumpur: MBRAS, 2004.

Khoo Salma Nasution, *More than Merchants. A History of the German-speaking Community in Penang, 1800–1940s*, Penang: Areca Books, 2006.

Khoo Su Nin, *Streets of George Town, Penang. An illustrated guide to Penang's city streets & historic attractions*, Penang: Janus Print & Resources, 1993.

Kratoska, Paul H., *The Japanese Occupation of Malaya and Singapore, 1941–1945: A Social and Economic History*, Singapore: NUS Press, 2018 (second edition, first published in 1998).

Lim Kean Siew, *Blood on the Golden Sands: The Memoirs of a Penang Family*, Subang Jaya: Pelanduk Publications, 1999.

Loh Kok Wah, Francis, Cecilia Ng and Anthony Rogers, *The Xaverian Journey: The Story of a Lasallian School in Penang, Malaysia, 1787–2019*, Penang: St Xavier's Institution, 2019.

Mahani Musa, *Malay Secret Societies in the Northern Malay States, 1821–1940s*, Kuala Lumpur: MBRAS, 2007.

Moussay, Gérard, *Les Missions Etrangères en Asie et dans l'océan Indien*, Paris: Les Indes Savantes, 2007.

O' Donovan, Patricius, *Jungles are Never Neutral: War-time in Bahau: An extraordinary story of exile and survival: The diaries of Brother O' Donovan fsc.*, Ipoh: Malaysia, Media Masters Publishing, 2008.

Patary, Bernard, *L'institution missionnaire en Asie (XIXe – XXe siècles) Le Collège Général de Penang: un Creuset Catholique à l'époque coloniale*, Paris: Editions Kartala, 2016.

Pilon, Maxime & Danièle Weiler, *Les Français à Singapour, de 1819 à nos jours*, Singapore: Editions Didier Millet, 2011.

Saravanamuttu, Manicasothy, *The Sara Saga*, Penang: Areca Books (1970) 2010.

Shennan, Margaret, *Out in the Midday Sun: The British in Malaya 1880–1960*, Singapore: Monsoon Books, (2000) 2015.

Sibert, Anthony E., *Bicentennial Souvenir Magazine 1811–2011*, Penang: Church of the Immaculate Conception, 2011.

Tan, Keith, *Mission Pioneers of Malaya: Origins, Architecture and Legacy of our pioneering schools*, Subang Jaya: Taylor's University, 2015.

Tan, Keith, *Mission Schools of Malaya: Architecture, Legacy and Conservation of our Landmark Schools,* Subang Jaya: Taylor's University, 2011.

Tsuji, Masanobu, *Singapore 1941–1942: The Japanese Version of the Malayan Campaign of World War II*, Singapore: Oxford University Press, 1988.

Wong Hong Suen, *Wartime Kitchen: Food and Eating in Singapore 1942–1950*, Singapore: Editions Didier Millet, 2009.

ARTICLES

Guillot Claude, 'A propos de François Albrand (1804–1867) et de son dictionnaire malais. Les Missions-Etrangères de Paris et la langue malaise au début du XIXe siècle', in *Archipel*, no. 54, Paris, 1997, pp. 153–172.

Reid, Anthony, 'Fr Pécot and the Earliest Catholic Imprints in Malay' in *Lost Times and Untold Tales from the Malay World*, Singapore: NUS Press, 2009, p.177–185.

Reid, Anthony, 'Regional Networks of Knowledge: The Penang Collège Général and Beyond' in *Penang and Its Network of Knowledge*, Penang: Areca Books, 2017, p. 60–81.

Wazir Jahan Karim, 'The "Discovery" of Penang Island at Tanjong Tokong before 1785: Bapu Alaidin Meera Hussein Lebai and Captain Francis Light', in *JMBRAS*, no. 304, Kuala Lumpur, 2013, p. 1–29.

WEB SOURCES

Diary of Charles Robert Samuel, 9 February 1883–15 December 1944 (With a preface of David Lewis in March 2015), http://www.far-eastern-heroes.org.uk/Charles_Robert_Samuel/

Index